REMAINING IN THE
TRUTH OF CHRIST

Remaining in the Truth of Christ

Marriage and Communion in the Catholic Church

Edited by
Robert Dodaro, O.S.A.

IGNATIUS PRESS   SAN FRANCISCO

Cover design by Devin Schadt, Saint Louis Creative

© 2014 by Ignatius Press, San Francisco
All rights reserved
ISBN 978-1-58617-995-3
Library of Congress Control Number 2014943997
Printed in the United States of America ∞

Because it is the task of the apostolic ministry to ensure that the Church *remains in the truth of Christ* and to lead her ever more deeply into that truth, pastors must promote the sense of faith in all the faithful, examine and authoritatively judge the genuineness of its expressions and educate the faithful in an ever more mature evangelical discernment.

—St. John Paul II, *Familiaris consortio*, no. 5 (emphasis added)

CONTENTS

ACKNOWLEDGMENTS

The Editor gratefully acknowledges the permission granted by the Libreria Editrice Vaticana to publish *Testimony to the Power of Grace: On the Indissolubility of Marriage and the Debate Concerning the Civilly Remarried and the Sacraments*, by Gerhard Ludwig Cardinal Müller, as well as the magisterial texts published in the appendix of this volume.

The Argument in Brief

Robert Dodaro, O.S.A.

The essays in this volume represent the responses of five Cardinals of the Roman Catholic Church and four other scholars to the book *The Gospel of the Family*, published earlier this year by Walter Cardinal Kasper.[1] Kasper's book contains the address he gave during the Extraordinary Consistory of Cardinals held on February 20–21, 2014. An important focus of that meeting was to prepare for the two sessions of the Synod of Bishops convened by Pope Francis for 2014 and 2015, concerning the theme "Pastoral Challenges to the Family in the Context of Evangelization". Toward the end of his address Cardinal Kasper proposed a change in the Church's sacramental teaching and discipline, one that would permit, in limited cases, divorced and civilly remarried Catholics to be admitted to Eucharistic Communion following a period of penance. In making his case, the Cardinal appealed to early Christian practice as well as to the long-standing Eastern Orthodox tradition

---

[1] Walter Cardinal Kasper, *The Gospel of the Family*, trans. William Madges (Mahwah, N.J.: Paulist Press, 2014).

of applying mercy to divorced persons under a formula by which second marriages are "tolerated"—a practice generally referred to by the Orthodox as *oikonomia*. Kasper hopes his book will provide "a theological basis for the subsequent discussion among the cardinals", and that the Catholic Church will find a way to harmonize "fidelity and mercy in its pastoral practice".[2]

The purpose of the present volume is to answer Cardinal Kasper's invitation for further discussion. The essays published in this volume rebut his specific proposal for a Catholic form of *oikonomia* in certain cases of divorced, civilly remarried persons on the grounds that it cannot be reconciled with the Catholic doctrine on the indissolubility of marriage, and that it thus reinforces misleading understandings of both fidelity and mercy.

Following this introductory chapter, the volume examines the primary biblical texts concerning divorce and remarriage. The subsequent chapter treats the teaching and practice prevalent in the early Church. In neither of these cases, biblical or patristic, do the authors find support for the kind of "toleration" of civil marriages following divorce advocated by Cardinal Kasper. Meanwhile, the fourth chapter examines the historical and theological background of the Eastern Orthodox practice of *oikonomia*, while the fifth chapter traces the centuries-long development in current Roman Catholic teaching on divorce and remarriage. The urgency of these chapters is made clear by Cardinal Kasper's assertions that in regard to the doctrine of the indissolubility of marriage, "the tradition in our case is not at all so unilinear, as is often asserted", and that "there

[2] Ibid., pp. v, 26–27.

are historical questions and diverse opinions from serious experts, which one cannot simply disregard."[3] Given the gravity of the doctrinal question involved, these historical claims require a scholarly response.

In the light of the biblical and historical findings of this first part of this volume, the authors of the remaining four chapters reiterate the theological and canonical rationale for maintaining the coherence between Catholic doctrine and sacramental discipline concerning marriage and Holy Communion. The studies included in this book thus lead to the conclusion that the Church's long-standing fidelity to the truth of marriage constitutes the irrevocable foundation of her merciful, loving response to the individual who is divorced and civilly remarried. This book therefore challenges the premise that traditional Catholic doctrine and contemporary pastoral practice are in contradiction.

The purpose of this first chapter is to summarize and highlight the principal arguments against Cardinal Kasper's proposal as they are presented in this book.

Divorce and Remarriage in Sacred Scripture

The New Testament records Christ as condemning remarriage after divorce as adultery. In Gospel passages that treat of divorce, the condemnation of remarriage is always absolute (see Mt 5:31–32; 19:3–9; Mk 10:2–12; and Lk 16:18; cf. Lk 5:31–32). Saint Paul echoes this same teaching and insists that it is not his, but Christ's: "to the married I give charge, *not I but the Lord*" (1 Cor 7:10; emphasis added).

[3] Ibid., p. 44.

The key biblical text from Genesis 2:24 ("Therefore a man leaves his father and his mother and cleaves to his wife, and they become one flesh") establishes the truth that marriage is between one man and one woman, that it is only found outside of one's family of origin, that it requires physical intimacy and closeness, and that it results in their becoming "one flesh". That this verse represents the true Christian definition of marriage is made clear when Jesus quotes it in his reply to the Pharisees that Moses had permitted divorce as a concession to "*your* hardness of heart, ... but from the beginning it was not so" (Mt 19:8; cf. Mk 10:5–6; emphasis added). In his explanation to the Pharisees on this occasion (Mk 10:6–9), Jesus alludes both to Genesis 1:27 (from the beginning of creation, "God created man in his own image, ... male and female he created them") and to Genesis 2:24. Taken together, these passages describe marriage in the original state in which God created it. Jesus' point is that the indissolubility of marriage between a man and a woman is founded on a divine law that overrides contemporary Jewish norms concerning divorce: "What therefore God has joined together, let not man put asunder" (Mk 10:9).

The Exception Clauses in Matthew's Gospel

If Jesus' teaching concerning divorce and remarriage is so clear, how are we to interpret the two passages in Matthew's Gospel that appear to allow divorce in the case of *porneia* (Mt 5:32; 19:9)? Two authors in this volume directly confront this question. Paul Mankowski, S.J., suggests on philological grounds that *porneia* may refer not to adultery, as is commonly supposed, but to incest, and perhaps also to polygamy (a practice then current among gentiles). In this case, Mankowski argues that these two passages may represent "diriment exceptives" inasmuch as they are not exceptions to the rule, but conditions under which the rule does not apply, given that separation between a man and woman in either of these cases does not constitute "divorce", there being no real marriage to dissolve.

John Rist, in his essay in this volume, offers a different explanation. He interprets *porneia* in these passages as "adultery" on the part of the wife. Jewish law not only permitted divorce in this case; it required it (Dt 24:4; Jer 3:1). In ancient societies, Hebrew and pagan, adultery on the part of the wife risked the introduction of the children of strangers into the family estate, because property passed from the father to his heirs. Jesus clearly rejects this logic, which he said Moses had allowed because of the "*your* hardness of heart", and points to the original divine command about marriage as a lifetime commitment. Hence, remarriage after divorce is not permitted as long as the other spouse continues to live.[4]

The Patristic Evidence

Cardinal Kasper seeks to ground his argument in the experience of the early Church. However, the few examples he cites will not support his conclusion, and the vast recorded experience of the early Church flatly contradicts it. His

---

[4]For further treatment of the scriptural basis for the Catholic Church's teaching on marriage, see the remarks at the beginning of the chapter in this volume by Gerhard Ludwig Cardinal Müller (chap. 6).

discussion of the patristic evidence is brief; he refers his readers to three published studies on divorce and remarriage in the early Church.[5] Yet, it is clear that he relies for the specific cases he mentions exclusively on one author and ignores the counterarguments of others. For example, he suggests that "there are good reasons for assuming" that canon 8 of the First Ecumenical Council held at Nicea in A.D. 325 confirmed an already existing pastoral practice in the early Church "of tolerance, clemency and forbearance" toward divorced and remarried Christians.[6] But the historical evidence for his conclusion, which has been advanced by Giovanni Cereti, is deeply flawed, as was demonstrated decades ago by Henri Crouzel, S.J., and another eminent patristic scholar, Gilles Pelland, S.J. In the third chapter of this volume, John Rist carefully reviews this and other cases and contends that Cereti has failed to this day to respond adequately to substantive objections to his arguments. It is not clear whether Kasper is aware of the level of detail in the scholarly objections, not only to Cereti's interpretations of this canon, but to those of the other patristic texts he cites. Nevertheless, the Cardinal employs them as evidence for his proposal.

Although Rist accepts that the "merciful" solution proposed by Kasper was not unknown in the early Church,

---

[5]See Kasper, *Gospel of the Family*, pp. 36–37, where the Cardinal cites Giovanni Cereti, *Divorzio, nuove nozze e penitenza nella Chiesa primitiva* (Bologna: Dehoniane, 1977; second edition, Bologna: Dehoniane, 1998; third edition, Rome: Aracne, 2013); Henri Crouzel, S.J., *L'Eglise primitive face au divorce. Du premier au cinquième siècle* (Paris: Editions Beauchesne, 1971); Joseph Ratzinger, "Zur Frage nach der Unauflöslichkeit der Ehe. Bemerkungen zum dogmengeschichtlichen Befund und zu seiner gegenwärtigen Bedeutung", *Ehe und Ehescheidung—Diskussion unter Christen*, ed. Franz Henrich and Volker Eid (Munich: Kösel-Verlag, 1972), pp. 35–56.

[6]Kasper, *Gospel of the Family*, p. 31.

he argues that it was generally condemned as "unscriptural" and that "virtually none of the writers who survive and whom we take to be authoritative defend it" (p. 82). Rist accuses Kasper of the "unfortunate practice all too common elsewhere in academia", whereby a "very few cases" are selected in order to claim the existence of a practice, even when the contrary historical evidence is "overwhelmingly superior" (p. 92). When this tactic fails to convince, Rist adds, the claim is then made that the scant evidence "at least leaves the solution open". Scholarly procedures such as this, Rist concludes, "can only be condemned as methodologically flawed" (p. 92). Pelland makes a similar point:

> In order to speak of a "tradition" or "practice" of the Church, it is not enough to point out a certain number of cases spread over a period of four or five centuries. One would have to show, insofar as one can, that these cases correspond to a practice accepted by the Church at the time. Otherwise, we would only have the opinion of a theologian (however prestigious), or information about a local tradition at a certain moment in its history—which obviously does not have the same weight.[7]

Eastern Orthodox Doctrine and Practice

Outside of the limited circles of a few specialists, the Eastern Orthodox practice of *oikonomia* as applied to divorce and remarriage is not well understood, even in general terms.

[7]Gilles Pelland, S.J., "Did the Church Treat the Divorced and Remarried More Leniently in Antiquity than Today?", *L'Osservatore Romano*, English Edition, February 2, 2000, p. 9.

Cardinal Kasper cites it as encouragement for the Catholic Church. In the fourth chapter of this volume, Archbishop Cyril Vasil', S.J., offers a rare up-to-date account of the history, theology, and law behind this practice. He locates the fundamental difference between Eastern Orthodox and Catholic positions on divorce and remarriage in a divergence over their understandings of Matthew 5:32 and 19:9. Historically, Orthodox authorities interpreted *porneia* as adultery and read these passages as providing an exception to Christ's prohibition of divorce. Catholic interpretations, on the other hand, held that Christ intended the marriage bond to remain intact even if, on account of adultery, the couple should separate.

During the first millennium the Church in both East and West resisted attempts by the emperors to introduce divorce and remarriage into ecclesiastical law and practice. The Council in Trullo in 692 marks the first sign of acceptance by the Church of motives for permitting divorce and remarriage (motives reducible, however, to the absence and presumed death of one of the spouses). A major change takes place in 883 when under Patriarch Photios I of Constantinople an ecclesiastical legal code incorporates a much longer list of reasons for permitting divorce and remarriage. A further complicating factor arises in 895 when the Byzantine Emperor Leo VI rules that in order to attain legal recognition marriages have to be blessed by the Church. By 1086 in the Byzantine Empire, only ecclesiastical tribunals were permitted to investigate marriage cases, and they were required to do so on the basis of imperial and civil law that permitted divorce and remarriage for a large number of reasons extending beyond adultery. Thus, from the ninth century the Eastern Church falls progressively under the sway of successive Byzantine political rulers, who persuade the bishops to accept liberalized divorce and remarriage rules. Patriarch Alexius I of Constantinople (1025–1043) for the first time permitted a Church ceremony (a blessing) for second marriages in the case of women who divorced adulterous husbands. As missionary efforts brought Christianity from Constantinople to other nations, these and similar marital customs and ethics developed within the Orthodox Churches in those lands.

Archbishop Vasil' illustrates these developments by looking closely at Russia, Greece, and the Middle East, observing similarities and differences between those churches. He notes the lack of a coherent basis—or even of a common terminology—for comparing the theological, canonical, and pastoral rationales behind practices associated with *oikonomia* among the different Orthodox Churches. This confused context explains, in part, the difficulty in locating a mature theological literature on *oikonomia* among Eastern Orthodox writers. Vasil' concludes that it may not be possible to determine a uniform "Orthodox position" on divorce and remarriage, and therefore also on *oikonomia*. At best, he fears, one can talk about the practices within a given Orthodox Church—although even here the practices are not always consistent—or one can speak about the shared position of a few bishops, or the viewpoint of a particular theologian. There are open disagreements among Orthodox bishops and theologians over the theology and law concerning these issues.

At the heart of the dilemma one finds the issue of the indissolubility of marriage. Roman Catholic theology, following Saint Augustine, views indissolubility in both a legal and spiritual sense as a bond (*sacramentum*) that binds the spouses to each other in Christ for as long as they live. However, Eastern Orthodox authors eschew the legal sense of this bond, and they view the indissolubility of marriage solely in terms of a spiritual bond. As has been stated, Orthodox authorities generally interpret Matthew 5:32 and 19:9 as permitting divorce in the case of adultery, and they insist that there are patristic grounds for doing so. If there is a common point of view among Eastern Orthodox bishops and theologians, this is it. But from this point on, Orthodox authors begin to take divergent views. Hence, while many hold the relatively strict position that divorce and remarriage are permissible only in cases of adultery, some, like John Meyendorff, suggest that the Church may grant a divorce on the grounds that the couple has refused to accept the divine grace that is offered to them in the sacrament of matrimony. Ecclesiastical divorce, in Meyendorff's view, is merely the Church's acknowledgment that this sacramental grace has been refused. Paul Evdokimov modifies this thesis, maintaining that because reciprocal love constitutes the image of the sacrament, once this love grows cold, the sacramental communion, which is expressed in the sexual union of the couple, dissipates. As a result, that relationship deteriorates into a form of "fornication".[8] Other Orthodox writers speak of the moral or spiritual "death" of a marriage and liken it to the physical death of one of the spouses, thus dissolving the bond and making remarriage possible.

[8] See John Meyendorff, "Christian Marriage in Byzantium: The Canonical and Liturgical Tradition", *Dumbarton Oaks Papers* 44 (1990): 99–107, esp. pp. 102–3; John Meyendorff, "Il Matrimonio e l'Eucaristia", *Russia Cristiana* 119 (1970): 7–27; 120 (1970): 23–36; and Paul Evdokimov, "La grâce du sacrement de mariage selon la tradition orthodoxe", *Parole et Pain* 35–36 (1969): 382–94.

In the light of their understanding of indissolubility, John Rist asks what relationship the Orthodox see between the first and second marriages in the case of divorce. Rist believes the question will be difficult to answer coherently because the Orthodox view of indissolubility leaves God's role in the sacrament ambiguous. If the evil actions of one or the other spouse (adultery, abandonment, etc.) can effectively destroy the bond, so that the second marriage should be celebrated with less ceremony and even in a penitential spirit, then are there two different grades of marriage in Orthodox thought? Given that Catholic theology indicates a clear role for God in the indissoluble marriage bond, Rist suggests that it would be even more difficult for Catholics to make theological sense out of the second marriage (a remark that calls to mind Cardinal Kasper's reference to "a willingness to tolerate something that, in itself, is unacceptable").[9]

Catholic Doctrine and Practice in the Middle Ages

In the fifth chapter Walter Cardinal Brandmüller sketches a concise overview of Western Church teachings on marriage and divorce from the Synod of Carthage (407) to the Council of Trent (1545–1563) that complements Archbishop Vasil's account of developments in the Eastern Church. Brandmüller notes that even during the evangelization of Germanic-Frankish peoples, among whom indigenous marriage customs deviated from Christian norms, bishops acting through Church councils gradually

[9] Kasper, *Gospel of the Family*, p. 31.

established the principle of the indissolubility of marriage. Despite this development, Brandmüller acknowledges that there were occasions in the Middle Ages in which Church synods and councils permitted remarriage after divorce, notoriously so in the case of King Lothair II (835–869). However, he examines some of these instances and finds in many of them compromising circumstances, such as the application of outside political pressure, that mitigate the doctrinal significance of the decisions taken by these councils. He holds that the outcomes of general councils and particular synods can only embody *paradosis* or tradition "if they themselves correspond to the demands of the authentic tradition in terms of both form and content" (p. 143). Hence during the Middle Ages, as in the patristic era, the existence here or there of highly dubious exceptions to the otherwise manifest standard teaching and practice of the Church concerning the indissolubility of marriage is more suggestive of anomalies than of parallel or alternative traditions that might be subject to retrieval today.

Current Catholic Teaching

Current teaching of the Church's Magisterium on divorce, remarriage, and Holy Communion can most concisely be apprehended by focusing on sections from the Apostolic Exhortations *Familiaris consortio* (paragraph 84), issued by Saint John Paul II in 1981, and *Sacramentum caritatis* (paragraph 29), issued by Pope Benedict XVI in 2007.[10] These

[10]See the collection of Magisterial texts at the back of this volume. The principal points of Catholic teaching are also spelled out in the *Catechism of the Catholic Church*, nos. 1644–51, included in the texts at the back of this volume.

are summarized by Gerhard Ludwig Cardinal Müller in the sixth chapter of this volume. The latter document belies the claim that Church doctrine relegates divorced and civilly remarried Catholics to second-class membership. Benedict XVI expressly urged that they "live as fully as possible the Christian life through regular participation at Mass, albeit without receiving communion, listening to the word of God, Eucharistic adoration, prayer, participation in the life of the community, honest dialogue with a priest or spiritual director, dedication to the life of charity, works of penance, and commitment to the education of their children." Cardinal Kasper has argued that this statement demonstrates a softening of attitudes toward divorced and remarried Catholics and a tendency toward a revision of the current discipline.[11] But Cardinal Müller explains, by quoting *Familiaris consortio* (no. 84), the irreformable nature of the teaching concerning the faithful whose "state and condition of life objectively contradict that union of love between Christ and the Church which is signified and effected by the Eucharist." The Cardinal continues:

> Reconciliation through sacramental confession, which opens the way to reception of the Eucharist, can only be granted in the case of repentance over what has happened and a "readiness to undertake a way of life that is no longer in contradiction to the indissolubility of marriage". (p. 155)

Yet as Müller points out, far from treating the divorced and civilly remarried with judgmental coldness and aloofness, pastors are obliged by the Magisterium "to welcome

---

[11] See Kasper, *Gospel of the Family*, p. 27.

people in irregular situations openly and sincerely, to stand by them sympathetically and helpfully, and to make them aware of the love of the Good Shepherd" (p. 165).

Marriage and the Individual Person Today

Cardinal Müller returns to an issue introduced in an earlier essay in this volume by John Rist: the nature of the individual person who seeks to marry in today's world. Both authors raise the question concerning the intentions or "mentality" of the spouses before, during, and after they exchange their marriage vows. What do they understand marriage to be? Do they understand that it is indissoluble, or do they expect only to try it out and see whether it works for them? How do they view the personal question of bringing children into the world? Do they understand that openness to children is a requirement for a valid sacramental marriage? And, more centrally, given the superficiality of relationships in the world today, are young Catholics even capable of understanding the Church's language about sacraments, fidelity, indissolubility, and openness to children?

John Rist also worries that people today are taken in by the concept of "sequential" or "serial" selves that has developed in contemporary philosophy. This concept encourages a shift in traditional belief about human nature; specifically it promotes the view that personal identity changes during one's lifetime. Rist observes that "many hardly believe themselves to be the same person from conception to death" because they "are subject to such ongoing and psychologically radical variations as they proceed through life" (p. 67). Hence, these people would conclude, "I am not the same person as I was when I married, and my wife is not the same person either", resulting in a belief that their marriage has become "a fictional relationship" (p. 68).

Cardinal Müller accepts that "today's mentality is largely opposed to the Christian understanding of marriage, with regard to its indissolubility and its openness to children", and that, as a consequence, "marriages nowadays are probably invalid more often than they were previously". He suggests that "assessment of the validity of marriage is important and can help to solve problems" (p. 157).

Nevertheless, in a Church in which the term "prophetic" has today become a catchword within movements that openly challenge prevailing cultural trends, Müller invites the Church to resist "pragmatically accommodating the supposedly inevitable" and to proclaim "the gospel of the sanctity of marriage" with "*prophetic* candor" (pp. 160–61; emphasis added). The difficulties involved in accepting Christ's teaching concerning the sanctity of marriage were first acknowledged not by a Synod of Bishops, but by the apostles who, when they heard this teaching directly from the Lord, responded with incredulity, "If such is the case of a man with his wife, it is not expedient to marry" (Mt 19:10). However, both Cardinal Müller and Paul Mankowski, S.J., in their respective essays in this volume, recognize that along with his "hard" teaching concerning the indissolubility of marriage, Christ also promised, in the words of Mankowski, "a new and superabundant afflatus of grace, of divine help, so that no person however fragile should find it impossible to do God's will" (p. 63).

Mercy and the Rules of the Church

But what about failure in a marital relationship, breakdown, and divorce? Does the Church's current teaching
and practice concerning divorced and civilly remarried
Catholics demonstrate the quality of mercy that Jesus
showed to sinners? Cardinal Müller replies that in order to
avoid an incomplete view of Jesus' mercy we need to look
at the entirety of his life and teaching. The Church cannot
appeal to "divine mercy" (p. 163) as a way of jettisoning
those teachings of Jesus that she finds difficult.

> The entire sacramental economy is a work of divine
> mercy, and it cannot simply be swept aside by an appeal
> to the same. An objectively false appeal to mercy also runs
> the risk of trivializing the image of God, by implying that
> God cannot do other than forgive. The mystery of God
> includes not only his mercy but also his holiness and his
> justice. (p. 163)

In the eighth chapter of this volume, Velasio Cardinal
De Paolis, C.S., echoes Cardinal Müller's view: "Mercy is
often presented in opposition to the law, even divine law.
But setting God's mercy in opposition to his own law is
an unacceptable contradiction" (p. 203). De Paolis notes
that Kasper does not propose "mercy" as a way to Eucharistic Communion for *all* divorced and civilly remarried
Catholics, but only for those who fulfill certain conditions.
He finds the reasoning behind Kasper's conditions illog-
ical. He asks what it is about *civil* marriage that qualifies
it as more morally sound than mere cohabitation. The
Church does not regard civil marriage following divorce

as a valid marriage. So the fact that Catholics in this situation are married according to the laws of the State does not make their behavior more morally respectable than a couple who live together outside of marriage. To Kasper's argument that the education of the children of spouses in a civil marriage makes it objectively a better moral option (a "lesser evil") than the alternatives, De Paolis replies that fictive marriages wear down the basic principles of marriage and family as well as of sexual morality in general, and he wonders what kind of moral education the couple in that condition would be passing on to their children:

> Respect for the moral rule that prohibits marital life between people who are not married cannot admit exceptions. The difficulty one encounters in respecting the moral law does not then permit that person to turn around and violate the same moral law. (p. 195)

Discipline and Doctrine

Cardinal De Paolis also observes that "a distinction is often made between doctrine and discipline in order to say that in the Church doctrine does not change, whereas the discipline does" (p. 206). However, a change in Church practice aimed at permitting divorced and civilly remarried Catholics to receive the Eucharist necessarily involves a change in doctrine. No one should be under any illusion about this. De Paolis points out that in Catholic theology, "discipline" refers to something broader than human laws. For example, "discipline includes the divine law, such as the commandments, which are not subject to change although they are not directly of a doctrinal nature.... Discipline often includes everything to which the believer must feel committed in his life in order to be a faithful disciple of our Lord Jesus Christ" (p. 206). Hence, the distinction between the discipline of the sacraments and Catholic doctrine is not as clear as many believe it to be or would like it to be.

In the seventh chapter of this volume, Carlo Cardinal Caffarra outlines reasons that Cardinal Kasper's proposal necessarily involves a change in doctrine and not just in sacramental discipline. He notes that according to "the tradition of the Church, founded on the Scriptures (see 1 Cor 11:28),...: communion with the Body and with the Blood of the Lord requires of those who participate therein that they not find themselves in contradiction with what they receive." The Cardinal concludes that "the *status* [emphasis in original] of the divorced and civilly remarried is in objective contradiction with that bond of love that unites Christ and the Church, which is signified and actualized by the Eucharist" (p. 175).

Caffarra explains that in the Catholic view, marriage consists of a bond that is not simply moral, but also ontological, because it integrates Christ into the marriage. "The married person is *ontologically* ... consecrated to Christ, conformed to him. The conjugal bond is put into being by God himself, by means of the consent of the two (spouses)." Caffarra concedes that if the marital bond were only moral and not ontological, it could be dispensed. However, given the ontological nature of the sacramental bond, "the spouse remains integrated into such a mystery, even if the spouse, through a subsequent decision, attacks the sacramental bond by entering into a state of life that contradicts it" (p. 175; emphasis in original). As a consequence, the admission of divorced and civilly remarried Catholics to the sacraments of penance and the Eucharist would not only mark a change in sacramental practice or discipline; it would introduce a fundamental contradiction into the Catholic doctrine concerning matrimony, and therefore also the Eucharist.

Caffarra sees in Kasper's proposal other consequences for the doctrine of the indissolubility of marriage. He argues that the admission of divorced and civilly remarried Catholics to the sacraments of penance and the Eucharist, even under the restrictive conditions that Kasper suggests, would essentially "recognize the moral legitimacy of living *more coniugali* [as husband and wife] with a person who is not the true spouse" (p. 176) and would "persuade, not only the faithful, but also any attentive person of the idea that, at its heart, there exists no marriage that is absolutely indissoluble, [and] that the 'forever' to which every true love cannot but aspire is an illusion" (p. 179).

In his book, Cardinal Kasper raises two other options for allowing divorced and civilly remarried Catholics to approach the sacraments of penance and the Eucharist: an appeal to *epikeia* (the presumption that the law should not be applied in a particular case because of extenuating circumstances), and the application of the moral principle of prudence. However, Cardinal Caffarra objects that an appeal to prudence cannot be made in this case, because "that which is in itself ... intrinsically illicit can never be the object of the prudential judgment." In other words, "a prudent adultery cannot exist". Caffarra holds that "the reference to *epikeia* is equally without a foundation" (p. 177). As a virtue, *epikeia* can only be applied to human laws, not divine laws. But the laws concerning the indissolubility of marriage, the prohibition of adultery, and access to the Eucharist are divine laws (see Mk 10:9; Jn 8:11; 1 Cor 11:28). The Church cannot excuse the faithful from their obligation to obey God's law.

Canonical Procedures Governing Declarations of Nullity

Cardinal Kasper also suggests that in the case of the faithful who are divorced and civilly remarried, the Church's judicial process governing declarations of nullity should be simplified. Specifically, Kasper suggests the adoption of "more pastoral and spiritual procedures".[12] He proposes that in lieu of diocesan marriage tribunals, "the bishop could entrust this task to a priest with spiritual and pastoral experience as a penitentiary or episcopal vicar."[13] In the ninth chapter of this volume Raymond Leo Cardinal Burke draws from extensive papal legislation and commentary, as well as from the experience of the Apostolic Signatura, to explain why Kasper's recommendations, if adopted, would weaken the Church's efforts to guarantee justice for the faithful.

Burke points out that the faithful are badly served by tribunals that fall "into a kind of pseudo-pastoral pragmatism", and he quotes Saint John Paul II, who "warned precisely against the temptation to exploit the canonical process 'in order to achieve what is perhaps a "practical" goal, which

---

[12] Ibid., p. 28.
[13] Ibid., p. 29.

might perhaps be considered "pastoral", but is to the detriment of truth and justice'"[14] (p. 215). Burke emphasizes that if tribunals give the impression that their main purpose is to enable those in failed marriages to remarry in the Church by offering superficial or erroneous explanations, or by employing incorrect procedures, the faithful could become "disedified and even scandalized" (p. 217).

At the heart of the canonical procedures that aim to establish the truth of a claim of nullity in a given case of marriage is a dialectic process known as the *contradictorium*. It embodies the principle *et audiatur altera pars* (and the other party is to be heard). Burke explains that this principle has historically determined the canonical procedures at use in issuing declarations of nullity, including the requirement of a defender of the bond and of a double conforming sentence. He defends these advances against the charge of a "burdensome juridicism" (p. 226) on the grounds that they strengthen the dialectic process that in turn guarantees that the tribunal can reach a "moral certitude" (p. 229) that the nullity of the marriage has been proven. Burke asserts that defenders of the bond too often have been manifestly negligent in fulfilling their obligations, resulting in a lack of integrity in the judicial process. Were all the ministers of the tribunal, including judges, to be more scrupulous in the performance of their responsibilities, "the process to arrive at a double agreeing decision, with the decree of ratification, will not take too long" (p. 236).

[14] Saint John Paul II, "Address to the Tribunal of the Roman Rota", January 28, 1994, *Acta Apostolicae Sedis* 86 (1994): 950, no. 5. English translation in *Papal Allocutions to the Roman Rota 1939–2011*, ed. William H. Woestman, O.M.I. (Ottawa: Faculty of Canon Law, Saint Paul University, 2011), p. 229, no. 5.

32

Sense of the Faithful (*Sensus fidelium*)

Toward the conclusion of his book, Cardinal Kasper cites
Blessed John Henry Newman's famous essay, "On Consulting the Faithful in Matters of Doctrine", and he discusses the canard attributed to Newman "that, in the Arian
crisis in the fourth and fifth centuries, it was not the bishops, but rather the faithful who preserved the faith of the
Church".[15] Kasper lionizes Newman as a "forerunner of
the Second Vatican Council" and links his essay with the
Council's affirmations concerning "the sense of the faith,
which is given to every Christian by virtue of baptism".[16]
Most commentators on Newman's essay mistake his
understanding of "faithful" as referring only to the "laity".
But as the eminent Newman scholar Ian Ker points out,
Newman included priests and monks among the "faithful"
in his argument, so that the distinction he drew was not
between clergy and the laity, as so many today believe.[17]

[15] Kasper, *Gospel of the Family*, p. 46. This English translation of Kasper's
book wrongly cites the title of Newman's article as "On Consulting the Faithful in Matters of Faith". See John Henry Newman, "On Consulting the
Faithful in Matters of Doctrine", *The Rambler*, 3rd Series, July 1859, pp. 189–
230; and John Henry Newman, *On Consulting the Faithful in Matters of Doctrine*,
edited with an introduction by John Coulson (London: Geoffrey Chapman,
1961), pp. 75–101.
[16] Kasper, *Gospel of the Family*, p. 46, referencing the Second Vatican Council, Pastoral Constitution on the Church, *Lumen gentium*, nos. 12 and 35.
[17] See Ian Ker, "Newman on the *Consensus Fidelium* as 'the Voice of the
Infallible Church'", *Newman and the Word*, ed. Terrence Merrigan and Ian
Ker (Louvain: Peters, 2002), pp. 69–89; Ian Ker, "Newman, the Councils, and
Vatican II", *Communio* 28 (Winter 2001): 708–28, esp. pp. 725–26. See also
Hermann Geissler, F.S.O., "Das Zeugnis der Gläubigen in Lehrfragen nach
John Henry Newman", *Communio* 41 (2012): 669–83, translated as *The Wit-
ness of the Faithful in Matters of Doctrine according to John Henry Newman* (Rome:
International Centre of Newman Friends, 2012). At p. 9, n. 22, Geissler offers
this clarification: "Newman's main desire is simply to say that pure belief

Moreover, historians disagree with Newman's version of this controversy and insist that insofar as the positions of the early Church faithful can be ascertained on the Arian question, in the main they tended to adhere to the view of their local bishop whatever his position was. It was not, therefore, the laity who were responsible for the victory of the Nicene faith over the Arians.[18] Nevertheless, Kasper forges an analogy between Newman's "faithful" and the married laity in today's Church, whom he contrasts with the "celibate" Cardinals in the Consistory, because the laity "live out their belief in the gospel of the family in concrete families and sometimes in difficult situations". He then pleads for the Church to "listen to their witness" and not to allow the question of the divorced and remarried to "be decided only by cardinals and bishops".[19]

However, "sense of the faithful" cannot be understood in Catholic theology as an expression of majority opinion within the Church, and it is not arrived at by conducting polls. It refers to an instinct for the authentic faith possessed by the faithful, understood as both the hierarchy and the laity together, as the one Body of Christ. Newman referred to this dynamic as *conspiratio*, a breathing together between pastors and laity. Hence, while it would be

---

during the Arian confusion was maintained by the faithful under the leadership of some influential confessing bishops, whilst many pastors, influenced by the Arian establishment at the imperial court, did not fulfil their responsibilities as teachers of the faith. All members of the Church count among the faithful, including also the pastors."

[18] See Yves M.-J. Congar, O.P., *Jalons pour une Théologie du Laïcat* (Paris: Éditions du Cerf, 1953), p. 395. English edition, *Lay People in the Church: A Study for a Theology of Lay People*, revised edition with additions by the author, trans. Donald Attwater (London: Chapman, 1965), pp. 285–86.

[19] Kasper, *Gospel of the Family*, p. 47.

erroneous to suggest that the lay faithful lack an instinct for the authentic faith, it is an abuse to employ the concept in an effort to pit a putative "voice of the laity" against either the bishops or Church teachings. Nor do these principles represent an isolated, conservative point of view. Each has been articulated by the Second Vatican Council and by successive popes thereafter, most recently by Pope Francis in his December 2013 address to the International Theological Commission.[20]

Conclusion

The authors of this volume jointly contend that the New Testament presents Christ as unambiguously prohibiting divorce and remarriage on the basis of God's original plan for marriage set out at Genesis 1:27 and 2:24. The "merciful" solution to divorce advocated by Cardinal Kasper is not unknown "in the ancient Church, but virtually none of the writers who survive and whom we take to be authoritative defend it; indeed when they mention it, it is rather to condemn it as unscriptural. There is nothing surprising in that situation; abuses may exist occasionally, but their mere existence is no guarantee of their not being abuses, let alone being models to be followed" (p. 82). The current Eastern Orthodox practice of *oikonomia* in cases of divorce and remarriage stems largely from the second millennium and arises in response to political pressure on the Church from Byzantine emperors. During

---

[20] See the collected statements of the Magisterium concerning *sensus fidelium* at the end of this volume.

the Middle Ages and beyond, the Catholic Church in the
West resisted such efforts more successfully and did so at
the cost of martyrdom. The Eastern Orthodox practice
of *oikonomia* is not an alternative tradition to which the
Catholic Church can appeal. *Oikonomia*, in this context,
rests on a view of the indissolubility of marriage that is
not compatible with Roman Catholic theology, which
understands the marital bond as being rooted ontologically in Christ. Hence, civil marriage following divorce
involves a form of adultery, and it makes the reception of
the Eucharist morally impossible (1 Cor 11:28), unless the
couple practice sexual continence. These are not a series
of rules made up by the Church; they constitute divine
law, and the Church cannot change them. To the woman
caught in adultery, Christ said, "[G]o and do not sin again"
(Jn 8:11). God's mercy does not dispense us from following his commandments.

2

Dominical Teaching on Divorce and Remarriage: The Biblical Data

Paul Mankowski, S.J.

This paper examines those biblical texts in which Jesus gives his teaching on divorce and remarriage, and those texts in view of which dominical teaching on divorce and remarriage may be better understood. Thus I look at 1 Corinthians 7:10–11, in which Paul claims to transmit the Lord's instructions, but I do not treat the so-called Pauline Privilege of 1 Corinthians 12–15, wherein Paul gives opinions explicitly said to be his own and not the Lord's. I do not engage source-critical or form-critical problems but take the *textus receptus* to be the governing word—in part because the sayings that the teaching Church has historically taken as dominical belong to this text (as opposed to a subset of *ipsissima verba* distinguished on scholarly grounds from *spuria*), and in part because I fail to understand how the Church, or one claiming to speak in her name, can call others to sacrifice and hardship on the basis of divine pronouncements that are intrinsically subject to deletion or change. The texts to be examined are (1) the nuptial teaching of Genesis 2:24, (2) Paul's tradition of

Jesus' teaching on divorce and remarriage (1 Cor 7:10–11), (3) the Lucan equation of divorce with adultery (Lk 16:18), (4) Mark's account of the Pharisees' testing of Jesus on divorce (Mk 10:2–12), (5) the corresponding episode in Matthew (Mt 19:3–9), (6) the divorce antithesis of the Sermon on the Mount (Mt 5:31–32), along with (7) a separate consideration of the diriment exceptive passages in Matthew.

Genesis 2:24

Located in the so-called second creation account, Genesis 2:24 is a key text in the biblical understanding of marriage, important in its own right and in the explication of subsequent passages, those reflecting Jesus' teaching in particular. Having recorded in the previous verse the man's reaction to the woman presented to him ("this at last is bone of my bones and flesh of my flesh"; RSV-2CE), the text continues, in verse 24,

> ʾAl-kēn yaʿăzob-ʾîš ʾet-ʾābîw wəʾet-ʾimmô wədābaq bəʾištô wəhāyû ləbāśār ʾeḥād.[1]

Therefore a man leaves his father and his mother and cleaves to his woman,[2] and they become one flesh.

---

[1] The Septuagintal, Vulgate, Syriac, Targum Yerusalmi, and Targum Neofiti renderings of this verse give "and *the two of them* become one flesh"—a reading also reflected in Jesus' citations of the text at Mt 19:5 and Mk 10:8 and by Paul at 1 Cor 6:16 (the Samaritan Hebrew gives *mšnyhm* "from the two of them"). The Masoretic Hebrew here is the *lectio brevior* and is probably original, but the predominance of the variant among the versional renderings points to an extensive parallel tradition.

[2] Here and throughout in my token translations I render the Hebrew *ʾiššāh* and the Greek *gunē* by "woman"—and so for similar terms—not because

While the verse has structural similarities to stereotyped expressions of folk wisdom, its content runs emphatically contrary to that expectation. As A. F. L. Beeston remarked, "In the Mediterranean-Near Eastern world, the norm of marriage is and always has been a virilocal arrangement, in which the wife moves into the household of the husband's family."[3] But here it is the man who leaves behind his parents, ruling out a notional connection to familiar domestic experience. By the same token the connective phrase *'al-kēn*, typically used to introduce folkloric explanations of name giving, customs, and so on, cannot be understood in this verse as "etiological thus",[4] for the reason that the maxim following corresponds to no recognizable convention. The meaning rather is extrahistorical and universal, focused on marriage *in se* and oblivious of ritual practices of wedding and courtship. It stresses that the marriage partner is found outside one's family of origin (one *leaves* father and mother); that the marriage is effected between a man and a woman; and that it is marked by physical proximity and intimacy (the Hebrew *dābaq* means "join", "cling", "keep close").

"wife" is not an appropriate or even superior translation in context, but in order to make clear the diction of the source text and to facilitate the passage from English to the transliterated Hebrew or Greek. Note: all translations are my own unless otherwise indicated.

[3] A. F. L. Beeston, "One Flesh", *Vetus Testamentum* 36 (1986): 116. Beeston claims to find in Gen 2:24 "the look of a fragment of an ancient law code, the editor being either unaware of its original meaning, or regarding it as irrelevant". I fail to see how Beeston's arguments do not weaken the plausibility of this hypothesis.

[4] For typical uses, see *multa inter alia* in Gen 11:9; 19:22; Deut 15:15; for the (mis-)application of "etiological thus" to Gen 2:24, see, e.g., Miriam Goldstein, *Karaite Exegesis in Medieval Jerusalem: The Judeo-Arabic Pentateuch* (Tübingen: Mohr Siebeck, 2011), p. 126.

Finally, it teaches that the man and the woman become "one flesh". While the theological, biological, and legal implications of this "one flesh" have been interpreted variously, it is clear that the phrase points to (1) the coming to be of a *new entity*, distinct from either of the constituent persons; (2) the fact that this entity is single, that is, not subject to recombination internally or externally; and (3) the fact that the entity is not an abstraction but an *organism*, enfleshed and endowed with life. Although the diction is pre-philosophical and the narrative is not speculative or analytic in form, the maxim is proffered as a universal truth, detached from local, historical, or even religious specificity, neither directed at a particular nation nor elicited from any nation's wisdom. Inasmuch as the verse in which it occurs is located in the prelapsarian episode—that is, before the act of disobedience and the consequent disfigurement of the husband-wife comity (Gen 3:16)—we are justified in taking this maxim as definitional, that is, not the expression of an unattainable ideal, but as a statement of the determinate nature or essence of marriage, whose outlines are unblurred by subsequent empirically influenced compromise, accommodation, and corruption. This seems to be precisely the way in which Jesus appeals to Genesis 2:24 in the dispute with the Pharisees at Matthew 19, where, after quoting the verse, he declares the Mosaic permission for divorce to be a concession to human obduracy, adding, "but from the beginning, it was not so" (19:8 [RSV-2CE]; see also Mk 10:5–6). The other biblical teachings on marriage, divorce, and remarriage, while at least implicitly cognizant of the varying sociolegal circumstances of its addressees, anchor themselves in this transhistorical certitude.

First Corinthians 7:10–11

Of particular interest for the Church's doctrine on marriage is 1 Corinthians 7:10–11, because of the comprehensiveness of Paul's concerns and the clarity with which he distinguishes divine command from self-evinced prudence. On the question of divorce he emphasizes that his pronouncements come from the Lord:

10 *Tois de gegamēkosin parangellō, ouk egō alla ho kurios, gunaika apo andros mē chōristhēnai* 11*ean de kai chōristhēi, menetō agamos ē tōi andri katallagētō, kai andra gunaika mē aphienai.*

10 To the married I command, not I but the Lord, that a woman not separate from her man, 11but if she should separate, let her remain unmarried or be reconciled to her man; also a man must not divorce his woman.

As Joseph Fitzmyer points out, the infinitive *chōristhē-nai*, though formally passive, may be translated either as a true passive ("a woman should not *be separated* from her man") or as having middle voice, as rendered above.[5] In the latter case it is the woman who is seen to initiate the separation; this reading, as Fitzmyer indicates, would be suited to a situation, such as obtained in Corinth, in which divorce initiated by the wife was much more common than in Jewish communities, and it has the added advantage of

[5]Joseph A. Fitzmyer, "The Matthean Divorce Texts and Some New Palestinian Evidence", *Theological Studies* 37 (1976): 199. Jerome Murphy-O'Connor, "The Divorced Woman in 1 Cor 7:10–11", *Journal of Biblical Literature* 100 (1981): 601–6, argues that the aorist passive infinitive should here be translated such that the verse reads "the wife should not allow herself to be separated from her husband", citing 1 Cor 6:7 and Rom 12:2 in support.

not making the last clause (prohibiting husband-initiated divorce) redundant. Further, were the wife here understood as the passive partner in a divorce effected by her husband, it seems odd to lay upon her the duty of reconciliation (*ē tōri andri katallagētō*) as the alternative to remaining unmarried.

The concessive syntax with which verse 11 begins ("if she [the woman] *should* separate"; *chōrristhēi* is subjunctive) has led some to argue that Paul countenances divorce "after the fact". But Paul does not suggest that one is free to act against the Lord's prohibition; indeed, such a liberty would be flatly contrary to the charge given at 7:10 and to his invocation of the Lord's authority in declaring it. The situation envisaged seems most likely to be that of a *fait accompli* in which the formerly pagan divorcée, newly desirous of instruction in the Christian way of life, is told she must be reconciled to her estranged husband or remain unmarried. Fitzmyer, echoing Hans Conzelmann, concludes that "the regulation is absolute."[6]

Luke 16:18

Luke 16:18 occurs at the end of a number of sayings of Jesus bracketed by the parable of the unjust steward (16:1–8) and the account of Dives and Lazarus (16:19–31), and it is given focus by the scoffing of the captious Pharisees (16:14). It is not strictly speaking a prohibition of divorce, but a condemnation of male remarriage after divorce by association with the stigma of adultery (see Ex 20:14; Deut 5:18; 22:22; Lev 20:10).

---

[6] Fitzmyer, "Matthean Divorce Texts", p. 200, quoting Hans Conzelmann, *A Commentary on the First Epistle to the Corinthians* (Philadelphia: Fortress, 1975), p. 120.

Pas ho apoluōn tēn gunaika autou kai gamōn heteran moicheuei
kai ho apolelumenēn apo andros gamōn moicheuei.

Everyone who divorces his woman and marries another
commits adultery, and he who marries a woman divorced
from her man commits adultery.

The use of the adjective *pas*, "all, everyone", with the par-
ticiple mimics the stereotyped Septuagintal legal formula,
but the new teaching conveyed is not legal but moral, and
hence universal in application.

What may be missed by its obviousness is the finality
with which Jesus refuses to recognize the second union
of a divorced person. The purported "marriage" simply
has no existence. As a consequence, the sexual relations
of the relevant parties are not marital but adulterous by
definition.

Because the verse treats only of the choices made by the
male, it may at first glance appear to be a continuation or
reflection of the androcentric language of Old Testament
law codes. In fact we have a departure from Near Eastern androcentrism precisely in focusing the opprobrium
of adultery on the male rather than the female offender.
Whereas the penalty for adultery was to be applied equilat-
erally (see Lev 20:10 and Deut 22:22), there is little doubt
that in reality the heavier reproach fell on the adulteress.[7]
For this reason it is significant that it is the male divorcée
(*pas ho apoluōn tēn gunaika autou*) attempting to remarry
to whom Jesus imputes a sin of particular odium, thus

[7] With the woman caught in adultery in the Gospel of John (8:3–11),
no interest is displayed by the scribes or Pharisees in apprehending the male
offender and, as required, putting him to death (cf. the ruse devised by the
traducers of Susanna in Dan 13:21, 37–40, Greek text).

apportioning blameworthiness to the freedom of choice of the moral agent. Here too the dictum is exceptionless.

Mark 10:2–12

Mark 10:2–12 is a passage in which the Pharisees are said to be testing Jesus, that is, attempting to maneuver him dialectically into a place where he will either contradict the law or contradict his own teaching, in either case to his discredit.

> *2 Kai proselthontes Pharisaioi epērōtōn auton ei exestin andri gunaika apolusai, peirazontes auton. 3Ho de apokritheis eipen autois, ti humin eneteilato Mōusēs? 4Hoi de eipan, epetrepsen Mōusēs biblion apostasiou grapsai kai apolusai. 5Ho de Iēsous eipen autois, pros tēn sklērokardian humōn egrapsen humin tēn entolēn tautēn.*

2 And Pharisees came up and asked him, "Is it lawful for a man to divorce his wife?" testing him. 3He answered them, "What did Moses command you?" 4They said, "Moses permitted one to write a bill of divorcement, and to divorce." 5But Jesus said to them, "For your hardness of heart he wrote for you this commandment."

Most scholars view the Mosaic permission here referred to as that reflected in Deuteronomy 24:1–4,[8] which is in

---

[8] "When a man takes a wife and marries her, if then she finds no favor in his eyes because he has found some indecency in her, and he writes her a bill of divorce and puts it in her hand and sends her out of his house, and she departs out of his house, and if she goes and becomes another man's wife, and the latter husband dislikes her and writes her a bill of divorce and puts it in her hand and

fact a complex specimen of case law in which the giving of the bill of divorcement is not commanded, but rather stipulated as one element in the lengthy and compound protasis.[9] That said, Jesus would appear to concede to the Pharisees both the existence of the commandment (*entolē*) permitting divorce and its authoritative standing in the Torah. But by the double occurrence of the dative plural pronoun *humin*—"for you"[10]—in verses 3 and 5, Jesus indicates that the directive force of the commandment applies to his addressees (however conceived) in a way from which he implicitly disassociates himself, and that he will explicitly replace it in verse 9 with a new and absolute commandment. Jesus attributes the Mosaic concession to *sklērokardia*, a rendering of the Hebrew

---

sends her out of his house, or if the latter husband dies, who took her to be his wife, then her former husband, who sent her away, may not take her again to be his wife, after she has been defiled; for that is an abomination before the LORD, and you shall not bring guilt upon the land which the LORD your God gives you for an inheritance" (Deut 24:1–4).

[9]Both Phillip Sigal, *The Halakah of Jesus of Nazareth according to the Gospel of Matthew* (Atlanta: Society of Biblical Literature, 2007), p. 17, and David Instone-Brewer, *Divorce and Remarriage in the Bible: The Social and Literary Context* (Grand Rapids: Eerdmans, 2002), p. 20, contend that divorce as a social reality was presupposed in the Pentateuch, whence the remarkably few pertinent passages (Deut 22:19, 29 may be added) concern casuistic case-specific restrictions on a widely tolerated practice. As Sigal remarks, "None of the [Old Testament] divorce passages provide for how the writ is to be composed, its wording, who is to preside, whether to require witnesses or how many, whether there is any liturgical element, and so forth" (p. 17, n. 58). Acquainted with a lengthy tradition of casuistic controversy, yet lacking a biblical proof text framed in the stereotyped syntax of a commandment, the Pharisees offer in reply to Jesus' question a summary statement that he accepts as correct.

[10]The referential target of the second person plural here is ambiguous and may be taken as "you Pharisees", "you Jews", "you men", "you married men", or "you human beings", with a different rhetorical force and different theological thrust in each case. For the present it is sufficient to call attention to Jesus' act of auto exclusion preceding his own new pronouncement in verse 9.

'*orlat lēbāb*,[11] literally, "foreskin (uncircumcision) of heart": contumacious—stubbornness in defiance of God's will.[12] In contrast to a sentimentalism current in our own day that views openness to divorce as a manifestation of charity, Jesus distances himself from the ostensible ground of the concession ("*your* hardness of heart") and proceeds to place himself in the paradoxical position of a new lawgiver vindicating the original and divinely ordained union of man and wife.

> 6 *Apo de archēs ktiseōs arsen kai thēlu epoiēsen autous.* [7]*Heneka toutou kataleipsei anthrōpos ton patera autou kai tēn mētera kai proskollēthēsetai pros tēn gunaika autou.* [8]*Kai esontai hoi duo eis sarkan mian; hōste ouketi eisin duo alla mia sarx.* [9]*Ho oun theos sunezeuxen anthrōpos mē chōrizetō.*

6 But from the beginning of creation, male and female he made them. [7]Because of this a man shall leave his father and mother and be joined to his woman, [8]and the two shall become one flesh. Thus they are no longer two but one flesh. [9]What therefore God has joined, let man not separate.

Continuing his reply to the Pharisees, Jesus makes reference to two texts from Genesis. The first is the final clause of 1:27,[13] prefaced by the phrase "from the beginning of creation"—not that the making of man and woman was

---

[11] See the Hebrew of Deut 10:16 and Jer 4:4, with the Septuagint (LXX).

[12] The connotations of uncircumcision in a Jewish context invest the term with a particularly pagan opprobrium, especially that of perversity and impurity in sexual matters.

[13] Whereas the Hebrew reads "male and female he created (*bārāʿ*) them", the LXX gives "he made (*epoiēsen*) them". The frequency with which Greek translators rendered forms of the Hebrew *bārāʿ* by equivalents of the Greek *poiein* (in preference to *ktizein*) makes it all but impossible to decide which Aramaic word of Jesus the Marcan passage reflects.

God's first act of creating, but that the created order itself included this dispensation from the time it was perfect and complete onward. The emphasis is on the state of the universe when the arrangement and operations of all things, including man and woman, conformed to God's sovereign, absolute, and as yet undefied will. This citation is followed immediately by another from Genesis 2:24, in the fuller form in which *hoi duo*, "the two", is included. In this discourse the logical connective *heneka toutou* (because of this) looks back not, as in Genesis 2:23, to the first man's exclamation ("this at last is bone from my bones"; RSV-2CE), but rather to Genesis 1:27, that is, to God's creative will. While the new anaphora does not contradict the meaning present in the original context, the focus changes from man's recognition of connaturality with the woman to the divinely designed purpose of the male-female duality. Jesus does not comment directly on the relation of the divorce commandment given by Moses to the will of God, but by explicitly connecting the marital becoming one flesh to the pristine order of creation, he is stating as emphatically as possible that the oneness of husband and wife is divine will and not a human contrivance.

The rhetorical power of Jesus' new commandment— "What therefore God has joined, let man not separate"—is considerable. In part, this is the effect of its occurrence at the climax of Jesus' discourse; in part, it is the effect of that combination of balance, pithiness, and sudden felicity of expression belonging to the most perfect epigrams—so great as to carry over into translation with minimal loss; in part it is the effect of the forceful cognitive contrast between God's work and man's that provides an irreducibly succinct summary of the preceding argument.

It is, moreover, propounded in absolute terms, extending beyond the concerns of Pharisees or Jews of any allegiance to those of all God-fearers—to anyone, that is, who believes the claims of God to override those of men. Thus any God-fearer who will concede that, in a given case, it is God who has effected the joining is eo ipso obliged to grant the conclusion and the force of the third-person negative imperative *mē chōrizetō*, namely, that man must not break the bond.

> 10 *Kai eis tēn oikian palin hoi mathētai peri toutou epērōtōn auton.* [11]*Kai legei autois, hos an apolusēi tēn gunaika autou kai gamēsēi allēn moichatai ep'autēn;* [12]*kai ean autē apolusasa ton andra autēs gamēsēi allon moichatai.*

> 10 And in the house the disciples asked him again about this matter. [11]And he said to them, "Whoever divorces his woman and marries another commits adultery against her; [12]and if having divorced her man she marries another, she commits adultery."

The conclusion of this episode takes place out of public earshot, either because the disciples feared the consequences of public expatiation on this teaching or because they were themselves shamefully dismayed by it, or both. In Jesus' reply the focus shifts from the question of the permissibility of divorce per se to that of remarriage. Here the language is similar to that of Luke 16:18, but with two differences. Verse 12 teaches that not only the husband who frees himself from a wife but the wife who frees herself from a husband commits adultery. Because the situation in which a woman was able to initiate divorce is rarely attested in Jewish communities in the first century, there is a sizable literature concerning the supposed *destinataires* of the Marcan writings and the authenticity of this verse. My own view is that such questions eclipse the more important consistency with which Jesus avoids treating problems within the terms of intra-Judaic casuistry but moves the discourse into the moral and spiritual realm pertinent to any human agent of any place and time (more of this on Mt 5:32 below). The second difference is the presence in verse 11 of the phrase *ep'autēn*, "against her".[14] It is not clear from the syntax of verses 11–12 whether the sin of adultery is here occasioned by divorce and remarriage considered as a single act or by remarriage simply. As with Luke 16:18, the imputation of adultery entails the claim that the attempted second marriage does not exist, and the responsibilities and obligations of the original marriage remain in full force. Yet the sin of adultery, as formulated by verse 11, is not, so to speak, intransitive but involves an injury against the first and only true wife (for the nature of this injury, see the section on Mt 5:32 below).

Matthew 19:3–9

The Matthaean pericope (Mt 19:3–9) corresponding to Mark 10:2–12 has a similar introduction, with Pharisees approaching Jesus in order to confound him on the disputed question of divorce.

---

[14] Gerhard Delling in "Das Logion Mark. X 11 [und seine Abwandlungen] im Neuen Testament", *Novum Testamentum* 1 (1956–1957): 270, regards the phrase as notionally superfluous in view of verse 12.

*3 Kai proselthon autōi Pharisaioi peirazontes auton kai legon-
tes, ei exestin anthrōpōi apolusai tēn gunaika autou kata pasan
aitian.*

3 And Pharisees came up to him testing him and asking,
"Is it lawful to divorce one's wife for any cause?"

The inclusion in the Pharisees' question of the phrase
"for any cause" (*kata pasan aitian*)—not attested in the
Marcan passage—is the subject of considerable discussion,
inasmuch as extrabiblical writings of the time show that it
had a role in a dispute waged between two schools of rabbinic interpretation, those of the first century B.C. rabbis
Shammai and Hillel, whose competing views on divorce
concerned the exegesis of Deuteronomy 24:1.[15] The Hillel school championed the view that not only proven
unseemly conduct on the wife's part but any defect in her
husband's eyes sufficed for divorce, whence the catchphrase
"for any cause" served as a kind of shorthand reference to
allegiance to the Hillelite school in this matter.[16] Thus it is
possible, as many scholars believe, that the Pharisees were
not simply asking Jesus' opinion of divorce tout court but
trying to see where he stands on the Shammai-Hillel controversy. That said, as striking as the verbal resonances of
kata pasan aitian are, and without denying the currency and

[15] An exceptionally lucid account of the controversy is given by Instone-
Brewer in *Divorce and Remarriage*, especially pp. 110–19.

[16] Apposite expressions in Hellenistic Jewish authors bolster this claim, e.g.,
Philo Judaeus, *De specialibus legibus* 3.30: "if the wife has left her husband for any
motive whatever ..." (*apallageisa gunē kath'hēn an tuchēi prophasin*); Flavius Josephus, *Antiquitates Judaicae* 4.253: "should his wife be living with him, the one
wishing to divorce her for any reason whatever ..." (*boulomenos diazeuchthēnai
kath'hasdēpotoun aitias*); see also Instone-Brewer, *Divorce and Remarriage*, p. 115,
and Sigal, *Halakah of Jesus*, p. 132.

pertinence of the dispute in the Judaism of Jesus' day, I am not convinced that the Pharisees' question gains intelligibility by relating it to the Shammai-Hillel dispute. Jesus' teaching on divorce, in these terms, was considerably more rigorous than the "rigorist" alternative held by the Shammaites, and it makes little sense to imagine that the Pharisees, if they were indeed out to entrap Jesus, would set the bait by asking if any reason were as good as another for a man to put away his wife. Any plausible doubts, after all, would concern the possibility that the doctrine of Jesus might be reconciled with the school of Shammai, which forbade divorce in all but a few circumstances. Thus the question as put in Matthew 19:3 is best understood as an alternative expression of that of Mark 10:2: Is there any cause that can be found for which divorce is permitted?[17]

4 *Ho de apokritheis eipen, ouk anegnōte hoti ho ktisas ap'archēs arsen kai thēlu epoiēsen autous?* [5]*kai eipen, heneka toutou kataleipsei anthrōpos ton patera kai ton mētera kai kollēthēsetai tēi gunaiki autou, kai esontai hoi duo eis sarka mia.* [6]*Hōste ouketi eisin duo alla sarx mia. ho oun theos sunezeuxen anthrōpos mē chōrizetō.*

4 He [Jesus] answered, "Have you not read that he who created them from the beginning male and female made them? [5]and said, 'Because of this a man shall leave his father and mother and be joined to his woman, and the two shall become one flesh.' [6]So they are no longer two

---

[17]While I would agree with Fitzmyer ("Matthean Divorce Texts", p. 223f) that "the Qumran evidence [viz., that some Essene Jews forbade divorce] supplies at least an intelligible matrix for the question posed in Mark", for the reasons given above I believe the vindication to be unnecessary.

but one flesh. What therefore God has joined, let man not separate."

In Matthew the reference to Pentateuchal permission for divorce is not elicited from the Pharisees by Jesus, as in Mark, but it is raised as an objection by the Pharisees after Jesus has given his pronouncement. But the passage in which Genesis 1:27 and 2:24 are cited is almost identical, as is the final commandment, and it is the implicit contrast between the life giving union belonging to God and the base and selfish individual motives for quashing this union that moves the dispute forward.

> 7 *Legousin autōi, ti oun Mōusēs eneteilato dounai biblion apostasiou kai apolusai autēn?* [8]*Legei autois hoti Mōusēs pros tēn sklērokardian humōn epetrepsen humin apolusai tas gunaikas humōn, ap'archēs de ou gegonen houtōs.* [9]*Legō de humin hoti hos an apolusēi tēn gunaika autou mē epi porneia kai gamēsēi allēn moichatai.*

7 They said to him [Jesus], "Why then did Moses command one to give a bill of divorcement, and to divorce her?" [8]He said to them, "Moses for your hardness of heart allowed you to divorce your women, but from the beginning it was not so. [9]But I say to you: whoever divorces his woman, except for wantonness, and marries another commits adultery."

It is noteworthy that the Pharisees bring up the bill of divorcement mentioned in Deuteronomy (24:1, 3) as a theological objection to the biblical teaching of Jesus ("*why then* did Moses command?") that would appear to ask for a theological answer: a reconciliation of scriptural teachings that at first glance point to contrary conclusions. The Pharisees' question may reflect sincere puzzlement on their part, but even if we take it as captious, it is clear that the focus of the conversation is no longer the theoretical preconditions for divorce but the connection of marriage to godliness and the problem of reconciling divorce with God's will.

As with the Gospel of Mark (10:3, 5), the referential scope of "you" and "your" in Jesus' response is ambiguous, yet here too it points to Jesus' disassociation of himself from the community in which the concession has force. In teaching "from the beginning it was not so", Jesus implicitly claims moral continuity with the prelapsarian order of creation, and God's superintendency over it, which provides the authoritative basis for his conclusion: "whoever divorces his woman, except for wantonness, and marries another commits adultery." (The phrase "except for wantonness" will be discussed together with Matthew 5:32 below.) The chief point to be noted is Jesus' theological explanation of the Mosaic provision; it is an accommodation to human *sklērokardia*, and, like God's decision to shorten man's lifespan to 120 years in order to limit the growth of his wickedness (see Gen 6:3), it does not augment human godliness but, in view of the persistence of human evil, merely sets constraints on the scope of that evil. In rejecting this accommodation, Jesus is negating the divine judgment on the persistence of human wickedness on which it was based—a claim that is only intelligible if Jesus had knowledge of a change in the potentialities of personal choice—if, that is, Jesus was aware of a radically new order of grace in virtue of which the life of man and woman "as it was from the beginning" had once more become a possibility.

Matthew 5:31–32

This passage on divorce and remarriage occurs as one of the antitheses proclaimed in the Sermon on the Mount, and it partakes of the formula "you have heard it said" (followed by a concise restatement of a provision of the Torah) and then "but I say to you" (followed by the teaching of Jesus).

> 31 Errēthē de Hos an apolusēi tēn gunaika autou, dotō autēi apostasion. 32Egō de legō humin hoti pas ho apolu-ōn tēn gunaika autou parektos logou porneias poiei autēn moicheuthōnai, kai hos ean apolelumenēn gamēsēi moichatai.

> 31 It was also said, "Whoever divorces his woman, let him give her a divorce certificate." 32But I [Jesus] say to you that every one who divorces his woman, except on the ground of wantonness, makes an adulteress of her; and whoever marries a divorced woman commits adultery.

The sermon (Mt 5–7) presents Jesus as a new Moses or, better, a Moses to end Moses, for he is not merely a trans-mitter of the law but a lawgiver in his own right—not standing in obedient alertness on Sinai but seated on the mountain and declaiming his commandments in the first person, saying, "Do not think that I have come to abolish the law and the prophets; I have come not to abolish them but to fulfil them.... I say to you" (5:17–18; RSV-2CE), announcing paradoxically that the Mosaic laws still have force, but that their force henceforth resides in his per-son, that their original function—namely, of connecting God's chosen people to the God who did the choosing—has been accomplished and replaced by his own activity.

In the Sermon on the Mount Jesus acts as a kind of antirabbi or rabbi in reverse.[18] His citations of the old law come from common parlance rather than memorized texts. He quotes no authorities on the controversies, offers no casuistry, and proposes no fines or penalties for non-compliance. In some sense the sermon is a de-Judaization of the law, but this view is incomplete. Jesus moves the focus of the law from a Jewish context to one of universal application, from a legal to a moral and spiritual framework, from a place of external action and verifiability to a place of interior deliberation, motive, and choice, whereof only God can judge with certainty. It may be called not only pre-Abrahamic but antediluvian, in that not only the circumcised but all men are arraigned under the same judgment—but this misses out on Jesus' teaching that discipleship creates a new commonwealth ("the salt of the earth ... the light of the world" [5:13–14]) with potentials unknown to the old dispensation. Jesus' authority locates itself in the aboriginal godliness of creation but is counternostalgic, pointing forward to new (and almost always more serious) possibilities.

Thus verse 31 begins with the abbreviated formula *errēthē* (aorist passive), "it was said". The divorce passage at Deuteronomy 24:1–4 is a plausible antecedent of the dictum

---

[18] This is not to deny but to affirm the situating of Jesus' teaching within the rabbinic/halakhic controversies of first-century Judaism, as expounded with painstaking precision by Sigal in *Halakah of Jesus*, especially pp. 61–140. I contend, however, that the more closely these rabbinic disputes are scrutinized, the more striking are Jesus' departures therefrom, not merely in legal-forensic language and protocol, but in his move to a vastly larger moral and intellectual world of discourse in which the predicament and ultimate fate of every individual person is considered with a seriousness the rabbinic literature scarcely ever approaches and never equals.

that follows, but it is not a direct scriptural quotation and may be a shorthand version of common legal doctrine refracted through ordinary speech. Matthew 5:32 begins with the adversative construction *egō de legō*, emphasizing the departure of the saying that follows from the statement preceding: "every one who divorces his woman ... makes an adulteress of her." The legal formula *pas ho apoluōn* echoes the Pentateuchal stereotype, but the conclusion is unexpected, almost certainly shocking to its hearers.

A word on the meaning of *poiei autēn moicheuthēnai*. The conventional rendering—"causes her to commit adultery"[19]—misses, I believe, the true force of the saying, imputing to the partner acted upon a sin of which she is in no way the agent. The syntax of the verb itself presents vexing problems,[20] but these problems can and, I contend, ought to be obviated. The reasons for this will require an excursus into the semantics of the Semitic verbal system.

---

[19] Translation according to the New American Bible, Revised Edition (1983), and the King James Bible (1611). The *Lutherbibel* (1545) reads "*dass sie die Ehe bricht*"; the *Reina-Valera Actualizada* (1983), "*hace que ella cometa adulterio*."

[20] The Greek verb *moixeuō/moixaō* (active voice) was used in the LXX with the meaning "commit adultery", and it coexisted with the middle voice form *moicheuomai* with the same meaning. Usually the active and middle forms were used of men as subjects, though in three instances women are used as the subject of the active voice (Hos 4:13,14; Jer 3:9) and once as the subject of the middle voice (Jer 3:8). Elsewhere in the LXX the woman (as one committing adultery) is the subject of the passive voice form. In the New Testament men are used as the subjects of the active and middle voice. In one instance (Mk 10:12) the woman is the subject of the middle voice form and elsewhere only of the passive. Limiting ourselves to the New Testament Greek usage, the most natural translation of *poiei autēn moicheuthēnai*—the infinitive is aorist passive— would be the conventional "he makes her commit adultery". By putting more weight on the active and middle attestations with female subjects, one might stretch the range of the passive infinitive to find a gentler nuance (cf. the RSV-2CE: "[he] makes her an adulteress").

The original words of the dictum given by Matthew were almost certainly Aramaic. In Semitic languages, the basic stem (*Grundstamm*) of a verbal root coexists with morphologically altered stems (conventionally but misleadingly called conjugations), including transitivizing stems (in Aramaic the *pael* and *haphel/šaphel*, in Hebrew the *piel* and *hiphil*).[21] Thus, to take a Hebrew example, "he forgot" is expressed by the basic stem *nāšāh*, whereas "he made me forget" is expressed by the transitivizing stem *niššeh*. In Greek translation, such transitivizing verbs are often rendered by a form of *poiein*, "to make", plus a complementary infinitive or verbal noun lexically correspondent to the Semitic verb. So, for example, the Septuagint (LXX) of Genesis 41:51, "God made me forget", is *epilathesthai me ho theos epoiēsen*.

But the semantics are not always so simple. The same transitivizing stems sometimes produce meanings that are not straightforwardly factitive or causal, but estimative, declarative, or ostensive. For example, the Hebrew *rāšaʿ* means "he was wicked", but the corresponding *hiphil* stem *hiršîaʿ* means not "he made (someone) wicked" but "he condemned, he declared guilty" (see 1 Kings 8:32). When the expression *poiei autēn moicheuthēnai* is examined with Semitic verbal semantics in view, and against the larger background of Synoptic teaching on adultery and divorce, the most plausible explanation in the Aramaic original was a transitivizing verb (*pael* or *haphel*) with an ostensive force, for example, "he turns her into (the equivalent of) an adulteress, he makes her subject to

---

[21] See, e.g., Gustaf Dalman, *Grammatik des jüdisch-palästinischen Aramäisch* (Leipzig: J. C. Hinrichs'sche Buchhandlung, 1905), pp. 250–51.

the stigma of adultery."[22] My surmise is that the use of *poiei* plus the infinitive in the Matthew passage represents a token translation in which the ostensive meaning was, via the Greek, forfeited to the causative.

How does a man by divorcing his wife make her an adulteress? Not by forcing her into sexual congress with other men. The point is that she cannot marry—at least not in righteousness—inasmuch as and as long as the man who has known her carnally as her true husband is still alive. Thus she bears the taint and the disqualifications of the adulteress in virtue of a decision made not by her but by her husband, and it is this injustice that Jesus condemns. Note that Jesus is not inveighing against Judaic restrictions against divorcées; nowhere does he suggest that a more equitable or godly dispensation would permit a divorcée to remarry. The weight of the opprobrium falls on the man who makes his wife subject to such hardship.

The Diriment Exceptives: Matthew 5:32; 19:9

In his condemnation of divorce as a form of adultery, Jesus makes a qualification recorded twice in the Gospel of Matthew, at 19:9, *mē epi porneia*, "except for wantonness", and at 5:32, *parektos logou porneias*, "except on the ground of wantonness". The phrases have given rise to a great amount of commentary and numberless speculations, yet documentary material that has come to light in the last fifty years can eliminate some of these from consideration

---

[22] The rendering of the *Nouvelle Édition de Genève* (1979), "*l'expose à devenir adultère*", approximates this ostensive nuance.

and may guide us to more satisfactory, if still provisional, answers.

We are told that Jesus' condemnation, or the application of his condemnation, holds except in the case of *porneia*. This noun is derivative from the Greek *pornē*, "prostitute, harlot", and refers to the behavior associated with prostitutes: harlotry in its broadest sense as well as its narrowest.[23] The Latin *fornicatio*, derived from *fornix*, "prostitute", is a typologically exact rendering, but in Christian writing "fornication" has a quasi-technical meaning sharing minimal semantic overlap with *porneia*, whence its use in translations almost always brings more confusion than clarity.[24] In the Septuagint the term *porneia* renders the Hebrew nouns *zǝnût*, *zǝnûnîm*, and *taznût*, all derived from *zônāh*, "prostitute". Examples of its application include commercial prostitution in a strict sense (Gen 38:24), wanton female promiscuity (Ezek 16:5), intemperate male lust (Tob 8:7), and very often figurative infidelity in the form of idolatry or apostasy (i.e., Num 14:33; 2 Kings 9:22). Although it is not easy to decide in some instances, the thrust of the revilement with which faithless Israel or Israelites are charged with *porneia* points not so much to the fault of calculating acquisitiveness, but rather

---

[23] The translation of *pornē* by "prostitute" and *porneia* by "prostitution" is lexically correct but overly restricts the meaning to the arena of sex for pay and imparts a somewhat genteel tone false to the actual usage. For *porneia*, "harlotry" is closer to the semantic range but too antique; the same is true of "whoredom". My own choice of "wantonness" was guided by its etymology (= ungoverned, unruly) and by its common application to a broad spectrum of sexual misbehaviors. No English equivalent is wholly satisfactory.

[24] See Bruce J. Malina, "Does *Porneia* Mean Fornication?" *Novum Testamentum* 14 (1972): 10–17, and especially p. 17, where he gives the definition of "fornication" as "pre-betrothal, pre-marital, heterosexual intercourse of a non-cultic or non-commercial nature".

to susceptibility to sensual enticements, a warm-blooded rather than a cold-blooded shamelessness.

The meanings of *porneia* in its New Testament occurrences are harder to pin down, inasmuch as it most often appears within a list of vices with little or no contextual specificity.[25] Setting aside the Matthaean exceptives, the clearest example is that of 1 Corinthians 5:1, where *porneia* is used unambiguously of an incestuous marriage (*hōste gunaika tina tou patros echein*). With somewhat less confidence we might find in the aphorism of 1 Corinthians 6:13, "the body is not for *porneia* but for the Lord, and the Lord for the body", the more general meaning of lust or inordinate sexual indulgence, and the same possibly holds for 1 Corinthians 6:18: "Flee *porneia*. Every sin that a man commits is outside the body, but he who commits *porneia* (*ho de porneuōn*) sins against his own body."[26]

The use of the word *porneia* in Acts (15:20, 29; 21:25) is of particular interest. The Christian community under the superintendency of the apostles discussed whether or not gentile converts should be required to observe the ritual provisions of the Torah, and they determined that gentiles should be free therefrom, with the proviso that they

---

[25] Such listings are found at Mt 15:19; Mk 7:21; 2 Cor 12:21; Gal 5:19; Eph 5:3; Col 3:5 (see also 1 Cor 6:9 and Heb 13:4). I am bracketing the occurrences of *porneia* in Revelation, for the reason that they are part of a mystical-oracular discourse in which the vituperative force of the word takes precedence over, even where it does not obscure, the exact nature of the sin referred to. The figurative equation of female harlotry with infidelity (and ungodliness, generally) is here so tight as to make it difficult to judge when *porneia* is metaphorical and when not.

[26] The same sense, i.e., unregulated lust or promiscuity of any sort, may be to the fore in 1 Cor 7:2 and 1 Thess 4:3–5, but the gentile background of both cases makes it also possible that the *porneia* contraposed to godly and honest marriage refers to pagan practices of concubinage or marriage within close degrees of kinship.

"keep apart (*apechesthai*) from what has been sacrificed to idols and from blood and from what has been strangled and from *porneia*". Fitzmyer argued that this instruction

> forbids, in fact, four of the things proscribed by the Holi-
> ness Code of Lv 17–18, not only for "any man of the
> house of Israel" but also for "the strangers that sojourn
> among them" (*ûmin haggêr 'áser yâgûr bĕtôkâm*, 17:8). These
> were the meat offered to idols (Lv 17:8–9), the eating
> of blood (Lv 17:10–12), the eating of strangled, i.e., not
> properly butchered, animals (Lv 17:15; cf. Ex 22:31), and
> intercourse with close kin (Lv 18:6–18).[27]

It is especially noteworthy that even within the so-called Holiness Code, often viewed as a manifesto of tribal distinctiveness signposted by ritual taboos, these provisions are incumbent not only on the circumcised Jews bound to the Sinai covenant but also on the gentile guest workers in their midst, which suggests that the earliest Christian community required their observance by gentile converts because they were viewed as belonging to a precovenantal, that is to say, universal, understanding of righteousness.

The equation of *porneia* with incest (or marriage within near kinship) might appear somewhat adventitiously applied to Acts but for extrabiblical evidence that Jews of the time condemned incest under the title of *zənût*, for which *porneia* was the Greek calque translation. The so-called Damascus Document,[28] produced by sectarian

---

[27] Fitzmyer, "Matthean Divorce Texts", p. 209.

[28] This document is partially extant in two scrolls discovered in the Cairo Geniza and dating from the tenth and twelfth centuries A.D. Small fragments of the same text were later found at Qumran, thus aggregating the composition to those of the Essene community. See John Kampden, "The Matthean Divorce

rabbis of the Essene community, includes an admonitory harangue addressed to Jews of lax or doubtful allegiance, whom it warns of three "nets of Belial" (*mṣwdwt blyʿl*), that is, demonic snares, by which wickedness is made to appear as righteousness. Mentioned first (before riches and profanation of the sanctuary) is *zənût*, which is expounded so as to include polygamy (or divorce and polygamy) as well as incest: "And each man takes to wife (*lwqḥym ʾyš*) his brother's daughter and his sister's daughter."[29] This specification of *zənût* in a religious document of Palestinian Judaism considerably strengthens the reading of *porneia* in Acts as applied to incestuous marriages, since it dovetails not only with Paul's concern expressed in 1 Corinthians 5:1 but with what we are told of the disciples' anxieties in respect of the lives of gentile converts.

This reading of *porneia* as a calque translation of *zənût* has permitted commentators to make sense of the Matthaean exceptive clauses. As argued above, Jesus' teaching on the Torah regularly moves the common dispute from the legal to the theological sphere, such that the pertinent choice is viewed in its universal moral and spiritual dimensions. Sent first to the "lost sheep of the house of Israel" (Mt 15:24), Jesus the lawgiver responded to Jewish questions with pronouncements equally applicable to gentiles.[30] In the case of gentiles already living in incestuous unions, who were

Texts Reexamined", in *New Qumran Texts and Studies: Proceedings of the First International Organization for Qumran Studies, Paris 1992*, ed. George J. Brooke (Leiden: Brill, 1994), especially pp. 154–61.

[29] Chaim Rabin, *The Zadokite Documents: I. The Admontions II. The Laws* (Oxford: Clarendon, 1954), pp. 17, 19.

[30] In "Matthean Divorce Texts", Fitzmyer takes *zənut/porneia* in the exceptive phrases to mean "incest" but believes it was not a genuine saying of Jesus but added by the evangelist in order to take account of changing social realities

prepared to do what was necessary to repent and live in righteousness, how were they (or the Jews among whom they lived) to understand Jesus' condemnation of putting away one's wife or husband? In keeping with Jesus' nuptial understanding of Genesis 2:24, the prohibition applied *parektos logou porneias*: except in the case of incest—except, that is, in those instances in which the prohibition *could not apply*, because there was from the outset no true marriage to dissolve, no true wife or husband to send away. For this reason the Matthaean qualifications may be termed diriment exceptives, inasmuch as they are not strictly speaking exceptions to a rule, but conditions under which the rule is logically otiose. The same holds true if the referent of *zƏnût* is broadened to include polygamy: one cannot divorce the second, third, and so forth spouse because, as long as the first is living, there is no marriage to dissolve.

Conclusions

Reacting to Jesus' pronouncement that remarriage after divorce is adultery, his disciples said to him, "If such is the case of a man with his wife, it is better not to marry" (Mt 19:10). From the first moment of its declaration, the teaching Jesus propounded as the will of God was deeply

---

not envisioned in the original statement: "Matthew ... would be making an exception for such marital situations for Gentile Christians who were living in a mixed community with Jewish Christians still observing Mosaic regulations" (p. 221). I am less confident that Jesus had no awareness of gentiles and no capacity to envision their difficulties. His encounters with the centurion and the Syro-Phoenician woman—who seek him out as a holy man—as well as his journeys in the Decapolis, point at minimum to exposure to gentile concerns.

distressing, even to men of good will. Subsequent centuries have shown no slackening in the energy and ingenuity devoted to weakening or nullifying the force of this teaching, and as long as it is expedient to circumvent the doctrine, there will be attempts to explain away its scriptural anchoring. But the doctrine is given as absolute in Matthew, Mark, and Luke, and even Paul goes out of his way to insist that, as a messenger of the teaching and not its author, he is not to blame for its rigor: "To the married I give charge, not I but the Lord" (1 Cor 7:10). There can be no serious doubt that the teaching is dominical.

Yet it is mistaken, or if not wholly mistaken seriously incomplete, to view Jesus as a disputant who championed the rigorist side of legal-moral controversy, and whose appeal was and is solely to the tough-minded. For he also promised a new and superabundant afflatus of grace, of divine help, so that no person however fragile should find it impossible to do God's will. John the Baptist was arrested and killed because Herod Antipas, after divorcing Phasaelis, the daughter of the Nabataean prince Aretas, went on to marry Herodias, ex-wife of his own brother Philip, whereupon John denounced the union as unlawful. Jesus said of John, "Truly, I say to you, among those born of women there has arisen no one greater than John the Baptist; yet he who is least in the kingdom of heaven is greater than he" (Mt 11:11). Under the old dispensation it may have required heroic moral and physical courage, as well as a love of godliness, to remain true in practice and conviction to God's creative will in the matter of nuptial fidelity—but under the new covenant, even *ho mikroteros*, the least in the Kingdom, will be given the strength to stay faithful, and to do greater things besides.

3

Divorce and Remarriage in the Early Church: Some Historical and Cultural Reflections

John M. Rist

> For the politically minded patriarchs, *oikonomia* was be-
> coming a form of realistic accommodation with the
> powers-that-be.
>
> —John Meyendorff

Introduction: Marriage in Contemporary Society

On February 20, 2014, Cardinal Kasper delivered an
address to the Extraordinary Consistory on the Family
in which he adduced evidence from the early Church in
the context of continuing debate about the remarriage of
divorced Catholics. Although in an interview on related
subjects in *Commonweal* magazine on May 14, 2014, discussing his book *Mercy: The Essence of the Gospel and the
Key to Christian Life*,[1] Kasper made no further reference to

[1] Walter Cardinal Kasper, *Mercy: The Essence of the Gospel and the Key to
Christian Life* (New York: Paulist Press, 2014).

those early years, his conclusions provide a suitable opportunity for a further review of the evidence for the beliefs of the early Church about Christ's teaching on marriage and divorce. For while no one would assert that we are in every particular bound by what was said by the Church Fathers—indeed we could not be since they disagree on some questions rather radically—Cardinal Kasper is right to assume that if we are to view Church teachings as developing coherently, rather than radically changing from one age to another, the evidence of the Fathers cannot simply be passed over.

It is easy to understand Kasper's concerns: among these, the "merciful" change he envisages would bring Catholic teaching on remarriage closer to that of the Orthodox Churches, thus making negotiations with them easier. But such "ecumenical" matters apart, there are more immediately pressing problems that Kasper hopes a change might help to relieve. Thus, in the interview with *Commonweal* he cites a remark of Pope Francis that some 50 percent of Catholic marriages are probably not valid, being undertaken by those Kasper calls "baptized pagans". The figure itself seems not implausible, since marriages now are contracted in a very different world from that of even the recent past.

As I survey the scene that young people are now confronting, I recognize that we live much longer (nostalgia for a lost youth at the male menopause is obviated if one dies at thirty-five)—and in the impersonality of large urban communities where the high costs of education and other economic pressures force women to work full-time during their childbearing years; and amid the individualism, sex idolatry, and consumerism of Western, and increasingly non-Western, societies; and where now the cyber revolution means parents can hardly prevent their children getting into "chat rooms" and texting (and "sexting") one another about their experiences there and elsewhere. All this puts increasing strain on family life and promotes an inevitable increase in marriage breakdown, not least among Catholics who have little understanding of Catholic marriage in the first place.

Such observations suggest that before we consider any reform or rewriting of Catholic teaching we should make very serious attempts to dispel the widespread ignorance of its character among those about to be married in the Catholic Church. Yet as presently dispensed the level of instruction may vary from the bureaucratic minimum to the patronizing and uninformative—uninformative in that the young couple learn little of how difficult Catholic marriage has now become, and how and why their loyalty to their marriage vows is likely to be sorely tested. And it will be "tested" the more either if the couple are ignorant of what Catholic marriage is and must be, or if those instructing them have little real idea of the perils of the non-Catholic (and increasingly too the "Catholic") world into which the intended marriage is about to be launched.

The Catholic doctrines of marriage grew up in the distant past and are ever developing, and it is not always safe to assimilate distant times to our own. In asking ourselves how we are to present Christ's teaching to the present age, we need to understand these new difficulties which confront our contemporaries—especially our Western contemporaries—when they attempt to face them while accepting the realities of Church doctrine. No one in touch with this age can deny that "commitment", whether to marriage or to anything else, has become peculiarly challenging in a way that is not to be recognized in earlier, let alone, patristic times. So before embarking on an investigation of the past, we need to ask some preliminary questions about human nature that may help us understand why demands to modify Church teaching about the indissolubility of marriage seem to have become more pressing.

An Example of Cultural Change

By way of recognizing the complexity of the situation, let us pause to reflect on a surprising feature of the contemporary social scene that encourages couples to abandon their marriage vows (and priests and religious their vows for a celibate life, the so-called late bloomers). This derives from a radical and increasingly popular change in beliefs about human nature, reinforced by contemporary academic thinkers and journalistic publicists. The change I refer to involves that many hardly believe themselves to be the same person from conception to death—that even though they may have a persisting name, and certainly a unique DNA, they are subject to such ongoing and psychologically radical variations as they proceed through life as to be what the philosophers who follow Hume would denote sequential selves.[2] In his retrospective autobiography Newman famously remarked, "Pass a number of years, and I find my mind in a new place";[3] many of our

[2] For an introduction to the philosophical problems in question see Derek Parfit, *Reasons and Persons* (Oxford: Oxford University Press, 1986), and Thomas Nagel, *The View from Nowhere* (Oxford: Oxford University Press, 1986). I shall examine some of the consequences of such Humean and similar projects, all dissolving the "self", in *Augustine Deformed* (Cambridge: Cambridge University Press, forthcoming).

[3] John Henry Newman, *Apologia pro vita sua*, ed. M.J. Svaglic (Oxford: Clarendon, 1967), p. 155.

contemporaries in effect gloss this as "pass a number of years, and I find that I am not the same person as I was."

Such questions about personal identity are, to my mind, the most serious theoretical issues being debated in the contemporary philosophical world, though Catholic thinkers take little part in the debate, typically concerning themselves more with the finer points of Catholic disputes in the past than with bringing the wisdom of the past, insofar as it can stand on its own feet, into direct confrontation with the radically antipersonalist and anti-Christian claims of present intellectual (and soon run-of-the mill) society. But if we are serial selves, gradually remaking ourselves like a ship whose parts are all replaced one by one but which in name and registration still remains the same ship, then it makes sense to say that I am not the same person as I was when I married, and my wife is not the same person either, so why should we continue, if we do not want to, in what is after all a fictional relationship? Arguments or assumptions of this sort, whether valid or not, will destroy responsibility for most, if not all, of our past actions—not only for the intelligibility of marriage vows or other promises. But for the moment we need only think about the problems of marriage.

The Original Teaching on Christian Marriage in Context

With such caveats in mind we can turn to the history. The early Christian Church grew up from its Jewish roots in a pagan world. In that world, as among the Jews, the purpose of marriage was the generation of legitimate children to replace their parents in society and eventually inherit their property. Among both Jews and pagans divorce was available—always for men, sometimes for women. Adultery by the wife, who thus might introduce the children of strangers as heirs to the family estate, was far more serious than adultery by the husband; and by a rule often retained by Christians, a husband was normally obliged to divorce his wife if she were caught in an adulterous act; Jeremiah (3:1) points to the impurity incurred if he does *not*. In such circumstances remarriage for the husband would be expected, and there were other grounds for divorce and remarriage, too—not least infertility, misunderstood as always a failure of the wife, since it frustrated the purpose of the original marriage contract. Jews in particular were expected to marry and be blessed with children, in accordance with God's commandments handed down in the Hebrew Bible—though in the first century A.D. Philo and Josephus indicate that at least briefly certain groups among them disagreed, perhaps believing that the end times were at hand.

When Christ was questioned about marriage he was asked to pronounce on the fact that Moses allowed divorce; he replied that it had been permitted because of the hardness of their hearts (see Mk 10:2–5). But for Christians the *original* command of God about marriage was to be obeyed (see Mk 10:10–12; Mt 19: 4–9; Lk 16:18; cf. Lk 5:31–32); it was to be a lifetime commitment, and although Matthew indicates the possibility of *separation* for *porneia*—presumably to be translated as the wife's playing the whore—there is no suggestion in the Gospels that even in that case was remarriage permitted during the other spouse's lifetime. On that we may also compare Paul at Romans 7:2–3, where the stricter Christian position rejects the rule for the remarriage of women of Deuteronomy 24, and again at 1 Corinthians 7:8–11, where Paul specifically cites the command of the Lord. Indeed, the rules against wifely adultery are to be applied in equal measure and strictness also to the husband—a radical change obviously related to Paul's insistence, again against Jewish custom (1 Cor 7:2–4), that each partner has identical rights over the body of the other, all this making a radical transformation of traditional marital practices that Christian males often found difficult to accept.

But Jesus also encouraged some—those who could receive this teaching—to be as "eunuchs for the sake of the kingdom" (Mt 19:12), for in heaven we shall be like the angels who "neither marry nor are given in marriage"— however that be interpreted (Mt 22:30; Mk 12:25; Lk 20:35–36). And perhaps in line with the ascetic ideas alluded to in Philo and Josephus, he lamented the fate of the married in the desperate last days (Mt 24:19; Mk 13:17; Lk 21:23) prefigured in the sack of Jerusalem in A.D. 70. In brief, then, ideally there are to be two kinds of Christians: those married once and those not married at all—hence a coming problem as to whether marriage in any form was a second-best option; and that brings us back to the purpose of marriage, and that it might seem no longer necessary now that the Messiah has come. Yet, as Paul is concerned to repeat (2 Thess 2:1–3), though the end might be near, no one knew how near—which meant that preserving the family and its property *must* remain a serious concern until further notice. What is more, as he told the Corinthians (1 Cor 7:8–11), it is better both for the unmarried and for the widowed to marry than to burn (whether with carnal lust or in hell—which might amount to the same thing in the longer term).

Avoiding some kind of burning hardly constitutes a ringing endorsement of the married state (though it was later explained as helping character formation), but in texts that the ancients regarded as unquestionably Pauline (Eph 5:22–26, 33; 1 Tim 2:11–13, 15; Col 3:18–19), Paul assumes that most Christians will be married with families, and he gives directions as to how, within such families, one can live a Christian life. Yet, as with the teaching of Jesus himself, one can again recognize the possibility of easy conflict about Christian living and more specifically about Christian perfection. Is it not the case that a spiritual athleticism of celibacy and preferably virginity distinguishes the practice of the "real" Christian? Should such asceticism be the goal of all?

In light of prevailing customs both among the Jews and in the Greco-Roman world more widely, such debate must have seemed largely unintelligible outside Christian circles (though a few eccentric and celibate philosophers—such as Plato and Plotinus—might have understood it), and Christian ideals look the more radical if we remember that it was assumed in society at large, indeed legally recognized, that since the master of a "family" owned the bodies of his slaves, he could use them, whether male or female, for sexual gratification as he (or less respectably she) saw fit. So Christians stood out then, as often later, for a strictness in sexual matters of which they boasted— even when they failed to live up to their own ideals— and which those around them often found bizarre, even, among males, unmanly.

Celibacy entails abstinence from genital acts, and insofar as such abstinence was often held laudable by Christians, it was inevitable that—apart from Paul's strictures about burning—the use of sexuality would become problematic even within the marriage bond. And the demand that it be used comparatively minimally affected the question of divorce and possible remarriage: How were Christ's ascetic words to be applied within a marriage, and how would a correct understanding of them affect a possible rigorism about divorce and a hostility to Jewish and pagan options of remarriage following divorce?

And then there is the question of civil law, which Christians had to accept and against which, except when it affected freedom of religion, they never protested—for we should remember that in early centuries there was, *legally*, no specifically Christian form of marriage. Getting too close to the pagan law codes, however, might encourage the introduction of pagan practices into primitive Christian attitudes to marriage through the back door[4]—a similar fear to that driving the expected nonappearance of the clergy at the raunchier and more erotic secular festivities that followed the completion of the legal (and when possible Christian) niceties of weddings.[5] Indeed, the legal problem, rather than that of mere prudery, became more rather than less serious when the law itself became gradually more Christian, especially in the Greek-speaking half of the empire, where the threat of caesaropapism and (not

[4] It was not till the publication of Justinian's Code (565) that legal (and of course un-Christian) acceptance of divorce by consent was outlawed.

[5] See Peter Brown, *The Body and Society: Men, Women, and Sexual Renunciation in Early Christianity* (New York: Columbia University Press, 1988), p. 313, on Christian Antioch in the fourth century.

least) of monarchical lust was the more palpable in the ongoing Byzantine world, as in the later Tudor period in England.

Among certain pagan groups, as well as for Jews like Philo who were influenced by Stoic or neo-Pythagorean ideas, genital activity, even among married couples, was reserved for the purposes of marriage, as traditionally defined, and, as we have noted, the primary such purpose was the begetting of legitimate children or, as the Greeks were more likely to put it, "of children for the city". For marriage was viewed as much the business of the family or of the society more widely as of the individual—after all with no children there would be no citizens and no soldiers—though Roman law codes always emphasized, often without being able to enforce it, that "not lying together but consent makes a marriage"; that is why slaves cannot marry, since they cannot give free consent. As for the individual, if male, he could console himself with courtesans or prostitutes (male or female), or slaves, and at least the latter option, as we have seen, might be available, though more disreputably, at least for widows.

Christian opinion on the purposes of marriage became more nuanced, though civil law had to be obeyed, and gradually means were discovered to harmonize Christian sensibilities with legal realities. In the earliest days of the new religion, of course, there was nothing like canon law in the modern sense, though it soon began to develop from accepted practices. That meant there would be Christian converts, the original form of whose marriage was entirely "pagan", and other cradle Christians who wanted to establish (and over time did begin to establish) practices whereby their marital union was not only legal but "in

the Lord" rather than "from lust"; the idea is already present in the second-century bishop Ignatius of Antioch (*Ad
Polycarpum* 5.2), formally recognized, that is, and blessed
by the Christian community, normally in the person of
its bishop. And there would also be a large third group,
those whose marriage was legally accepted by the passage of time in what the Romans would call *usus*, a word
indicating something like a common-law marriage, and
perhaps the only type of union many could afford. These
too might require to be formally recognized within
the Christian group. We do not hear much about such
people in Christian communities, not least, presumably,
because their status must have seemed anomalous if not
marginal and potentially threatening to the civil order. In
Christian terms Augustine could have "married" his concubine, but his career—so dear to Monica—would probably have been over if he had done so. As for Christian
slaves, as we have noted, they could not be legally married
at all, until 1095 by Byzantine edict.

As we have noticed, the growth of Christian abstinence went hand in hand with a growing belief, among
more serious Christians, that the generation of legitimate
children was no longer mandated as it had once been—
and still remained—for the Jews; since the Messiah had
come, the command to be fruitful and multiply no longer
had the same urgency. That changed more than might
appear; Christians of a more rigorist stripe might talk not
just about the begetting of offspring as a consolation for
the endless cycle of births and death, as did, for example, Gregory of Nyssa in the fourth century, but physical love making could and should develop ever more
into a form of affective charity, what Augustine was

eventually to call the "affection of a respectful love" (*piae caritatis*)—a benevolent friendship between the spouses— though that part of the story should not be exaggerated or romanticized.

In the spirit of the love poetry of the Song of Songs, Paul had declared marriage (Eph 5:25–30) between a man and a woman a symbol of the relationship between Christ and his Bride, the Church, applying to it the term *mysterion* (Latin: *sacramentum*) and thus revealing what was later identified as a "sacramental character" that, especially in the West, radically distinguished it from its pagan counterparts and added significantly substantial weight to objections to the normal Jewish and Roman practice of divorce. As we have seen, an important reason for divorce among non-Christians—namely, the inability of the original couple to have legitimate children—could hardly provide any similarly compelling counterweight in Christian circles, at least officially.

Jesus' teaching that marriage is indissoluble in that it cannot be repeated (certainly, that is, during the continuing life of an earlier spouse) is reemphasized by Paul (1 Cor 7:10–11, 39; Rom 7:2–3), though the imprecision of some of his letters—letters indeed, not tracts—might suggest a less strict application to men than to women, that is, if his insistence on the equal physical rights of both partners is neglected. The reasons for that less strict application are not difficult to discern, and we can find evidence of its problematic effects in various influential writers, including most significantly Basil. One of the reasons for the less strict application, a particular concern of the male-dominated societies of the ancient world, as we have noted, is that women, if unchaste or even allowed to remarry, may complicate or even disrupt the customary processes concerning the inheritance of property.

Interestingly, however, Paul says nothing very specific about the appropriate reasons for genital activity—whether only for procreation or otherwise—within the marriage, though, of course, those married would generally be assumed to hope to procreate. Nevertheless, at least by implication, he partially fills the gap: if marriage is to avoid "burning", we need not conclude that in every marriage act he assumes there should be a conscious attempt to generate children. The matter is alluded to more euphemistically by John Chrysostom, who says that the purposes of marriage are *first* "to make us better"[6] (that is, by enabling us to control our physical lusts, which may be eventually superseded), then to beget children—in that order of priority for reasons we have already noticed.

Thus far we have identified two possibly "gray areas" in early Christian teaching: Although marriage is indissoluble, partners are allowed to separate—but are they ever to be allowed remarriage? And what is the role of genital activity, and when is it appropriate, within the marriage itself? Only the first of these is our immediate concern, but since questions of divorce cannot be separated from questions about the nature and purpose of marriage, it is necessary to recognize a more generally and often excessively critical attitude to sexual activity, even in marriage, among the Fathers than would be normal in our own secularized, or insufficiently thoughtful, Christian society. And the notion of indissolubility too might seem ambiguous: it was often held, especially but not only in the

[6]John Chrysostom, *Homily on the Writ of Divorce*, PG 51.221.

East, that not only death but the adultery of the wife dissolved the marriage,[7] while developing Western accounts
of the sacramentality of marriage further complicated
the problem of the nature of indissolubility itself, as we
shall see.

Sufficient for now, however, is to indicate that the
most effective and helpful discussion of problems about
the "use" of marriage in the ancient Church, indeed perhaps anywhere, is by Augustine, who points to at least
three serious problems that should give us pause in face of
the apotheosis of sex as currently practiced even in marriage: the tendency in fallen humanity—more open in
antiquity, more concealed (*occultior non melior*) in our own
world—to substitute the desire to dominate a partner,
especially but not only the female partner, for the mutual
exchange of a joyful surrender of self; the tendency to
turn the partner into a romantic idol "to enjoy her/him
as 'divine' in contempt of God", as Augustine would put
it; and the temptation to pursue pleasure for its own sake
rather than as an accompaniment of activity or as part of
a wider project (as Aristotle explains in book 10 of the
Nicomachean Ethics).[8]

[7] A perhaps not entirely anachronistic view of this is offered by Peter L'Huillier, "The Indissolubility of Marriage in Orthodox Law and Practice", *St.
Vladimir's Theological Quarterly* 3 (1988): 210: "One does not find in the Eastern Patristic tradition the idea that the marriage bond persists after divorce."
Perhaps not in the Western sense, but note, for example, John Chrysostom's
repeated comments (*On Repudiation* 3) that whatever the behavior of the husband, the wife is bound to him during his lifetime.

[8] For a good introduction to Augustine's great merits in the matter, which,
however, sometimes seems to stumble upon the carefulness of Augustine's
account rather than setting them out as I have sketched them here, see Cor-
mac Burke, "Saint Augustine: A View of Marriage and Sexuality in Today's
World", *Angelicum* 89 (2012): 377–403.

78

A Methodological Caution

Such preliminaries behind us, we can now turn to the more immediate question of the attitude of the Fathers to second marriages after divorce. But first a further note of caution: we cannot allow ourselves to be guided uncritically in this inquiry by practices later regularized in the Eastern churches, there regarded as in accordance with patristic behavior, for two reasons. First, as already indicated, Eastern Christianity came to accept a very different account of the nature of the indissolubility of the marriage bond (the *sacramentum*) from that of the West (which has largely followed Augustine),[9] but it claims in doing so not to have betrayed the original scriptural notion of indissolubility; secondly, and more basically, we must resist *all* attempts uncritically to read later practices back into the patristic age, whether by scholarly malpractice or for ideological reasons, the latter often deriving from a misguided notion of ecumenism pursued in disregard of historical truth. Obviously reflection on any reform of the Western position must start from what it is and why it is, not from what it might have been or become, or from what one might have wished it to have been or become.

First let us discuss indissolubility. Writers in the Orthodox tradition normally stress that the Church must teach that so long as it lasts, the marriage bond, as a sacrament, is indissoluble, but that indissolubility is not a legal but only a theological or spiritual bond, which in reality ceases to exist

[9] In later accounts of the seven sacraments, seemingly first formally recognized as such at the Second Council of Lyon (1274), although, unlike, for example, baptism, marriage does not impress a sacramental character on those committed to it, the permanence of the marital bond is always emphasized.

after adultery or similar sins.[10] The difficulty with that is
that the role of God in the sacrament seems to be neglected;
hence the bond can be snapped (despite the apparently clear
sense of the words of Jesus and Paul) by an appeal to the
principle of "economy", whereby for merciful reasons, or
to avoid worse sins, a second marriage can be permitted in
the lifetime of the earlier spouse. The liturgical celebration
of this now nonsacramental arrangement must, however,
be distinct, and more penitential, than that which sancti-
fied the original marriage, and those entering into such a
second marriage must do penance; over the centuries these
penances have varied in severity. It is clearly to this principle of economy that Cardinal Kasper and others refer in
hoping for a more "merciful" solution to the problem of
the divorced and remarried within the Catholic Church.[11]

---

[10] "Similar" sins might include homicide (perhaps of the children or spouse)
or apostasy, the latter understood in Old Testament terms as spiritual fornication. I take John Meyendorff as a characteristic and responsible advocate of the
Orthodox position; see his "Christian Marriage in Byzantium: The Canonical
and Liturgical Tradition", *Dumbarton Oaks Papers* 44 (1990): 99–107, especially
pp. 102–3, and more generally, *Marriage: An Orthodox Perspective* (Crestwood,
N.Y.: St. Vladimir's Seminary Press, 1978), p. 60. Note the clear statement in
"Christian Marriage", pp. 102–3: "The Byzantine Church, though proclaiming
and cherishing the principle of the indissolubility of marriage, as affirmed by
Jesus according to the Synoptics' accounts ... never understood indissolubility
to be a *legal* absolute. It condoned the famous exception found in Matthew ...
and recognized adultery as a legitimate cause of divorce, covering other situations, where the mystical union of husband and wife had, in reality, ceased to
exist, that is, situations practically equivalent to the death of one of the partners
(disappearance, insanity, violence). However, even in cases when divorce was
admitted, remarriage was, in principle, only tolerated and subject to penitential
conditions." Yet the Orthodox view of marriage was that it might continue
even after the death of the parties, and the extension of *porneia* to other situations might seem gratuitous.

[11] It should be noted that many prominent Orthodox have been worried
about such developments, not least Theodore of Stoudios, who protested the
divorce of Constantine VI from Mary the Paphlagonian (in 795) in favor of

Kasper is right to point out that Eastern practice about divorce and remarriage was not condemned at the Council of Trent. That Council, however, was primarily concerned with Protestantism, so there was no pressing reason to discuss Eastern attitudes. In any case, the Fathers of Trent believed that those attitudes—and consequent practices— had already been condemned in the Profession of Faith proposed to the apparently converted Byzantine emperor Michael VIII Palaeologus (who was seeking Western help against the Turks) and read out (but not ratified) at the Second Council of Lyon (1274).[12]

The legal as well as the spiritual bond of the Catholic sacrament of marriage would make Cardinal Kasper's revised Catholic position even stranger than that of the Orthodox. It might appear to a Catholic that in Orthodox theology, since the first marriage is somehow indissoluble

---

Theodote. According to Theodore "economy" could only be allowed to Constantine if he abandoned his adulterous union with his new "wife", that is, if action accompanied "repentance". See J. H. Erickson, "*Oikonomia* in Byzantine Canon Law", in *Law, Church and Society: Essays in Honor of Stephan Kuttner*, ed. Kenneth Pennington and Robert Somerville (Philadelphia: University of Pennsylvania Press, 1977), pp. 225–36. But decisive moves toward what Theodore disapproved had already been taken, first in the mid-sixth century when Basil's Letter 188 (= canon 9) was read as tolerating second marriages after divorce (it will be discussed below) and was accepted as part of the legal canon of the Byzantine Church. That was confirmed in a more explicit form by canon 87 of the Council in Trullo (691 or 692). See G. Nedungatt and J. M. Featherstone, eds., *The Council in Trullo Revisited* (Rome: Pontificio Istituto Orientale, 1995). Thus on the basis of the disputed texts of Basil, L'Huillier, "Indissolubility of Marriage", p. 204, concludes: "It is evident that in this case the Church tolerates remarriage", and Meyendorff, *Marriage*, p. 49, comments that "St. Basil the Great (+379), in his canon 4, defines that those who enter a second marriage after either widowhood or divorce must undergo penance", implying, in accordance with the Eastern tradition, that Basil accepted second marriages for the divorced whether their original partners were alive or not.

[12] See Denzinger-Hünermann, *Enchiridion Symbolorum*, 37th edition (Freiburg im Breisgau: Verlag Herder, 1991), no. 860.

but supposedly dissolved by evil actions of one or other of the partners—so that the second, if inferior version, can be accepted—divorced and remarried individuals are somehow involved in two distinct kinds of marriage at the same time, or at least they would be if God's role in the sacrament were taken into account. If a similar system were to be adopted in the West, the situation would be even stranger since the specific account of indissolubility and the role of God in the sacrament must compel a more demanding doctrine—for the indissolubility lasts till the physical, not just to the possibly more "spiritual", death of one of the spouses. (There may, however, be a problem as to why it should entirely end even then!)

It should be noted that some Eastern writers seem to avoid our dilemma by failing to mention indissolubility at all, or by implying that it hardly exists.[13] Be that as it may, the revision along "merciful" lines of the Catholic position would probably entail a much more far-reaching rewriting of the entire account of Catholic sacraments. Fortunately, as I shall argue, no such dilemma could have faced patristic theologians of the first five centuries, since

[13] Thus in L'Huillier's article, "Indissolubility of Marriage", there is little analysis of indissolubility, though it is implied in the title. The author remarks, however (p. 210), that "one does not find in the Eastern Patristic tradition the idea that the marriage bond persists after divorce", and (p. 207) that Augustine who offers the more "legal" account normally accepted in the West was probably unsure of his own position (which the author seems to suppose Augustine must have found defective for the same reasons as he does). Thus he writes (p. 207): "For the Bishop of Hippo, this characteristic (viz., the 'intangibility' of the marriage bond) derives from the *sacramentum*, that is, the irrevocable engagement pronounced by the spouses before God. Was Augustine convinced in his innermost thoughts of the solidity of these arguments? One cannot be entirely sure, for in his *Retractationes* he admits that the question is obscure and difficult." But that sort of self-indulgent psychologizing must be viewed with great suspicion.

for the overwhelming majority of them, as for the New Testament writers, second marriages (except, with some reservations, for widows and widowers) are forbidden during the lifetime of the original spouse. Among identifiable sources the only immediately obvious exception to that rule is Ambrosiaster.[14]

Early Christian Texts on Remarriage and Divorce

It is time to turn to the very limited number of texts that might be recognizable as debatable. In doing so, I do not intend to argue that the "merciful" solution is unknown in the ancient Church, but that virtually none of the writers who survive and whom we take to be authoritative defend it; indeed when they mention it, it is rather to condemn it as unscriptural. There is nothing surprising in that situation; abuses may exist occasionally, but their mere existence is no guarantee of their not being abuses, let alone being models to be followed. Nor can I claim much originality in what I shall argue in the following pages. Most of the texts relevant to the remarriage of those divorced or separated have been examined by substantial scholars,

---

[14]Ambrosiaster was a priest in late fourth-century Rome whose uniquely ultra-Pauline position—he thinks the Christian partner can remarry after the collapse of a "mixed" marriage—also includes denying that women are created in God's image (and on unusual grounds). For Ambrosiaster on sexual difference see David G. Hunter, "The Paradise of Patriarchy: Ambrosiaster on Women as (Not) Created in God's Image", *Journal of Theological Studies* 43 (1992): 447–69; for the wider problem of such (non-)creation see John M. Rist, *What is Truth? From the Academy to the Vatican* (Cambridge: Cambridge University Press, 2008), pp. 18–103. For Ambrosiaster on divorce see Henri Crouzel, S.J., *L'Eglise primitive face au divorce: Du premier au cinquième siècle* (Paris: Editions Beauchesne, 1971), pp. 269–74.

especially by the French Jesuit Henri Crouzel,[15] and it must be recognized, with regret, that those who have continued to maintain much of what Crouzel denied, especially Giovanni Cereti[16] (apparently Cardinal Kasper's principal informant), have failed to reply adequately to their arguments—or to reply, in many cases at all, to the objections of Crouzel and others, especially Gilles Pelland.[17] Indeed Cereti has groundlessly insinuated that Crouzel—conveniently now dead—had had second thoughts.[18]

Kasper cited no evidence in favor of his position from the first 150 years of Christianity, presumably aware both that the evidence is very limited and often unclear, and

[15] There is no need to rehearse earlier "literature", but for Crouzel see especially "Les digamoi visés par le Concile de Nicée dans son canon 8", *Augustinianum* 18 (1978): 533–46; "Un nouvel essai pour prouver l'acceptation des secondes noces après divorce dans l'Eglise primitive", *Augustinianum* 17 (1977): 555–66; and "Le remariage après séparation pour adultère chez les Pères latins", *Bulletin de Littérature Ecclésiastique* 75 (1974): 189–204. In the latter two articles Crouzel outlines a set of principles for the interpretation of ancient texts that he argues, successfully, have been ignored by his critics, especially by Cereti. See further (by the same author) "Divorce et remariage dans l'Eglise primitive: Quelques réflexions de méthodologie historique", *Nouvelle Revue Théologique* 98 (1976): 891–917.

[16] Primarily in *Divorzio, nuove nozze e penitenza nella Chiesa primitiva* (Bologna: Dehoniane, 1977; second edition, 1998; third edition, Rome: Aracne, 2013), reviewed by Crouzel in *La Civiltà Cattolica*, no. 3046 (May 1977): 304–5.

[17] In particular, see Gilles Pelland, S.J., "La pratica della Chiesa antica relativa ai fedeli divorziati risposati", in *Sulla pastorale dei divorziati*, ed. Congregation for the Doctrine of the Faith (Vatican City: Libreria Editrice Vaticana, 1998), pp. 99–131.

[18] In comments on Kasper's address published as "Il Vangelo della famiglia", *Il Regno* 15 (2014): 148–50, at p. 150, note 4, Cereti thanks Cardinal Kasper ("in conformity, I think, with the desire of the Pope") for singling out for praise his own work on remarriage for those divorced, indicating that in his view the key text in the debate is canon 8 of the Council of Nicea (to be discussed later). He graciously concludes that he hopes that his opponents will not become out and out Novatianists, deniers, that is, even of second marriages for the widowed, and more generally of the power of the Church "to absolve all sins"—thus outside ecclesial communion.

that in those early times a substantial number of the Fathers disliked and discouraged *any* form of remarriage, even for widows and widowers. Typical, as noted by Meyendorff,[19] is the designation by Athenagoras (late second century A.D.) of a woman divorced and remarried as an adulteress, with the further comment that "he who rids himself of his first wife, although she is dead, is an adulterer in a disguised manner" (*PG* 6.968). But, as Kasper notices, clearly different attitudes become visible in the better-recorded third century when Origen, in his *Commentary on Matthew* (14.23) informs us that certain bishops allowed a second marriage to women whose first husbands were still living. That decision, says Origen, is intelligible, but, he adds on three occasions, it is wholly contrary to the teaching of the Scriptures. So occasionally at that time remarriage after divorce was tolerated, but, however it might be defended by argument, it was understood by Origen to be opposed not only to the Bible itself but, presumably, also to traditional interpretations of the relevant texts—hardly a commendation from so biblical a theologian. In sum, there already existed in the third century what Origen stigmatized as abuses in the handling of Christian marriage by bishops, but as I have already observed, the present investigation is not about whether improper practice occasionally occurred but about what seriously learned theologians (and later Councils) thought of them.

Nevertheless, it is worth considering why the bishops acted as they did, and why Origen was prepared to say that their actions were not unreasonable—perhaps in that they make pagan but not Christian sense. It seems very likely

[19] Meyendorff, *Marriage*, p. 60.

that the cases the bishops had to deal with were of a sort where the husband had committed adultery (and perhaps also others in which the wife was the guilty party). The Matthaean text allowing separation in such cases might obviously provoke the following question: Why should not the *innocent* party be able to remarry if he so wished? And we should remember again that the marriage itself would have been according to Roman law, where remarriage after divorce was permitted; so it seems plausible that an appeal to, or toleration of Roman legal practice, for whatever reason, lay behind the unscriptural attitudes of a few bishops in a limited number of cases of remarriage after divorce. Indeed it seems that an innocent party in such cases might induce a limited leniency even among the recognizably strict—that may explain the notorious passage of Basil to which we have already alluded, and also a single but uncertain text of Augustine.

In the period I have just considered the views examined are those of "private" theologians. With the beginning of the fourth century we meet Church councils and thus more "official" rulings, so it is very significant that attitudes do not change. Thus from the Council of Arles (canon 10) in 314 we hear that husbands of adulterous wives (from whom they are allowed to separate) are told they are forbidden to marry again, in that remarriage is impossible so long as the wife remains alive. Judged more significant in recent debates is canon 8 of the Council of Nicea, which some, including Cardinal Kasper[20] (again following the discredited Cereti), think is perhaps the best

[20] See the address published as "Bibbia, Eros e Famiglia", *Il Foglio*, March 1, 2014. For the English translation, see Walter Cardinal Kasper, *The Gospel of the Family* (Mahwah, N.J.: Paulist Press, 2014), pp. 31, 37.

evidence that remarriage after divorce was accepted in the early Church, if with regret. But that hypothesis, as Crouzel[21] and Pelland[22] have shown, is a serious misreading of the canon, and their arguments to that effect have not been refuted, though at times they have been ignored. For the canon is directed against the Novatianists who (in the spirit of earlier rigorist groups) refused remarriage under any circumstances, even for widows and widowers.

Crouzel and Pelland have also rightly objected to attempts to explain the canon with reference to an unjustifiably emended text of Bishop Epiphanius of Salamis, who treats of the need to correct the Novatianists in chapters 34 to 64 of his *Panarion* (*GCS* 31). According to *Panarion* 59, as emended by Karl Holl (1922)—but against perfectly good sense and all the manuscripts—the Novatianists are reproved for disallowing remarriages, not only for widows and widowers but also for the divorced during their partners' lifetime. Without the unnecessary and ideologically driven emendations, however, Epiphanius can be seen to be thinking, as were the Fathers of the Council of Nicea, of those whose wife or husband has died and who, unless they are clergy, are allowed to remarry. Behind the text of Epiphanius, Crouzel and Pelland have recognized references to 1 Corinthians 5:1–5, 1 Corinthians 7:8–9, and 1 Timothy 5:14.

In considering *Panarion* 59 we should recall that Holl's reading of it gives a sense *directly contrary* to what Epiphanius holds elsewhere in treating of the Novatianists. And we should also be aware of Crouzel's observation that

---

[21] Especially in Crouzel, "Les digamoi".
[22] See Pelland, "La pratica della Chiesa".

Holl's reckless treatment of the text enables him to follow those in the early modern period who, influenced by the marital theories of Luther, looked for support from the ancient bishop of Salamis.[23]

Apart from the important and much controverted text of Basil to which I have already referred, there are two further authors of the post-Nicene period to whom appeal is sometimes made about the divorced and remarried:[24] Gregory of Nazianzus and Augustine, though neither provides a compelling argument for revisionism. Gregory's *Oratio* 37, on Matthew 19:1–2, was preached at Constantinople in 380. Speaking of sequential marriages, he notes that the first is by law, while the second is by indulgence and the third outside the law—presumably Christian law; the fourth, he adds, is for *pigs*. Again, however, there is no reason to suppose that Gregory is discussing second marriages after divorce rather than what we have seen to be the traditional problem of remarriage after the death of a spouse, and Gregory repeats the traditional teaching that a husband should divorce his adulterous wife (but not vice versa). As Crouzel has shown,[25] Gregory's position on the substantive issue can be clarified if we look at *Letter* 140, where he argues that although divorce and remarriage are possible under civil law, "our laws", that is, the "laws" of

[23] See Crouzel, "Un nouvel essai", p. 564.

[24] We should recall that with the acceptance of Christianity by Constantine, the number of new converts must have increased pressure for a more lenient attitude to divorce. George D. Gallaro, in "Oikonomia and Marriage Dissolution in the Christian East", *Folia Canonica* 11 (2008): 97–124, rightly draws attention to the dissatisfaction of Patriarch Timothy of Alexandria (about A.D. 380) with the increasing laxity, of which he still strongly disapproves.

[25] Crouzel, *L'Eglise primitive*, pp. 155–56.

the Church, forbid it. Thus although in *Oratio* 37 Gregory's intent is not totally transparent, there is no reason to enroll him (along with Ambrosiaster) among those allowing remarriage after divorce.

So next we can turn to Augustine, who in *On Faith and Works* (19.35) discusses a man who, after discovering the adultery of his wife, repudiates her and marries another woman. His fault, says Augustine, is pardonable—note the comparison, as we shall see, with the language of Basil. There is no indication, however, that Augustine does not expect separation from the second wife. But, as an argument from silence, that is not entirely compelling.

Finally, we can return to the passages of Basil, in particular to *Letter* 188, which, as we have seen, had no inconsiderable impact on the Eastern tradition. Again, these texts have been treated at length by Crouzel,[26] whose interpretation should largely be followed—without immediate reference, that is, to what subsequent centuries made of them. For later Eastern interpretations assume that Basil is speaking generally of remarriage after divorce, so that in our own times, as we have noted, Meyendorff can write: "St. Basil the Great (+379), in his canon 4, defines that those who enter a second marriage after either widowhood or divorce must undergo penance, i.e., abstain from communion for one or two years."[27] In light of all this, this text of Basil clearly demands careful consideration, though the difficulties of interpreting it are compounded by the fact that it is informal, being a reply to questions put to Basil by Bishop Amphilochius of Iconium. When

---

[26] Ibid.

[27] Meyendorff, *Marriage*, p. 49. Basil adds, we note, that a third marriage is adultery, demanding double penance.

it took its place in the Orthodox tradition of canon law, however, it was treated as though it were a quite formal document.

Perhaps Basil is discussing a situation similar to that treated by Augustine, and certainly both of them say that the man's second union is pardonable; but unlike Augustine, as Crouzel noted, Basil does not speak of a second *marriage*, referring only to "the woman who lives with him" after his divorce. So perhaps in Christian terms we have a case of fornication, but of a second marriage according to civil law, rather than of adultery, and which is to be pardoned—a less serious offense for Christians, as is revealed by much earlier disputes in the third century about what the Church is empowered to pardon that centered on the cardinal sins of murder, adultery, and apostasy, not on fornication. And we remember that the scrupulous Monica urged the young Augustine at least not to get involved with *married* women (*Confessions* 2.3.7).

So it might seem that Basil's case deals with a normal possibility in Roman civil law: a Christian has divorced his wife for adultery, and has entered into a new relationship (perhaps legally by *usus*). Legally, then, and in accordance with Jewish as well as Greco-Roman practice, he is not guilty of adultery; indeed he may have entered into a "common-law marriage" with a previously unmarried woman. But when Basil says he can be pardoned, what is he recommending him to do, now that he is clear that the man is not, by civil law, an adulterer? Is he to be pardoned for his fornication, or for his second "marriage", and what is expected of him by the Church? In any further inquiry, we must remember that we have little detail of the precise circumstances of the case.

In *Letter* 188 more generally Basil shows a certain unease in his responses to Amphilochius. He tells him that the logic of Jesus' teaching about marriage is that similar obligations are imposed on both husband and wife, but he admits that by Church custom (at least in Cappadocia) a husband is supposed to separate from his adulterous wife while she is not similarly instructed in relation to her husband. Basil seems in effect to admit that the bishops of the local church have compromised with the strict teaching of Christ, probably to accommodate social norms about the inequality of the sexes. He then proceeds to discuss the case of the Christian who has been abandoned by his wife and is now living with another woman. In this situation he is to be treated indulgently, presumably therefore being admitted, eventually, to the Eucharist; nor is the woman with whom he lives to be condemned.

But surely Basil would not recommend that someone he considered a mere fornicator be admitted to Communion if the "fornication" continued, so that the only solution to the dilemma would appear to be that he thinks of the new couple as somehow "married" (as seems also to be the interpretation adopted in canon 87 of the Council in Trullo). For his part Crouzel quotes and approves the judgment of Fulbert Cayré, A.A., to the effect that Basil condones this second "marriage" while not approving of it.[28] Certainly at this time there would be no question of any Christian rite for such a marriage (as eventually there was in Byzantium). Nevertheless, Basil's name must be added to that of Ambrosiaster as a man prepared, less willingly though more fatefully, at least to tolerate a second

---

[28] Crouzel, *L'Eglise primitive*, p. 147.

marriage after divorce in limited circumstances.[29] Pelland tries to avoid this conclusion by pointing first to the discussion of penances that he holds to be the core of Basil's letter, then to the fact that Basil says elsewhere (*Moralia*, rule 73) that "a man who has put his wife away is not allowed to marry another".[30] But the first of these arguments is not compelling, and the second deals with a different sort of case. Granted that Basil is generally strict in such matters, however, we have to admit that he is, in at least this one passage, prepared to tolerate a second marriage after divorce, but in circumstances that are largely unknown to us and in a text that reveals unease about departing from biblical norms.

Conclusions

Those who argue that the ancient evidence in favor of change is quite inadequate must be careful not to overstate their case; some of the evidence brought forward in favor of the *status quo*, while in no way supporting an alternative position, is ambiguous and its interpretation uncertain. It is important that those who argue against change themselves avoid the very ideological interpretations and wishful thinking that often nullify the claims of their opponents. There is some reason to conclude that the fateful text

[29] Among other cases Basil also treats of women who go through a form of marriage with a man abandoned by his wife whom they suppose to be unmarried. They are strictly guilty of fornication but ignorantly so, and therefore there is no penalty. They can (re)marry, but Basil does not advise it.

[30] Gilles Pelland, S.J., "Did the Church Treat the Divorced and Remarried More Leniently in Antiquity than Today?" *L'Osservatore Romano*, English Edition, February 2, 2000, p. 9.

of Basil is often subjected to mistreatment of this kind, but the only proper guide in historical studies is a sincere determination to understand what happened and why.

Nevertheless, the conclusion of this inquiry can be expressed quickly and succinctly; although among ancient Christians second marriages during the lifetime of a spouse were normally forbidden and those who were engaged in them were denied Communion, there were a very small but noticeable number of exceptions to the rule that, however, were almost invariably condemned. Although we do not know and can only speculate about the reasons for these exceptions, we can certainly be clear that they are exceptions and must be treated as such, because Christians in antiquity viewed any more "merciful" treatment of the divorced and remarried as directly opposed to the instructions of Christ himself. That being the case, whatever the merits or demerits of changes in current practice in the Roman Catholic Church, it is clear that such changes cannot be supported by significant evidence from the world of the first five centuries of Christianity.

If we ask how it can be the case that there are those who appeal to the ancient evidence as part of an argument *in favor of change*, we can only conclude that they (or the sources on which they rely) are guilty of an unfortunate practice all too common elsewhere in academia; the evidence in favor of one view is overwhelmingly superior, but there are a very few cases—and perhaps even these largely of uncertain determination—that point to the contrary conclusion. It is then claimed that the evidence, if not in favor of change, at least leaves the solution open. Such a procedure can only be condemned as methodologically flawed.

4

Separation, Divorce, Dissolution of the Bond, and Remarriage: Theological and Practical Approaches of the Orthodox Churches

Archbishop Cyril Vasil', S.J.

Introduction

Until some decades ago, the Orthodox Churches' theological and practical attitudes toward the separation of spouses, the dissolution of the marriage bond, divorce, and the possibility of remarriage with an ecclesial blessing were topics of interest only within a restricted circle of Catholic theologians and canonists. However, in these last years, this argument has become a matter of concern for a wider audience. There are two principal reasons for this change.

Following the growing phenomenon of migration, pastors of the Catholic Church in the West have been increasingly confronted with the need to respond to requests for permission for mixed marriages, in which one of the parties is Catholic and the other is Orthodox. In the course of planning and preparing the marriage, it frequently happens that the Orthodox party admits to having previously contracted a marriage in the Orthodox Church in his home country, a marriage that did not last. After a civil divorce, the religious marriage was then dissolved by the competent authority of his respective Orthodox Church. In some cases this ecclesiastical authority may have released documents declaring that the marriage was no longer valid, that it has been dissolved, that the blessing has been removed (or something similar—the terms used vary and do not always have a clear canonical meaning), and that permission to remarry has been granted to the person in question. An urgent question emerges for the Catholic party and for the Catholic Church in general when this happens. How are they to understand and interpret the practice of the Orthodox Churches? What are the moral, canonical, and pastoral consequences for the Catholic party who wishes to marry a divorced person whom the Orthodox Church has subsequently declared "free to marry"?

Another motive for increasing interest is the debate in Catholic circles about the practice of the Orthodox Churches concerning *oikonomia* in the context of divorce and remarriage. For this reason, we will seek to analyze the historical origins of the different approaches of the Orthodox Churches regarding the solutions of "matrimonial causes". In this context, "matrimonial causes" refers to all the circumstances in which marriages between two of the faithful are considered null, invalid, dissolved, and so on. In this essay, we wish to present a brief synthesis of the theological reflection and the pastoral and juridical processes that these Churches have adopted throughout the centuries.

Finally, we will attempt to point to a response to two questions concerning this topic: What should be the position of Catholic officials and tribunals that are competent in evaluating decrees or documents released by Orthodox Churches that declare the invalidity, dissolution, or divorce of the contracted marriage in the Orthodox Churches along with permission to contract a new marriage? Could the practice of the Orthodox Churches be considered "a way out" for the Catholic Church in the face of the growing instability of sacramental marriages, by providing a pastoral approach toward those Catholics who, after the failure of a sacramental marriage and a subsequent civil divorce, contract a second, civil marriage?

East and West on the Indissolubility of Marriage: Common Sources and Diverse Interpretations

In examining how the idea of the indissolubility of marriage formed among Christians of the first centuries, we must recognize that the ancient Church did not elaborate a specific theory of matrimonial law. Saint Paul's texts, as well as the Synoptic tradition, represent a desire to offer the teaching of Christ regarding the dignity of marriage within the concrete situations of their respective societies— both for the Christianity that grew out of Jewish roots and also for the Christianity that was born and developed in the Roman and Greek social contexts.

In the view of biblical exegetes, it is precisely for this reason that in the text of Matthew that prohibits divorce, one finds the clause regarding the cases of concubinage, illegitimate union, and fornication (Mt 5:32; 19:9). In fact, in the mindset of that age, it was socially, psychologically, and even practically unthinkable that the husband would continue to live with a wife who was unfaithful to him.

This approach is derived from an Old Testament conception documented in Jeremiah. The woman who committed adultery is rightly divorced by her husband, and he does not return to her, nor can she return any longer to her husband. This woman is considered impure, and any husband who would accept her in this way participates in her sin: "If a man divorces his wife and she goes from him and becomes another man's wife, will he return to her? Would not that land be greatly polluted?" (Jer 3:1). In the same tone, we find in Deuteronomy:

> [A]nd if she goes and becomes another man's wife, and the latter husband dislikes her and writes her a bill of divorce and puts it in her hand and sends her out of his house, or if the latter husband dies, who took her to be his wife, then her former husband, who sent her away, may not take her again to be his wife, after she has been defiled; for that is an abomination before the Lord. (Dt 24:2–4)

The Matthean clause—except for the cases of fornication, concubinage, and illegitimate union—over the course of successive exegetical and canonical interpretations has contributed to the process of differentiation in the understanding of the absolute indissolubility of matrimony. Here we do not want to analyze the various exegetical interpretations of the phrase; it is sufficient to be aware that adultery, in particular, adultery committed by the wife, was considered a grave sin against the marriage bond, and that, in general, even among the first Christians, it was considered a sufficient cause to break the bond and to lead the spouses to separate. At any rate, it is an open question whether a separation caused by adultery opened the way for both parties, or at least the innocent party, to a new marriage or not.

Basilio Petrà observes that the true problem stems from the commandment not to separate what God has united (cf. Mk 10:9). The tradition that developed in the Orthodox East interprets this commandment as a moral imperative that sinful individuals will ignore or violate. In this case *porneia* is interpreted as a true exception to the indissolubility of marriage. The tradition accepted in the West and common in the Catholic Church, both Latin and Eastern Catholic, tends to see in this commandment an indication of the objective nature of a marriage bond that may not be dissolved by the spouses even as a consequence of their subsequent behavior. In fact, the Lord's words establish that the marriage constitutes a bond so stable that it remains intact even after separation so that any attempt to contract another marriage is considered equal to adultery.[1]

Let us also be aware of a terminological difficulty. Today, in the spirit of the Western canonical tradition as accepted also by the Eastern Catholic Churches, we are accustomed to distinguish among various terms:

- Separation of the spouses with the continuation of the marriage bond
- Dissolution of the marriage bond, for example, in a case that deals with a marriage *ratum et non consummatum*, the case of the Pauline privilege, or the Petrine privilege

---

[1] See Basilio Petrà, *Divorzio e seconde nozze nella tradizione greca: Un altra via* (Assisi: Cittadella Editrice, 2014), 183–84.

- Declaration of nullity of the marriage: a pronouncement that the marriage *de facto* had never been truly and legally contracted, for example, due to an impediment or lack of consent
- Divorce: intervention of civil authorities on account of which, from the civil point of view, the marriage bond is dissolved and the parties are permitted to contract another civil marriage. However, for the Catholic Church, in the case of a sacramental marriage, civil divorce is considered irrelevant both from the spiritual point of view and in respect to the permanence of the sacramental marriage bond. In this case any new cohabitation, even in the form of a new civil marriage, is considered a *grave sin* that impedes access to Eucharistic Communion.

This terminological distinction results from a long historical development. We would be mistaken to expect to find it being used by early Christian authors or in legal texts from the first centuries. We need to be aware of a certain terminological disparity especially among ancient and modern authors in Eastern Christian traditions.

Among Church Fathers of the first five centuries there are many strong supporters of the principle of indissolubility of marriage who held for the illegitimacy of new marriages in cases in which the commission of adultery by one partner led to the separation of a married couple. The general patristic principle that favors the indissolubility of the marriage bond and rejects divorce and second marriages, even in the case of adultery in the first marriage, holds true despite those rare texts that are open to ambiguous interpretations or that signal the admission of a certain rational comprehension and eventual pastoral tolerance of isolated cases of divorce and remarriage in contradiction to the gospel. This radical position in favor of Christian marriage was also confirmed by ecclesiastical legislation in the first centuries, formulated at synods as well as at local and ecumenical councils.

Influence of Roman and Byzantine Civil Law on Divorce and Second Marriages

In the pre-Christian era Roman law permitted divorce in general for two sets of motives: upon agreement of the parties (*dissidium*), or on the basis of a fault by one of the parties (*repudium*). One motive for divorce was the loss of one of the party's personal liberty or civil position.

Christian emperors were cautious about changing Roman law. In an imperial constitution promulgated in 331, Constantine specified the reasons for which divorce on the grounds of *repudium* was permitted.[2] These were, in the case of the wife, adultery, attempted poisoning, and prostitution; in the case of the husband, homicide, the desecration of graves, and attempted poisoning. The constitution did not permit other reasons for divorce, and every violation of it was subject to a penalty.

This innovation in marriage law was suppressed in 363. Subsequently, the norms of 421 issued by the emperors Theodosius II and Honorius introduced a new series of motives for divorce, ranging from *magna crimina* (great

---

[2] *Codex Theodosianus* 3.16.1.

crimes) and *mediocres culpae* (minor faults).[3] Another step in the development of Roman divorce legislation occurs with the emperor Theodosius II in 449, who established that divorce is permissible only if a just cause exists, indicating some examples such as adultery, the attempted assassination of the partner, and the desecration of graves, among others.[4]

The greatest reformer of Roman law, the emperor Justinian (527–565), personally desired that his reform of marriage law be applied also within the Church. Justinian, in *Novella* 111 and, especially, in *Novella* 117 of 542, suppressed the possibility of divorce by mutual agreement. The transgression introduced by this latter *Novella* was confirmed in 556 by *Novella* 134, which prescribed the punishment of reclusion in a monastery. Justinian's attempt, although well-intentioned, created many difficulties and tensions. Thus his successor, Justinian II (685–695 / 705–711), reintroduced the possibility of divorce through mutual agreement of the parties. Other emperors, most of all those of the Isaurian dynasty, Leo III (711–741) and Constantine V (741–775), attempted to eliminate this kind of divorce. This finally happened in Leo III's *Eclogues* in 740 as well as in the legislation of Basil the Macedonian (867–886) and his son Leo VI (886–912).

The legislation of Justinian specified the possible causes of divorce in the following way:

- *First Group*. Reasons: *bona gratia*. The spouses may separate and divorce if for at least three years

---

[3] Ibid., 3.16.2.
[4] *Codex Iustinianus* 5.17.8.

no conjugal act has taken place, or if, in the case of imprisonment of the husband during war, he should not return home within five years. The only possible cause for separation or divorce by reciprocal agreement was the desire of one of the partners to enter a monastery.

- *Second Group.* Reasons: *iusta causa* or *cum damno.* The husband may divorce his wife if she participates in a plot against the emperor; if she commits adultery; if she puts the life of her husband in danger; if she attempts to murder or if she collaborates with anyone who attempts to murder her husband; if she unjustly and abusively accuses her husband of adultery while she herself continues to live in concubinage. The wife may obtain a divorce if her husband pressures her to commit adultery; if he puts her life in danger; if he accuses her of adultery without evidence; or if he himself conducts a scandalous life.

Leo VI added to this list prepared by Emperor Justinian the following causes: insanity and voluntary abortion.[5]

Novella 117 of Justinian was a compromise between the tradition of the Eastern Church, which permitted separation for reasons of adultery or in order to enter a monastery, and Roman law, which permitted divorce for many more reasons. It is often asserted that the Eastern Church, in its desire to live in harmony with civil authorities, often made concessions at the cost of compromising

---

[5] See Luigi Bressan, *Il divorzio nelle Chiese orientali: ricerca storica sull'atteggiamento cattolico* (Bologna: Edizione Dehoniane Bologna, 1976), pp. 22–23.

the message of the gospel. However, during the first millennium we can say that even in the East the Church adhered to the axiom of Saint Jerome: "aliae sunt leges Caesarum aliae Christi" (the laws of Caesar are one thing, the laws of Christ another).[6] In the case of *Novella* 117, for a few centuries the Byzantine Church refused to incorporate it in Church law. After the second half of the sixth century, canonical collections appear in the Church that combine civil and ecclesiastical legislation, for example, the *Collectio in 85 Chapters*, the *Collectio tripartita*, the *Sintagma in 50 chapters* of John Scholasticus, and the first redaction of the *Nomocanon in 14 titles*. However, it is noteworthy that Justinian's *Novella* 117 does not appear in any of these collections. The Byzantine Church, quite radically and often at the cost of conflicts with the will of emperors, justified the distinction between the application of civil and ecclesiastical laws. The first sign of the acceptance of multiple causes for divorce is canon 87 of the Council in Trullo in 692. The Council allows divorce in the case of soldiers who have been imprisoned. However, this Council is more concerned with granting the possibility of a new marriage on the basis of the presumed death of one of the spouses than it is with permitting divorce per se.

We first notice a real change in the *Nomocanon in 14 titles* compiled by Patriarch Photius of Constantinople in 883. This collection affirms the indissolubility of marriage while it also provides a list of causes for divorce introduced by Justinian's legislation. The successive development in the Byzantine Empire reinforced the role of the Church,

---

[6] Saint Jerome, *Epist.* 77.3 (PL 22.691).

while the Church accepted a new relationship to the State. A new compilation of civil legislation, Emperor Basil I's *Basilica*, sought in its re-elaboration of Justinian's *Corpus Iuris Civilis* to omit some of the problematic points of the latter's legislation that were in contrast with the position of the Church. However, Patriarch Photius' so-called *Nomocanon*, which at the Synod of Constantinople in 920 was approved as the official collection of laws in Byzantium, accepted some possibilities for divorce for reasons indicated by the law.

Up until the end of the ninth century, it was still possible to contract a civil marriage, but by the year 895, on the basis of Emperor Leo VI's *Novella* 89, the Church was declared the only institution with legal competence for the celebration of matrimony. In this way, the priestly blessing became a necessary part of the legal act of marriage. Thus, the Church became the guarantor of marriage as a social institution. Following this, ecclesiastical tribunals gradually, and then in 1086 definitively, received exclusive competence for the examination of marriage cases. As a consequence the Eastern Church had to conform its practices to State and civil legislation. Then once civil legislation began to allow divorce and successive remarriages, the Eastern Church was obligated to recognize these practices.

The first patriarch who seems to have looked upon divorce benevolently was Alexius I of Constantinople (1025–1043). He prohibited marriage with a woman who had been divorced because she committed adultery. Priests who dared to bless second marriages involving such women were threatened with suspensions of their priestly faculties. However, he ordered that his ruling not be applied to those who had separated from a guilty party, and he allowed blessings of the second marriages of women who sought divorce due to the immoral life of their husbands.[7] However, commenting on this norm, Pietro Dacquino warns that, in this case,

> it [Patriarch Alexius' ruling] could refer to "fiancés" because the fourth decree punishes severely a priest who performs the nuptial blessing for those who divorce by mutual consent, even in violation of civil law. In fact, in view of the severity demonstrated by the eastern Churches regarding the second marriages of widows, it is clear how those who had dissolved previous engagements to marry (considered in the East as a first marriage) could create a problem for the ideal of strict monogamy, which had been developed at that time. A more severe practice placed these separated fiancés on the same level as widows, depriving them of a marriage blessing if they married.[8]

Later, the famous commentators of the twelfth century Zonaras, Aristenes, and Balsamon emphasize the fact that marriage cannot be dissolved by anyone for any sort of reason, but that in the case of divorce, conditions established by the law must be fulfilled. Practically speaking this interpretation relies on an expansion of a paragraph in canon 48 of the *Canons of the Apostles*, which punishes with excommunication a layman who divorces his wife for motives other than those recognized by law.[9] These three commentators did not reflect on the fact that the Church

---

[7] See Bressan, *Il divorzio*, p. 28.

[8] Pietro Dacquino, *Storia del matrimonio cristiano alla luce della Bibbia. 2. Insepa-rabilità e monogamia* (Leumann: Elle Di Ci, 1988), pp. 298–99.

[9] See Pierre L'Huillier, "L'indissolubilité du mariage dans la droit et la pra-tique orhodoxes", in *Studia Canonica* 21 (1987): 251.

was compelled to accept a larger list of legal reasons for a divorce. This list was not inspired by the Holy Spirit but rather by civil law that often based itself on the hardness of hearts.

The successive spread of Christianity from its center in Constantinople to other missionary territories and nations brought about the geographical extension of the judicial-disciplinary practices of this tradition as well as the diffusion of the theological principles that founded such practices. In this context today, we see diverse Orthodox Churches, which, despite the fact that they are institutionally and hierarchically separate, nevertheless follow most of the same disciplinary and spiritual principles.

Divorce in the Russian Orthodox Church

Once Christianity arrived in Russia from ancient Byzantium, the provisions of Byzantine law regarding divorce were incorporated into its laws along with some modifications regarding the Russian situation.[10] Sterility on the part of the wife was considered a concrete motive for divorce, while her entrance into monastic life was treated as a formal cause. Neither in Russia nor in Byzantium was the chronic sickness of a spouse considered a reason for divorce. Jaroslav the Wise (ca. 978–1054), in a collection

[10] In what follows concerning the practices of the Russian and Greek Orthodox Churches, we rely heavily on the work of Jiří Dvoráček, in "Il divorzio del vincolo matrimoniale nelle Chiese ortodosse e le sue conseguenze giuridiche per la Chiesa cattolica", *Rodina, konflikt a možnosti mediace*, eds. Slávka Michančová and Lenka Pavlová (Křtiny: Evropský smírčí institut, 2011): 25–67. The article was originally part of a doctoral thesis defended in the Pontifical Oriental Institute, Rome.

of laws called the "*Ustav*", established that even if a wife were blind or suffering from a long-term illness, she could not be divorced for these reasons.[11] In practice, however, these conditions constituted a motive for divorce on the part of the husband, even though the official reason given was that the wife had entered monastic life. According to the "*Ustav*" the husband could divorce

- if the wife did not inform the husband about the intention of a third party regarding a plot against a czar or prince;
- because of the wife's adultery;
- because of a plot, both by the wife and by others, against the husband;
- if the wife ate with other men or slept outside of the home;
- in the case of the wife's gambling obsession;
- if the wife, by herself or with accomplices, robbed the husband or the Church.[12]

Notwithstanding this list of causes for which divorce was permissible, during the following centuries, especially in the sixteenth and seventeenth, mutual-consent divorces were also common, as is evidenced by cases in southwest Russia. The case for divorce was presented to the municipal courts through a request for divorce drafted by the

[11] See *Ustav velikago knaza Jaroslava, prostrannaja vostočnorusskaja redakcia*, art. 12, cited in Vladimir Nikolaevich Beneševič, *Sbornik pamjatnikov po istorii cerkovnogo prava, preimuščestvenno russkogo, končaja vremenem Petra Velikago* (Petrograd, 1914), p. 80.

[12] See *Ustav velikago knaza Jaroslava, vostočnorusskaja redakcia*, art. 55, cited in Beneševič, *Sbornik*, pp. 85–86.

parish priest. Frequently, the woman entered a monastic community in order to consent to the husband's remarriage. In such cases, one can raise doubts about the free choice of the woman's entry. In judicial practice, the causes for divorce were principally adultery committed by the wife, attempted homicide, cruel treatment of the wife, and—beginning in the eighteenth century under the influence of Western canon law—the disappearance of a spouse and criminal conviction.

In the so-called synodal period (1721–1917), a fixed number of reasons for divorce was established and clarified by State authorities in collaboration with ecclesiastical authorities. In a decree of Czar Peter I in 1720, imprisonment was considered a "civil death" and likewise caused the marriage to cease. In 1722, Peter I limited the concessions of divorce to three motives: adultery, absence of a spouse for five years, and exile in Siberia. Only the czar could grant divorce in other cases, and these had to be indicated in the request. In special instances, the ecclesiastical consistory and the synod dissolved marriages even for permanent mental illness, although this cause was not admitted by law.

The most frequent cause for divorce in this period was the commission of adultery by either the wife or husband. A spouse could also request divorce if he converted to Christianity while the other remained an unbeliever (decree of January 12, 1739); however, this case was not a direct application of the so-called Pauline privilege.

At the end of the nineteenth century, divorce by mutual consent was no longer permitted, and clergy were prohibited from making requests for divorce on these grounds. Following long discussions, on March 18, 1905, the

Russian Synod consented to second marriages even in the case of a spouse guilty of adultery.[13]

For Orthodox marriages or for mixed marriages between Orthodox Christians with non-Orthodox, various motives were considered valid for divorce,[14] some of which, in the Catholic Church, fall under the category of impediments (e.g., previous and chronic impotence), reasons for nullity, or the application of the Pauline privilege.

Practical concerns subsequently pressured the Holy Synod to introduce other motives for divorce. Divorces were also obtained through appeal to the State, outside of the normal judicial procedures. This so-called right of the State in the matters of divorce was founded on the legislative power of the monarch. The reason for this practice derived from the fact that the ecclesiastical tribunal was constrained by civil regulations, while the legislator was not.[15]

[13] See Ivan Žužek, S.J., *Kormčaja kniga: Studies on the Chief Code of Russian Canon Law* (Rome: Pontifical Oriental Institute, 1964), p. 249.

[14] The following were considered valid motives: (1) adultery: the law did not speak about the possibility of second marriages in this regard, but in practice they were permitted; (2) bigamy; (3) impotence prior to the marriage (not *impotentia superveniens*): a request for divorce in this case could be presented only after three years of the celebration of the wedding; (4) the condemnation of one of the spouses into forced labor or exile with the stripping of all civil rights: divorce in this case could be requested by the innocent spouse who did not want to follow the condemned spouse into exile and who wanted to remarry (however, this right could only be exercised immediately following the sentencing of the guilty party); (5) the disappearance of one of the spouses: divorce in this case could be sought only after five years had passed since the disappearance; (6) in a mixed marriage, the desire of the spouse who was not a believer to separate from a spouse who had converted to the Orthodox faith, as well as the unbeliever's resistance to the obligation to encourage the Orthodox faith for the children; (7) the profession of monastic vows by both of the spouses, and therefore without the possibility of remarriage: it was otherwise not permitted that either spouse should enter a monastery while both spouses were living.

[15] See Nicolaj Semenovič Suvorov, *Učebnik cerkovnogo prava*, 4 izdanie (Moscow: Jakovlev, 1912), p. 390.

In 1917–1918 the Pan-Russian Council (*Vserossijskij Pomestnij Sobor*) of the Russian Orthodox Church adopted new regulations concerning divorce. Reacting to recent secular laws established by the Soviets, the Holy Synod established the following principles:

- A marriage blessed by the Church cannot be the object of a divorce granted by the State, nor would the Church recognize civil divorces.
- Orthodox faithful whose marriage was blessed by the Church and who subsequently were granted a divorce by the State but not by the Church, should they then contract a civil marriage, live *de facto* in a state of bigamy and adultery.
- The registration of the spouses by civil officials does not substitute for the blessing of the Church. Hence, such marriages require the rite of crowning in order to be blessed by the Church.[16]

The Synod established on April 7 and 20, 1918, that marriage blessed by the Church is indissoluble. Divorce "is admitted by the Church only in condescension to human weakness and out of care for the salvation of man", on the conditions that there has been a breakup of the marriage and that reconciliation is impossible. The decision to concede an ecclesiastical divorce falls under the competence of the ecclesiastical tribunals, which work at the request of

---

[16]See Dvoráček, "Il divorzio", pp. 40–41. This author's source consists in the deliberations of the Holy Synod of the Russian Orthodox Church, February 19/March 4, 1918, published by the Svjaščennyj Sobor Pravoslavnoj Rossijskoj Cerkvi in *Dejanija Sobranie opredelenij i postanovlenij*, vol. 2, part 2 (Moscow: Izd. Sobornogo Soveta, 1918), pp. 21ff.

the spouses, provided that the reason presented for divorce conforms to those approved by the Holy Synod.[17]

In 2000 the Russian Orthodox Church promulgated new motives for permitting divorce:

- Contraction of AIDS
- Alcoholism or chemical dependence attested to by a medical examination
- Abortion procured by the wife without the consent of the husband

The Russian Orthodox Church today admits fourteen valid reasons for permitting divorce. The 2000 Synod document recalls that in marriage preparation with young couples it is important to emphasize the principle of the indissolubility of marriage as well as the fact that divorce is only an extreme solution and can only take place under the conditions established by the Church. The document insists that ecclesiastical divorce cannot be conceded frivolously or as a mere consequence of civil divorce. It reiterates the ancient principle that permits the innocent party

[17] These reasons are as follows: (1) apostasy from Orthodoxy; (2) adultery or homosexual acts: cause for divorce must be presented within three years of the discovery of the adultery; (3) impotence: it must be permanent and prior to the marriage, in which case the request for divorce must be presented no less than two years after the celebration of the wedding; (4) leprosy or syphilis; (5) the disappearance of one of the spouses for a period of two years if the disappearance is due to war-time imprisonment, otherwise three continuous years; (6) conviction of a crime with the consequent loss of civil rights; (7) threat to the life of the other spouse or of the children; (8) sexual relations with the father-in-law or with the mother-in-law, pimping, and the manipulation of the spouse's state of need; celebration of a second marriage. To these causes, the Holy Synod in its deliberations of August 20/September 2, 1918, added two others: incurable insanity of one of the spouses who does not agree to continue cohabitation; abandonment of the other spouse. See Dvoráček, "Il divorzio", pp. 41, nos. 43, 44.

in a divorce to contract a second marriage, while the guilty party may do so only after he fulfills the *epitimie* (assigned, rigorous penances). In the exceptional case of a third marriage, these penances are more severe.[18] Recent norms of the Russian Orthodox Church leave it to the competence of the bishops to deal with questions regarding divorce and new marriages. Such work is done either personally by the bishop or by the eparchial council. The Russian canonist Vladislav Cypin explains that in making his decision the bishop takes into consideration the declarations of the spouses, their spiritual father, witnesses of good faith, even the civil judgment expressed by the judge or official of the State regarding the case.[19]

However, from the study of actual divorce decrees or declarations issued by the bishops of the Russian Orthodox Church, it seems that it is not possible to deduce any particular method for conducting a canonical investigation, or to understand clearly the reasoning behind the application of a given motive for granting divorce. Often one simply finds in this documentation an ecclesiastical divorce decree, together with the request presented by the interested party, a statement that the couple has not been living together, and an indication that a civil divorce has been granted. Following this, the dissolution of the religious marriage and permission to remarry is granted.[20]

---

[18] *Osnovy social'noj koncepcii Russkoj Pravoslavnoj Cerkvi* (Moscow: Izdatel'stvo Moskovskoj Patriarchii, 2000). See especially chapter 10: *Voprosy ličnoj, semennoj i obšestvennoj nravstvennosti*, paragraph 3.

[19] Vladislav A. Cypin, *Cerkovnoje pravo Izdatel'stvo* (Moscow: Moskovskogo universiteta, 1996), p. 386.

[20] See the recent study of Edouard Sheshtak, *Divorce and Remarriage in the Orthodox Churches of the Tradition of Kiev* (Užhorod: Lira, 2011), pp. 260–61, 280–85.

Divorce in the Greek Orthodox Church

Regarding the indissolubility of marriage, among Byzantine authors, there has yet to be published a systematic treatment.[21] Beginning in the twelfth century, divorce was received in canonical legislation and in practice by the Greek Church. Slowly, causes for divorce were introduced that were modeled on the morals and the situation of society. The unjustified absence of a spouse for five years, an invincible aversion to one's spouse caused by a defect that was previously hidden, or the wife's hatred toward the husband were considered causes for divorce.[22] In the sixteenth century, other causes for divorce were introduced, for example, grave and chronic illness, serious incompatibility, and the abandonment of the conjugal bed for three years, as well as mutual consent. In this latter case, however, the divorce could be granted only by the patriarch.[23] Beginning in the seventeenth century, divorce was made more difficult; marriage could only be dissolved for the reasons mentioned in the Gospels.[24]

At the end of the eighteenth century the compilation of laws known as the *Pedalion* allowed only one motive for divorce—adultery. Canon 48 of the *Pedalion* states that if a man marries a divorced woman, both of them will be

---

[21] See Pierre L'Huillier, "L'indissolubilité", p. 252. On divorces in the late Byzantine period, a detailed treatment can be found in the article of Patrick Viscuso, "Late Byzantine Canonical Views on the Dissolution of Marriage", *Greek Orthodox Theological Review* 44:1–4 (1999): 273–90.

[22] See Jean Dauvillier and Carlo de Clerq, *Le marriage en droit canonique oriental* (Paris: Sirey, 1936), pp. 91–92.

[23] See Jean-Baptiste-Marie Mayaud, *L'indissolubilité du mariage, étude historico-canonique* (Strasbourg/Paris: F.-X. Le Roux, 1952), p. 74, n. 96.

[24] See L'Huillier, "L'indissolubilité", p. 254.

excommunicated. According to the commentary on this canon, in accord with the gospel, divorce for reasons of adultery is not subject to excommunication. However, both husband and wife are excommunicated if they are divorced for reasons other than adultery and then take a new spouse. Such persons are subject to the canonical punishment of seven years' prohibition from the Eucharist. The *Pedalion* recalls that according to the Council of Carthage (407), spouses divorced for reasons other than adultery must reconcile or never remarry.[25] The *Pedalion* was published with the consent of the patriarch and became above all the recognized text in the Greek Church. However, it did not have a strongly restrictive influence regarding the practice of divorce.[26]

Greece obtained its independence in 1832; matrimonial affairs were regulated by a royal decree issued in 1835. The decree states that civil laws contained in the *Hexabiblos* will remain in effect until the promulgation of a civil code.[27] The *Hexabiblos* contained marriage laws dating from the emperor Justinian and his successors. The Greek State recognized the sacramental character of marriage and entrusted marital affairs to the competence of the

[25] See *The Rudder (Pedalion) of the Metaphorical Ship of the One Holy Catholic and Apostolic Church of the Orthodox Christians, or All the Sacred and Divine Canons*, trans. Denver Cummings (Chicago: Orthodox Christian Educational Society, 1957), pp. 76–80.

[26] See L'Huillier, "L'indissolubilité", pp. 254–55.

[27] The *Hexabiblos* was composed in the fourteenth century by the Greek canonist Constantine Harmenopoulos. *Hexabiblos* is the name of the six books of the *Procheiron*, a collection of *novellae* and civil laws of the Macedonian emperors from Basil I until the fourteenth century. See Andréa Belliger, *Die wiederverheirateten Geschiedenen. Eine ökumenische Studie im Blick auf die römisch-katholische und griechisch-orthodoxe (Rechts-)Tradition der Unauflöslichkeit der Ehe* (Essen: Ludgerus Verlag, 2000), pp. 160–61, and n. 187 (with bibliography).

Greek Orthodox Church, except for questions of divorce, which remained an affair of the State. It was then up to the bishops to examine the presuppositions of the marriage contract and the impediments, while civil divorces were provided by the State. Later, the Church obtained the role of mediator in divorce cases. Prior to the case's arrival before the civil judge, the bishop was obligated to try to reconcile the couple. Only after three months could the acting party bring the case before the civil court. If this tribunal decreed a divorce, the bishop was obliged by civil law to grant a "spiritual divorce".[28]

The causes for divorce in this period were divided into the categories of *cum damno* (with fault) and *bona gratia* (without fault).[29]

In 1920 a new law on divorce was promulgated (Law no. 2228/1920). The causes of divorce were divided again into two groups: absolute causes (for which divorce had to be granted without exception) and relative causes (for which divorce could be granted only if the motives for divorce so influenced the relationship between the spouses that their cohabitation was judged impossible).[30]

Until 1982, when the new law on marriage (Law no. 1250/1982) went into effect in Greece, the State did not

[28] See ibid., pp. 160–61, 195–96.

[29] To the first group belonged the following: (1) adultery; (2) attempted homicide of the spouse; (3) abortion; (4) conspiracy with one's child. The causes *bona gratia* were the following: (1) impotence; (2) abandonment of the spouse; (3) insanity; (4) apostasy from the Orthodox faith; (5) monastic vows; (6) refusal of the wife to follow her husband to another place.

[30] Absolute causes were (1) adultery; (2) bigamy; (3) attempted homicide of the spouse; (4) abandonment of the spouse for more than three years. The relative causes' *raison d'être* is due to the fact that, if by the fault of a spouse, the other spouse's life was threatened, for both it was no longer possible to remain married (Article 5 of Law no. 2228/1920). Concretely, this is an issue of madness, insanity, and disappearance.

recognize the existence of any "civil marriage" for its citizens (it was invalid even if it was contracted outside of the country). A law of March 15, 1940 (Law no. 2250/1940), decreed that marriage was an exclusively ecclesiastical institution. However, divorces were regulated solely by civil laws and were the exclusive competence of the civil courts. The ecclesiastical authority was left with the obligation to carry out the process of mediation. The civil code of 1940 lists five motives for divorce with fault and four without any fault.[31]

In practice, however, the majority of divorces were motivated along the lines of article 1442 of the legal code, according to which each spouse could ask for divorce if, owing to the fault of the other, an irreconcilable estrangement occurred between them. The law did not recognize mutual consent as grounds for divorce.

The divorce procedure took place in the following manner: the divorce case was presented to the bishop who sought to reconcile the two spouses. If after three months, reconciliation did not occur, the bishop would inform the civil court and it would accept the case. However, the court could accept the case even without being informed by the bishop, provided there had been an attempt at reconciliation and the bishop had been involved in it. The civil court then pronounced the sentence. A court official would then notify the bishop who would instruct the eparchial tribunal to release its sentence, one that would automatically conform to that of the civil court.

---

[31] The motives with fault were (1) adultery; (2) bigamy; (3) attempted homicide of the spouse; (4) abandonment of the spouse; (5) disruption of the conjugal life. The causes without fault were (1) insanity; (2) leprosy; (3) long absence; (4) impotence. See Belliger, *Die wiederverheirateten Geschiedenen*, pp. 200–201.

The divorced spouse (whose civil divorce was recognized by the ecclesiastical authority) who wished to contract a new marriage had first to perform an assigned penance (*epitimia*). Following this, the Church ritual for the second marriage had a penitential character. If this newly remarried spouse had earlier been declared guilty during his divorce proceeding, he was prohibited from approaching the priest who officiated at the second marriage, nor was he permitted to participate in the wedding banquet. A third marriage was conceded only to those previously divorced persons who were at least forty years old and without children. However, these individuals were prohibited from receiving the Eucharist for five years. An exception was conceded to petitioners who were at least thirty years old and who had children. These persons were permitted to remarry; however, the assigned penance in their cases would last four years. Fourth marriages were prohibited.[32]

After 1950 Greece witnessed a vigorous discussion of so-called dead marriages, in other words, marriages between persons who had lived separately for a long time with no hope of reconciliation, but who were nevertheless unable to find a valid motive for securing a divorce. In 1965, a legislative proposal was introduced to the Chamber of Deputies concerning "automatic divorce". Strong opposition from the Greek Orthodox Church delayed approval of this measure until March 1, 1979 (Law no. 868/1979).[33]

---

[32] See Elie Melia, "Le lien matrimonial à la lumière de la théologie sacramentaire et de la théologie morale de l'Église orthodoxe", *Revue de Droit Canonique* 21 (1971): 189–90; cf. also Dimitrios Salachas, "Matrimonio e divorzio nel diritto canonico orientale. Spunti e riflessioni", *Nicolaus* 1 (1973): 64–65.

[33] See Salachas, "Matrimonio e divorzio", pp. 65–66; Belliger, *Die wiederverheirateten Geschiedenen*, pp. 202–4.

In 1982 a further reform of family law took place in Greece. This reform introduced an option between civil and religious marriage and at the same time rescinded a series of impediments to marriage that were present in the civil code (Law no. 1250/1982). The Greek Church, however, retained these impediments.

In the case of divorce, only the civil courts have competence, according to the actual Greek judicial structure. Only after the civil decree of divorce has been issued can the Church decide whether to grant a religious divorce. This canonical dissolution of matrimony pertains only to those who have celebrated a canonical marriage and wish to contract another. The obligatory period for mediation and reconciliation prior to the granting of divorce was abolished once civil marriages were permitted by law.[34]

After the new law of 1982, two principle motives remained for civil divorce: the grave disturbance of the conjugal life and disappearance. Furthermore, divorce is also possible by mutual consent.

In the Greek Orthodox Church, the following are valid motives for divorce on the part of the husband:

- Adultery committed by the wife
- Threats to the husband's life by the wife
- Voluntary abortion, after which the wife remains so mutilated that she is no longer capable of conjugal relations

[34] See Charalambos Papastathis, "Staat und Kirche in Griechenland", *Staat und Kirche in der Europäischen Union*, ed. Gerhard Robbers (Baden-Baden: Nomos, 1995), pp. 125–50; See also Eleftherios J. Kastrissios, "Länderbericht Griechenland", *Internationales Ehe- und Kindschaftsrecht mit Staatsangehörigkeitsrecht*, ed. Alexander Bergmann, Murad Ferid, and Dieter Henrich, 6th ed. (Frankfurt/Berlin: Verlag für Standesamtswesen, 2001), pp. 39–62.

- The wife's unmotivated abandonment of the house, against the will of the husband
- Frequenting clubs without the consent of the husband

Following are the causes for divorce on the part of the wife:

- Adultery committed by the husband
- The husband's public and unjustified accusation of adultery on the part of the wife
- The husband's defamation of the wife

Following are the causes for divorce common to both spouses:

- Apostasy from the Christian faith
- The deliberate refusal of the baptism of the children
- The episcopal ordination of the husband
- The choice in favor of monastic life

Because it is recognized as a valid reason for divorce in civil law, the Greek Orthodox Church also recognizes the disappearance of one of the spouses due to deliberate abandonment as a valid motive for religious divorce.[35]

Looking now at both the Russian Orthodox and Greek Orthodox Churches' policies and practices, we see that valid motives for divorce can be divided in three groups:

1. Adultery and other similar immoral acts
2. Physical or legal situations similar to death (disappearance, attempted homicide, incurable illness, detention, separation for a long period, etc.)

[35]See Melia, "Le lien", p. 188.

3. Moral impossibility of a common life (encouragement of adultery)

Juridical Procedures in Countries with "Personal Statutes"

In 2001 in the Pontifical Oriental Institute's Faculty of Eastern Canon Law, Giuseppe Said Saad defended his doctoral thesis on the theme "the Dissolution of Marriage in Orthodox Communities of Lebanon". The author presented the juridical norms and the practices of five Eastern, non-Catholic Churches: the Greek-Melkite, Armenian, Syrian, Coptic, and Assyrian Church of the East. In Lebanon, as in other countries in the ex-Ottoman Empire, the life of these single, Christian communities is governed by so-called personal statutes. In these personal statutes, each Church defines itself and its relationship to the other ecclesial communities. Given the delicacy involved in the question of marriage law insofar as it affects the public and social life of individuals, the personal statutes are required in order to clarify certain procedural questions and juridical criteria. In this way, each Church was "obligated" to define reasons and conditions for the declaration of nullity of a marriage, the dissolution of the marriage bond, the separation of the spouses while remaining in the bond of marriage, and divorce, as well as the possibility to contract a new marriage.

A look at these approaches to marriage questions in some Orthodox Churches leads us to conclude that, in concrete practice, the Orthodox Churches either endorse civil divorces or recognize them more or less covertly. Although these Churches do not legitimate divorce, they tolerate it.[36] In theory these Churches reject divorce by mutual consent, but when the faithful obtain civil divorces in this way, they are in the end able to receive a declaration of the dissolution of their marriage bond by their Churches, and they are then able to enter into new marriages.

In actual practice, long-term separation of spouses is considered the equivalent to divorce because in Orthodox theology, common life is the essential element of marriage, and the conception of separation *manente vinculo*, as it is applied in the Catholic Church, is unknown in the Orthodox Churches.

Indissolubility of Marriage: Does a Common Orthodox Doctrine Exist?

In seeking a common Orthodox doctrine regarding the indissolubility of marriage, divorce, and the marriage of divorced persons, we confront the question of whether it is possible to speak of a common doctrine or of a "magisterium" of the Orthodox Churches, or if we are left with just the practices of individual Churches or of certain bishops, or even with the opinions of a few theologians. In this essay, we do not pretend to have a definitive response to this question. However, we will seek to present in summary form a number of themes that emerge from the Orthodox Churches and writers. We refer here to the work of Luigi Bressan, whom we have already mentioned.[37] The first difficulty we encounter is the fact that

[36] Pierre L'Huillier, "L'attitude de l'Eglise orthodoxe vis-à-vis du remariage des divorcés", *Revue de Droit Canonique* 29 (1979): 57.

[37] See Bressan, *Il divorzio*, pp. 39–46.

in the past, few Orthodox authors attempted a profound theoretical reflection on the question of common Orthodox doctrine. This is compounded by the fact that the quantity and quality of theological and canonical reflection on these issues is currently quite low.

True theological reflection by Orthodox authors begins only in the nineteenth century, and often only in reaction to the position of Catholic authors. Even the noted Orthodox theologian Alexander Schmemann (1921–1983) indicates that the individual aspects of marriage have not acquired the character of a completed or systematic doctrine.[38] We note that the profession of faith of Jeremiah, Patriarch of Constantinople in 1574, emphasizes that Christ came to perfect the Law of Moses, prohibiting the separation of that which God had united. In the profession of the Orthodox faith in 1695, it is demanded of each of the betrothed not to abandon the other, and that they maintain fidelity, love, and matrimonial honor until the end. In 1727 the confession of faith of three patriarchs—Paisius II of Constantinople, Silvester of Antioch, and Chrysanthus of Jerusalem—acknowledges divorce as permissible in certain cases defined by law, yet it also recalls the principle of the indissolubility of marriage. The aforementioned manual of canon law, the *Pedalion*, still published today with the approval of the Patriarch of Constantinople, permits the possibility of divorce only in the cases of adultery, heresy, and the attempt on the life of the partner.

In general, we can say that on the basis of the Gospel text, all the Orthodox authors at heart recognize the

[38] Alexander Schmemann, "The Indisolubility of Marriage: The Theological Tradition of the East", *The Bond of the Marriage. An Ecumenical and Interdisciplinary Study*, ed. William W. Basset (Notre Dame: University of Notre Dame Press, 1968), pp. 97–112.

indissolubility of Christian marriage as one of its characteristics and teach this doctrine to all Christian spouses as an ideal toward which to aim. It seems that in evaluating the positions of certain Orthodox authors, divorce is viewed as a possibility only in the case of adultery; whereas other Orthodox authors who have a more canonical approach indicate diverse reasons and motives for permitting divorce. At any rate, even as Orthodox bishops acknowledge the possibility of divorce and remarriage, they admit this only as an exception that confirms the rule of the unity and indissolubility of marriage.

Among Orthodox authors and bishops, opponents to divorce are not lacking. Some of these authorities uphold the complete observance of the indissolubility of marriage and the impossibility of divorce for any reason. For example, the Russian Archbishop Ignatius (in the Russian Orthodox Church, Saint Ignatius Brianchaninov [1807–1867]) did not permit divorce for any reason, not even for adultery. More moderate, but nevertheless appreciable opposition to divorce has also been evidenced both by Archbishop Iakovos (Coucouzis) (1911–2005), the Orthodox Metropolitan of North and South America (1959–1996), who insisted already in 1966 that concessions of divorce should be limited, and by the Coptic Patriarch Shenouda III (1923–2012), who following his enthronement in 1971 reduced the many reasons considered valid for granting divorce in the Coptic Church to one—adultery.[39]

---

[39] See Bressan, *Il divorzio*, p. 40. See also Luis Glinka, "Indisolubilidad y divorcio en las Iglesias ortodoxas. Una contribucíon al dialogo ecuménico", *Teología* (Buenos Aires) 51 (1988): 67.

Reasons for Divorce: Attempts at Systematization

We shall attempt to group together the reasons for which Orthodox authors and bishops, who seek to maintain the indissolubility of marriage as a universal ideal, nevertheless also consider certain situations as justifying divorce and remarriage.

Adultery and fornication. As has been stated, Orthodox authorities generally interpret Matthew 5:32 and 19:9 as permitting divorce in the case of adultery. If there is a common point of view among Eastern Orthodox bishops and theologians, this is it. Many theologians and bishops hold the relatively strict position that divorce and remarriage are permissible only in cases of adultery.

In cases of adultery, the Orthodox Church can permit both the innocent and guilty party to contract another marriage, but in the latter case, only after the performance of a long and demanding penance. The Greek Orthodox theologian Panagiotis Trembelas considers inadmissible the marriage of the adulterous woman to the person with whom she committed adultery.[40] Angelo Altan, on the other hand, adds that a single act of adultery is not sufficient cause to justify a divorce decree, but a long-term period of marital infidelity is.[41]

The theory of refused grace. For John Meyendorff, marriage, considered as a sacrament, involves the spouses not only in

[40]Panagiotis N. Trembelas, *Dogmatique de l'Eglise orthodoxe catholique*, vol. 3 (Chevetogne-Bruges: Desclée de Brouwer 1968), pp. 358–59.

[41]Angelo Altan, "Indissolubilitá ed oikonomia nella teologia e nella disciplina orientale del matrimonio", *Sacra Doctrina* 49 (1968): 87–112.

their earthly life, but also in eternal life, and the sacramental grace received does not come to an end, not even with death. Marriage is at the same time a gift of personal liberty. Hence, grace must fall on fertile ground; it has to be received. This reception (acceptance) of grace also requires personal effort. To renounce the effort involved results in the refusal of the grace offered.[42] In this sense, ecclesiastical divorce, in Meyendorff's view, is merely the Church's acknowledgment that this sacramental grace has been refused.

Paul Evdokimov develops the idea of grace refused or not received in concluding that if the unity of the spouses and their reciprocal love is the image of the sacramental grace, then in the event that this love ceases or diminishes, so too does the spiritual communion that is signified and realized in the corporal union—*una caro*. The continuation of marital cohabitation under these conditions approximates fornication more than it does the image of spiritual unity, and "fornication" of this kind indicates the termination of a marriage.[43]

The spiritual and moral death of a marriage. At the beginning of the twentieth century, the great Serbian canonist Nikodim Milaš elaborated and developed the theory of the moral death of a marriage.[44] This theory was later developed by the Greek theologian Hamicar S. Alivisatos.[45] According

---

[42]John Meyendorff, "Il Matrimonio e l'Eucaristia", *Russia Cristiana* 120 (1970): 23–24.

[43]Paul Evdokimov, "La grâce du sacrement de mariage selon la tradition orthodoxe", *Parole et Pain* 35–36 (1969): 382–94.

[44]Nikodim Milaš, *Das Kirchenrecht der morgenländischen Kirche* (Mostar: Verlag der Verlagsbuchhandlung von Pacher & Kisić, 1905), pp. 629–41.

[45]Hamicar S. Alivisatos, *Marriage and Divorce in Accordance with the Canon Law of the Orthodox Church* (London: Faith Press, 1948), p. 12.

to this theory, if the physical death of one of the spouses ends the marriage bond and the remaining spouse has the possibility to contract a new marriage, then it is possible to speak not just of a physical death of marriage, but also a spiritual death.

Concluding Considerations

In Pierre L'Huillier's view, the Orthodox Church usually does not make a decision concerning the dissolution of the marriage, except in those cases in which the Church itself bears a civil responsibility. For the Catholic canonist accustomed to reasoning according to categories of matrimonial procedural law, it is often difficult to understand the fact that in the Orthodox Church, there is no talk ever about procedural questions about marriage cases per se, that is, there are no roles for an advocate, a promoter of justice, a defender of the bond, and there are no instances of appeal, among other juridical structures.

L'Huillier also indicates that the Orthodox Churches have practically never elaborated a clear doctrine regarding the indissolubility of marriage that could bring the New Testament requirements to the judicial level. This fact is the key that allows us to understand why the Orthodox Churches, even through the expressions of their supreme authorities—oftentimes only passively—accept the sociological reality. This laxity reveals not only the inadequate expansion of the legitimate causes for divorce compared with the criteria that are indicated in the *Nomocanon*, but also the total disappearance of the differences between the divorce conceded *bona gratia* and the divorce conceded

cum damno. We also see this laxity in the acceptance of
the possibility of a second marriage for a divorced person, where the difference is practically eliminated between the party that caused the breakdown of the marriage
and the innocent party, thereby creating the impression
that a decree of divorce automatically concedes the right
to contract a new marriage.[46]

Another Orthodox author, Alvian Smirensky, commenting on the decrees of the Synod of Moscow in
1918, with a hint of sadness, indicates that unfortunately
in these decrees only fifteen lines are dedicated to the
question of indissolubility, while seven subsequent pages
describe the ways in which it is possible to dissolve the
indissoluble bond.[47]

The Position of the Catholic Church

The Catholic Church does not recognize the procedures
involved in the declaration of the dissolution of a marriage
bond, or those applied in the case of a divorce on account
of adultery, in the manner in which these procedures are
employed by a number of Orthodox Churches, nor does
it recognize the Orthodox application of the principle
of *oikonomia* (which, in this case, is considered contrary
to divine law), because these dissolutions presuppose the
intervention of an ecclesiastical authority in the breakup of
a valid marriage agreement.

[46] See L'Huillier, "L'attitude", p. 57.
[47] See Alvian Smirensky, "The Evolution of the Present Rite of Matrimony
and Parallel Canonical Developements", *St. Vladimir's Seminary Quarterly* 8.1
(1964): 45.

In the decisions in these matters reached by the authority of the Orthodox Churches, the distinction between a "declaration of nullity", "annulment", "dissolution", or "divorce" is usually lacking or is practically unknown, and often in these declarations the underlying motivations of the decision are not indicated. Furthermore, a fundamental uncertainty exists regarding the seriousness of the canonical process in verifying the eventual validity or nullity of a marriage in the Orthodox Churches. This produces a true doubt regarding the motivation and the legitimacy of these declarations as far as their applicability in the Catholic Church is concerned.

From the point of view of Catholic matrimonial law, we are bound to consider a marriage valid until there is certain contrary proof (cf. can. 1060 *Codex Iuris Canonici* [CIC] and can. 779 *Canonum Ecclesiarum Orientalium* [CCEO]). Many Orthodox Churches do little more than simply ratify the divorce sentence issued by the civil court. In other Orthodox Churches, as, for example, in the Middle East, in which ecclesial authorities hold exclusive competence in matrimonial matters, declarations dissolving religious marriages are issued solely by applying the principle of *oikonomia*.

At the beginning of this essay we asked whether the Orthodox practice could represent "a way out" for the Catholic Church in the face of the growing instability of sacramental marriages, by providing a pastoral approach toward those Catholics who, after the failure of a sacramental marriage and a subsequent civil divorce, contract a second, civil marriage.

Before responding to this question, another question should be posed. Is it thinkable to resolve the difficulties that Christian marriages must confront in the contemporary world by lowering the demands of indissolubility?

Will we have helped to cultivate the dignity of matrimony, or do we offer it only a *placebo*, as in the Old Testament, for the hardness of hearts?

Christ brought his new, revolutionary message, one that was "countercultural" to the pagan world. His disciples announced his good news, fearlessly presenting near impossible demands that contradicted the culture of that age. The world today is perhaps similarly marked by the neo-paganism of consumption, comfort, and egoism, full of new cruelties committed by methods ever more modern and ever more dehumanizing. Faith in supernatural principles is now more than ever subject to humiliation.

All this brings us to consider whether "hardness of heart" is a convincing argument to muddle the clearness of the teaching of the gospel on the indissolubility of Christian marriage. But as a response to the many questions and doubts, and to the many temptations to find a "short cut" or to "lower the bar" for the existential leap that one makes in the great "contest" of married life—in all this confusion among so many contrasting and distracting voices, still today resound the words of the Lord: "What therefore God has joined together, let not man put asunder" (Mk 10:9), and the final consideration of Saint Paul: "This is a great mystery ..." (Eph 5:32).

5

Unity and Indissolubility of Marriage: From the Middle Ages to the Council of Trent

Walter Cardinal Brandmüller

When in the fourth and fifth centuries the Western Church spread from the Mediterranean basin northward beyond the borders of the Roman Empire, missionaries were confronted with the social structures and ways of life of the people who were living there. The laws and customs of the Celts and the Germans did not encompass a concept of the unity and indissolubility of marriage. This factor introduced unfamiliar problems in terms of the evangelization of these nations, which were the subject of several synods during that period.

The Synod of Carthage in 407 had already instructed that spouses were not allowed to enter into a new marriage following a separation. Likewise, the Synod of Angers in 453 (canon 6) imposed the penalty of excommunication on any man who attempted to marry the wife of a man who was still alive. The same legislation appears in an Irish synod at the same time (canon 19). Canon 2 from the Synod of Vannes (465) excluded those men from Holy

Communion who dismissed their wives because of adultery without providing evidence for it and who subsequently married another woman. A similar decision was reached at the Synod of Agde (506), called by Caesarius of Arles. It excommunicated any man who separated from his wife because of her crimes and married another one without having obtained a favorable judgment from a provincial synod. Finally, the Council of Orléans (533) forbade divorce for reasons of illness under pain of excommunication.

Following the rise of the Carolingian dynasty, some remarkable developments can be noted. Pope Zacharias insisted with Pippin in 747 that a man who dismissed his wife for adultery and married another woman was excommunicated. Only ten years later the Synods of Verberie and Compiègne allowed the remarriage of a spouse in the case of adultery on the part of the other spouse, with the proviso, however, that the innocent party should practice continence. In particular, the separation of spouses was permitted in the following instances: if a man had sexual relations with his stepdaughter or a woman with her stepson; if a woman attempted an assault on her husband's life; if a woman refused to follow her husband into a foreign territory; or if a man had sexual relations with his wife's cousin. It should be noted that in all three manuscripts containing these dispositions the following words were added: "hoc aecclesia non recipit" (the Church does not acknowledge [these regulations]).[1]

---

[1] This comment refers to canon or chapter 18 of the *Decretum Vermeriense I* from the Synod of Verberie of 756: "Qui cum consobrina uxoris suae manet, sua careat et nullam aliam habet. Illa mulier quam habuit faciat quod vult. Hoc aecclesia non recipit." See PL 96.1508. (The man who stays [the night] with the

The structure of Frankish society, which included free men and slaves, introduced further problems. A way had to be found to reconcile the Church's demand for the indissolubility of marriage with the social status of married slaves, as, for example, when one of the spouses was sold, resulting in their separation. In more general terms synodal legislation soon adopted stricter regulations within the Frankish kingdoms that cannot be discussed in detail here. However, while the separation of the spouses was considered a possibility, as in the case of adultery, a second marriage was not permitted. The *Decretum Gratiani* of circa 1140 led to a standardization of marital legislation, removed existing inconsistencies, and gave a definitive expression to the Christian principle of unity and indissolubility of marriage.

An Exceptional Case: King Lothair II against Pope Nicholas I

The difficulties that had to be overcome especially in the Germano-Frankish world are vividly illustrated by the life of Charlemagne, who did not care for the unity and indissolubility of marriage. A particularly striking instance occurred in the dispute over the marriage of King Lothair II and Theutberga, which involved Pope Nicholas I in the years 860–869 and caught much attention in the Church

---

cousin of his wife has to leave her and not have any other. That woman he had may do what she wants. [But] this, the Church has never received.) Wielfried Hartmann in *Die Synoden der Karolingerzeit im Frankenreich und in Italien* (Paderborn: Verlag Ferdinand Schöningh, 1989), p. 75, has pointed out that the final phrase, "*Hoc aecclesia non recipit,*" is probably a gloss that was added to the text only in course of history.—ED. Unless indicated otherwise, all translations are my own.

1

and in the world. The question, which occupied several synods, was whether the king could separate from his legitimate wife, Theutberga, for lack of offspring in order to marry his former concubine Waldrada, with whom he had lived earlier in a so-called *Friedelehe* (love marriage) and with whom he already had had a son, Hugo, along with several daughters. The disputes became so fierce that at one point a Frankish army even invaded Rome and threatened the Pope.

Lothair II's marriage with Theutberga had a political background. With this union the king joined a noble dynasty that controlled the important posts for crossing the Alps. Thus, his marriage placed him in a better position for intervening in the Burgundian territories. Theutberga's brother was the lay abbot of the monastery Saint-Maurice d'Agaune, which had a strategically significant location. Moreover, the king hoped to remove his younger brother, Charles, from Burgundy and to ascend to its throne. However, his plan was thwarted when, in the year after his wedding to Theutberga, Pope Benedict III achieved a peaceful mediation between the two brothers.

Hence the political reason for the marriage no longer existed. In addition, the king had a personal aversion to Theutberga and had probably found himself for some time in conflict with her family. He then turned back to Waldrada. The question arose concerning the legal and sacramental quality of his prior union with her. If it were a legally valid and hence sacramental marriage, it should have been impossible for the king to have married Theutberga in the first place. Yet this solution seems unlikely, since his marriage with Theutberga took place without any opposition on the part of the Church.

What then was the nature of Lothair's *Friedelehe* with Waldrada? The literature in the field of legal history does not present a clear picture, but the following can be ascertained: a *Friedelehe* (derived from *friedila*, meaning "lover" or "spouse") was constituted by the consent of a man and a woman, by the bridelope (*Brautlauf,* a term also used for wedding customs in general) and by sexual intercourse (*Beilager*). In this form of relationship the husband did not have legal guardianship (*Munt*) over the wife. The bride's father was not given the bridewealth (*Muntschatz*), but the bride did receive the dower (*Morgengabe*).[2] In the Germanic legal realm a couple opted for *Friedelehe* when they were of different social status, for example, when a man sought a woman of means for economic reasons (*Einheirat*), or in the case of elopement, or as a form of concubinage. Lothair and Waldrada were living together in this kind of relationship.

Friedelehe thus differed fundamentally from the so-called *Muntehe* (dowered marriage) that was based on a contract between the two extended families (*Sippe*) or between the bridegroom and the bride's father or guardian. In this case, the groom received disciplinary power over the bride (*Munt*) and in exchange for it provided the bridewealth (*Muntschatz*, also called *Wittum*). The contract was forged through a series of legal acts, the solemn handing over of the woman, her being taken into the home of the husband or bridelope (*Brautlauf*), and the consummation of the sexual relationship (*Beilager*). Through a *Muntehe* the

[2] Bridewealth refers to the payment made by the groom's family to the bride's family in order to ratify the marriage. Dower refers to the share of the husband's estate to which the wife is entitled as a consequence of her marriage to him, not to be confused with dowry.—ED.

wife became the lady of the house and received her dower (*Morgengabe*) on the morning after the wedding.

Such was the situation in the Germano-Frankish legal realm that the Church was facing when she tried to implement Christ's demand for the unity and indissolubility of marriage. The struggle to establish the Christian understanding of marriage began relatively late for reasons that cannot be discussed here. Only Saint Boniface, in conjunction with the Frankish rulers Carloman and Pippin, managed gradually to bring the law of God to bear. The many reform synods convoked by Boniface provided an adequate forum for this effort. From then on the principle formulated by Benedictus Levita came into force: "Nullum sine dote fiat coniugium nec sine publicis nuptiis quisquam nubere praesumat." (No marriage should be held without a dower, and no one should dare to get married without a public wedding.)[3]

Though it would seem that the *Muntehe* or dowered marriage had won the day, it remains unclear whether *Friedelehe* was in fact abandoned. Paul Mikat sees unresolved questions for further research here, and Werner Ogris holds that whatever differences in detail there may be, there can hardly be serious doubt about the existence of a marriage without dower and without guardianship (*Minderehe*) in the Germanic realm.[4]

---

[3] Benedictus Levita, Liber II, ca. 133, cited in *Monumenta Germaniae Historiae: Leges*, ed. George Heinrich Pertz, vol. II. 2 (Hanover: Hahn, 1837), p. 80. Benedictus Levita is thought to be a pseudonym for a ninth-century forger.—ED.

[4] See Paul Mikat, *Dotierte Ehe, rechte Ehe: Zur Entwicklung des Eheschliessungsrechts in fränkischer Zeit* (Opladen: Westdeutscher Verlag, 1978); and Werner Ogris, "Friedelehe", in *Handwörterbuch zur deutschen Rechtsgeschichte*, vol. 1, ed. Adalbert Erler and Ekkehard Kaufmann (Berlin: Erich Schmidt Verlag, 1971), 1295.

However, under ecclesiastical influence there was a tendency to distinguish ever more clearly between *Muntehe* and *Friedelehe*, and hence to associate the latter by force with nonmarital sexual relations. This is shown in the indiscriminate use of the word *concubina* to indicate both a *Friedelfrau* and a concubine in the proper sense (*Kebsfrau*).

Under these circumstances it was an urgent requirement in the case of Lothair to examine whether before his marriage with Theutberga he had entered into a marriage with Waldrada *secundum legem et ritum* (according to law and custom or rite). The Pope insisted on a dower and a public blessing of the marriage.

Actually, we have no sources at all indicating that the Church ever recognised a *Friedelehe* as a marriage in the proper sense. This would be consistent with the fact that there were no objections from the Church when Lothair married Theutberga after his separation from Waldrada.[5]

[5] See Mikat, *Dotierte Ehe*, pp. 76–77:

The development of marriage law in Franco-Merovingian times and in subsequent centuries displays the difficulties the Church encountered in asserting its concept of, and its laws concerning, marriage among the Germanic peoples. Although the Church approached this issue fairly late and with hesitation, nevertheless, during this process of implementing the Church's teaching on marriage in these regions, the laws about contracting marriage were of special significance. The Church did not have ready to hand an ecclesial model for contracting marriage; it was willing to accept the indigenous laws concerning contraction of marriage provided they stood for a form of marriage that the Church theologically could accept without reservation, meaning that the form of marriage corresponded to the principle of indissolubility and of monogamous partnership for life. The development since the middle of the eighth century clearly confirms the fact that, from the Church's point of view, laws about contracting marriage had a merely functional character, and that the Church's influence on laws concerning the contracting of marriage was connected to its endeavour to assert its concept of marriage." (Translated from German; my translation.)

Under these circumstances it cannot but be called logical when Nicholas I called the attempt to contract a *Muntehe* with Waldrada a grave sacrilege. Nonetheless he wanted to establish justice and therefore ordered a detailed examination of the case at the Synod of Metz (863) through his legates Radoald and John. Their commission was to determine the accuracy of Lothair's claim that he had received Waldrada from her father as wife. This would hold if Lothair had indeed taken Waldrada as wife according to law and custom after having given the bridal dower in the presence of witnesses. If this were true, the question would arise why he then dismissed her and married Theutberga. If, however, Lothair claimed to have married Theutberga for fear, then the question had to be asked why such a powerful king would despise God's commandment and fall so low for fear of a single man.

Pope Nicholas ordered that if in the course of the investigation it emerged that Waldrada was not his legitimate wife, because she had not married Lothair with the priestly blessing according to custom, the legates were to make the king understand that he had to take back Theutberga, provided that she was without any guilt in the matter. He should not heed the voice of the flesh, but should rather obey the law of God. He should abhor perishing in the mud of fornication by following his own will, and rather be mindful that he would have to render an account before the judgment seat of Christ one day. The Pope also told his legates that Theutberga had already had recourse to the Apostolic See three times, that she was complaining about her unjust dismissal and insisted that she had been forced by Lothair to make a false admission of incest with her brother. Should Theutberga now obey the Pope's summons before the synod, the legates should examine her case conscientiously.

If she persisted with the charge that she was forced to make this admission and was sentenced by unjust judges, the legates should decide according to law and equity, so that she would not be crushed by the weight of injustice.

It is interesting to note that Nicholas does not ignore the fate of Waldrada. In fact, he accuses Lothair of acting sacrilegiously toward her too. Subsequently, several bishops received letters from the Pope calling upon them to use their influence on Lothair and make him return to the right path. Nicholas wrote to Lothair in person toward the end of the year 863: "You have yielded to the urging of your body so much, that you have slackened the reins of your lust. Thus you, who were made the guide of your people, have become the cause of ruin for many!"[6] After these and similar admonitions proved to be in vain, both Lothair and Waldrada were excommunicated, the latter not until June 13, 866. In the subsequent course of events, which could not be rectified during the king's lifetime, the Pope's position did not change in any way.

Taken as a whole, the statements of Nicholas I, as well as those of the eminent Archbishop Hincmar of Reims, regarding the case become a part of the continuous development of canonical tradition and of the Church's faith, which asserts the unity and indissolubility of a sacramental marriage. Another point emerges clearly: the more the Church succeeded in promoting this understanding of marriage, the less marriage was instrumentalized for other purposes.

In no historical period could it be excluded that marriages would be subservient to political, dynastic, or even financial interest; in such situations the personal dignity and rights of the women concerned were often sacrificed,

[6] See PL 119.869.

and men were provoked to break a marriage contracted with a woman they did not love. Nonetheless, Hincmar of Reims and, above all, Nicholas I highlighted the dignity and rights of the wife against the arbitrariness of the powers that be. Hincmar explicitly emphasized with reference to canon law that even the infertility of the wife was no reason for dissolving a valid marriage, and certainly not for a remarriage.

On the other hand, Nicholas, though not ignoring Waldrada's guilt, considered her also the victim of Lothair's passions. His most impressive explanations, which are contained in a letter to Lothair's uncle, Louis the German (October 30, 867), give witness to an understanding of marriage that could almost anachronistically be called "personalist". In this letter he asks Louis to try to influence his nephew Lothair not only to receive Theutberga again with honors and restore her rights, as had already been achieved by the legate Arsenius, but also to treat her as his wife in a real sense. What good would it be, Nicholas asks, if Lothair did not go anymore to Waldrada with the feet of his body, while his mind would rush to her; and what use would it be if he was separated from Waldrada externally, but internally still fused with her? After all Theutberga could not be satisfied with the physical proximity of her husband if there were no spiritual communion between them, given that Waldrada still exercised her power over Lothair as if *she* were the queen.

Further Development

Everything about this episode shows that a process had begun by which the Christian understanding of marriage gradually was to prevail over received, pre-Christian forms and norms of marriage among those peoples that had now been converted to the Christian faith.

If we look at the stages of this process, we find that there were no doubts regarding the theological foundations, but there were considerable uncertainties regarding the application of the Christian teaching of marriage to concrete cases, which emerged in social conditions that still bore the stamp of pre-Christian traditions. In fact, in this process of "inculturation" of the gospel we encounter individual bishops and even synods that believed they could dissolve marriage and allow remarriage, as had happened several times in the aforementioned case.

Around the year 1000, this process was largely completed, and the *Concordantia discordantium canonum* of Gratian (c. 1140), which has since been normative for ecclesiastical practice, shows that previous uncertainties had by then been overcome.

In the year 1184 the Synod of Verona under the presidency of Pope Lucius III numbered marriage among the sacraments of the Church as a matter of course; this was confirmed by the Second Ecumenical Council of Lyon (1274), and when Pope John XXII defended marriage against contemporary heretics as *coniugii venerabile sacramentum.*

The Ecumenical Council of Florence in 1439 pronounced extensively on the matter in the bull of union for those Armenians who returned to the Catholic Church. The reason given here for the indissolubility of marriage is that it represents the indissoluble union of Christ and the Church. The conciliar text continues: "But, although it is permitted to separate on account of fornication, nevertheless it is not permitted to contract another marriage since the bond of a marriage legitimately contracted is perpetual."[7]

It is remarkable that the text emphasizes the illicitness of remarriage with the words: "non tamen aliud matrimonium contrahere fas est." The phrase "non ... fas est" or "nefas est" does not simply signify an "injustice"; it denotes a "sacrilege".

This text corresponds to the teaching on marriage of the Council of Trent. Against the backdrop of the matrimonial scandals of King Henry VIII and the double marriage of Philip of Hesse, which was "permitted" by Luther, the Council in canon 2, *De matrimonio*, defined explicitly: "If anyone says that it is lawful for Christians to have several wives at the same time and that this is not forbidden by divine law, let him be anathema."[8]

History as a *Locus Theologicus*

Reviewing the different stages of this history could prompt us to remember a formula forged by canon law in the age of the Enlightenment: "olim non erat sic" (once it was not as it is today).

Applied to our present question, we would acknowledge that there were once occasions in which it *was* permitted to remarry after divorce. Given this fact, is there some reason in the current situation and in the face of present pastoral difficulties that would prevent us from returning to a doctrinal position already taken in the past

[7] See Denzinger-Hünermann, *Enchiridion Symbolorum*, no. 1327.
[8] Ibid., no. 1802.

and from accepting a "more humane" practice—as one would put it today—concerning divorce and remarriage?

This was also the reasoning of Martin Luther when he referred to the examples of polygamy in the Old Testament in his notorious "confessional advice", in order to justify the scandalous double marriage of Philip of Hesse in 1540. The reformer who found himself lacking in arguments failed to notice that, after the patriarchs of the Old Testament, Jesus Christ proclaimed the New and Eternal Covenant with God.

Similar arguments have been made in the field of ecumenical theology. Could one not convince the Orthodox of reunification much more easily if there were a return to the understanding of the Petrine primacy as it prevailed in the first millennium, and a return to the state of relations between East and West before their separation?

Already around the middle of the seventeenth century, there was a Protestant appeal—to be precise, by the theologians of Lutheran orthodoxy and the school of Helmstädt, which was closer to Melanchthon—to a model of reunification according to the so-called *consensus quinque-saecularis*, a return, that is, to the state of the doctrine of the faith and of the Church as it existed in the first five centuries, and about which there were no controversies at that time.

Truly fascinating ideas. But do they really offer a key to resolving the problem? Only in appearance. It is not for nothing that history has moved beyond them—their theological legitimacy does not rest on solid foundations. Tradition in the technical-theological sense of the term is not an antiques fair where one can look for and acquire particular desired objects.

Traditio-paradosis is instead a dynamic process of organic development according to—if I may use this comparison—the Church's given genetic code. This process, however, does not find adequate counterparts in the history of forms of societies, states, dynasties, and so on. Just as the Church herself is an entity *sui generis* with no analogies, so also its vital manifestations cannot be compared *sic et simpliciter* with those of purely humane and worldly communities. What is decisive here, instead, is divine revelation. This is the source of the indefectibility of the Church, or the fact that the Church of Jesus Christ, as far as its patrimony of faith, sacraments, and hierarchical structure founded on divine institution are concerned, cannot undergo any development that would threaten its identity.

As soon as one takes seriously the action of the Holy Spirit, who dwells within the Church and who, according to the promise of Jesus Christ, will lead her into all truth, it becomes clear that the principle *olim non erat sic* is not appropriate to the essence of the Church and therefore cannot be a determining factor for it.

But if the synods mentioned above effectively authorized Lothair II to remarry, was that not also a decision guided by the Holy Spirit? Was it not perhaps an expression of *paradosis*?

The answer to this lies in the concrete form and competence of those synods. While they did not pronounce on doctrinal questions or pass laws, they claimed to administer justice, and this not only in a narrowly juridical but also in a sacramental matter. In the case of Lothair these synods were not at all free of interference, and given the pressure exercised by the king they must undoubtedly be considered as biased, if not in fact corrupt. Their dependence on

Lothair II led to such compliance with the wishes of the king that the bishops even violated the law and corrupted the pontifical legates.

Taking into account these circumstances and other irregularities, it was evident that those synods had done anything but administer justice. It was precisely this kind of experience that led to the norm in canon law that deprives territorial ecclesiastical tribunals of competency over cases concerning the highest authorities of the State, and that indicates as the only competent forum the tribunal of the pope. In our case there is another decisive criterion: the uncompromising no of the pope to these synods, their procedure, and their judgment.

One can therefore not even remotely hold that such assemblies—and similar ones—could be a place to find the authentic and binding tradition of the Church.

Of course, not only general councils but also particular synods can formulate *paradosis* in a binding manner. Nonetheless, they can do so only if they themselves correspond to the demands of the authentic tradition in terms of both form and content. This, however—it is good to reiterate—was not the case with the assemblies of bishops examined here.

Following my argument, an objection may be raised from the perspective of Marxist historical interpretation that would see here an instance of a "history of the victors". According to this hermeneutic, the development of doctrine, sacraments, and the constitution of the Church by no means occurs as a consequence of some necessity or inner logic. Instead, the fact that other, perhaps contrary, approaches to doctrine and Church practice did not prevail was simply the result of accidental historical constellations or structures of power. This kind of Marxist perspective on the events of Church history permits one to view the outcomes of historical events within the Church as mere casual products of their own relativity. In other words, they could be tossed aside at any moment, and other directions could be followed.

But this is not possible if one takes as the foundation for reflection an authentically Catholic understanding of the Church, as expressed most recently in the Second Vatican Council's Dogmatic Constitution on the Church, *Lumen gentium*. It belongs to this understanding that the Church—as already mentioned—may be assured of the constant assistance of the Holy Spirit, who is her most intimate vital principle, establishing and guaranteeing her identity in spite of all the changes of history.

Thus the development of doctrine, sacraments, and the hierarchy of divine law does not come about as the casual product of history, but it is guided and made possible by the Spirit of God. For this reason, this development is irreversible and is open only toward a more complete understanding. Tradition in this sense thus has a normative character.

In our case, this means that there is no way out of the teaching of the unity, sacramentality, and intrinsic indissolubility of a marriage between two baptized persons—except the way into error.

The Example of the Martyrs

At what cost the Church defended the unity and indissolubility of sacramental marriage, and hence showed her faithfulness to the gospel of Jesus Christ, is witnessed not least by those saints who suffered martyrdom for it following the example of Saint John the Baptist. A few other examples may suffice.

In the early Germanic-Frankish Middle Ages, the age in which the conflicts about the Christian understanding of marriage were most intense, we encounter the Irish pilgrim monks Kilian, Kolonat (Colman), and Totnan, who had come as missionaries to the court of the Frankish Duke Gozbert. Their attempt to assert the norms of ecclesiastical law on marriage failed because of the resistance of Geilana, his illegitimate wife, who had the cumbersome protestors murdered around the year 689.

A similar experience was shared by Corbinian, probably of Breton nobility, who was consecrated a bishop in Rome around 714 and soon afterward went to Bavaria, where he introduced himself to Duke Theodo in Regensburg and to the co-regent Duke Grimoald in Freising. Corbinian's friendly relationship with Grimoald was shattered, however, when he declared the latter's marriage with Pilitrud as forbidden and demanded its annulment. Corbinian was forced to flee from Pilitrud's revenge and was able to return to Freising only after Grimoald's death.

Surely the most famous case is that of King Henry VIII of England, who desired the annulment of his undoubtedly valid marriage with Catherine of Aragon so as to be able to marry the maid of honor Anne Boleyn. In order to achieve this, he demanded in 1534 the consent of bishops, clergy, and the faithful of his realm to the so-called Act of Supremacy, by which he declared himself the supreme head of the Church of England in order to remove himself from the jurisdiction of the Pope, who was not able to comply with his request.

While almost the entire higher clergy submitted to the king, there was resistance from Bishop John Fisher of Rochester, previously chancellor of the University of Cambridge; from Thomas More, who resigned as lord chancellor because of the matter; from the Carthusians of London; from the observant branches of friars; and from some noble families. Fisher, More, and the London Carthusians soon felt the king's revenge. After spectacular trials, the verdict of which had been decided already before their start, they suffered martyrdom. The other faithful witnesses suffered violent persecution, which cost not a few of them their lives and many of them the loss of their property.

In this context the position of Pope Clement VII was remarkable. Notwithstanding strong political pressure and the danger of England's schism from the Catholic Church, he insisted on the validity and hence the indissolubility of the marriage between Henry and Catherine. To be sure, he tried by means of some hesitation, diplomatic initiatives, and procedural steps—some may call them dodges—to leave Henry time for reflection and repentance, but this was futile. Even the threat of England's separation from the unity of the Church did not shake the Pope.

It was a moment of glory in the history of the papacy when Clement VII, regardless of the consequence, upheld the truths of the faith and responded to the demands of the king with his famous "non possumus" (we cannot).

Bibliography

Angenendt, Arnold. *Geschichte der Religiosität im Mittelalter.* 2nd ed. Darmstadt: Primus Verlag, 2000.

Bedouelle, Guy, and Patrick Le Gal. *Le divorce du roi Henri VIII: Etudes et documents*. Geneva: Droz, 1987.

Brandmüeller, Walter, ed. *Handbuch der bayerischen Kirchengeschichte*. Vol. 1. St. Ottilien: EOS, 1998.

Gaudemet, Jean. *Conciles gaulois du IV siècle, texte et traduction*. Paris: Éditions du Cerf, 1977.

——. *Les canons des conciles merovingiens (VI–VII siècles)*. Texte latin de l'édition C. de Clercq. Introduction, traduction et notes par Jean Gaudemet et Brigitte Basdevant. Paris: Éditions du Cerf, 1989.

Hartmann, Wilifried. *Die Synoden der Karolingerzeit im Frankenreich und in Italien*. Paderborn: Verlag Ferdinand Schöningh, 1989.

Heidecker, Karle. *The Divorce of Lothar II: Christian Marriage and Political Power in the Carolingian World*. Translated by Tanis M. Guest. Ithaca: Cornell University Press, 2010.

Mikat, Paul. *Dotierte Ehe, rechte Ehe: Zur Entwicklung des Eheschliessungsrechts in fränkischer Zeit*. Opladen: Westdeutscher Verlag, 1978.

Ogris, Werner. "Friedelehe". In *Handwörterbuch zur deutschen Rechtsgeschichte*. Vol. 1. Edited by Adalbert Erler and Ekkehard Kaufmann. Berlin: Erich Schmidt Verlag, 1971.

Pontal, Odette. *Die Synoden im Merowingerreich*. Paderborn: Ferdinand Schöningh, 1986.

6

Testimony to the Power of Grace:
On the Indissolubility of Marriage and
the Debate concerning the Civilly
Remarried and the Sacraments

Gerhard Ludwig Cardinal Müller

The problem concerning members of the faithful who
have entered into a new civil union after a divorce is not
new. The Church has always taken this question very seriously and with a view to helping the people who find
themselves in this situation. Marriage is a sacrament that
affects people particularly deeply in their personal, social,
and historical circumstances. Given the increasing number
of persons affected in countries of ancient Christian tradition, this pastoral problem has taken on significant dimensions. Today even firm believers are seriously wondering,
can the Church not admit the divorced and remarried to
the sacraments under certain conditions? Are her hands
permanently tied on this matter? Have theologians really
explored all the implications and consequences?

These questions must be explored in a manner that is
consistent with Catholic doctrine on marriage. A responsible

pastoral approach presupposes a theology that offers "the full submission of intellect and will to God who reveals, freely assenting to the truth revealed by him".[1] In order to make the Church's authentic doctrine intelligible, we must begin with the word of God that is found in sacred Scripture, expounded in the Church's Tradition and interpreted by the Magisterium in a binding way.

The Testimony of Sacred Scripture

Looking directly to the Old Testament for answers to our question is not without its difficulties, because at that time marriage was not yet regarded as a sacrament. Yet the word of God in the Old Covenant is significant for us to the extent that Jesus belongs within this tradition and argues on the basis of it. In the Decalogue, we find the commandment "[y]ou shall not commit adultery" (Ex 20:14), but elsewhere divorce is presented as a possibility. According to Deuteronomy 24:1–4, Moses lays down that a man may present his wife with a certificate of dismissal and send her away from his house, if she no longer finds favor with him. Thereafter, both husband and wife may embark upon a new marriage. In addition to this acceptance of divorce, the Old Testament also expresses certain reservations in its regard. The comparison drawn by the prophets between God's covenant with Israel and the marriage bond includes not only the ideal of monogamy, but also that of indissolubility. The prophet Malachi expresses this clearly: "[S]he

---

[1] Second Vatican Council, Dogmatic Constitution on Divine Revelation, *Dei Verbum*, November 18, 1965, no. 5.

is your companion and your wife by covenant.... [L]et none be faithless to the wife of his youth" (Mal 2:14–15).

Above all, it was his controversies with the Pharisees that gave Jesus occasion to address this theme. He distanced himself explicitly from the Old Testament practice of divorce, which Moses had permitted because of man's "hardness of heart", and he pointed to God's original will: "[F]rom the beginning of creation, God made them male and female. For this reason a man shall leave his father and mother and ... the two shall become one flesh.... What therefore God has joined together, let not man put asunder" (Mk 10:5–9; cf. Mt 19:4–9; Lk 16:18). The Catholic Church has always based her doctrine and practice upon these sayings of Jesus concerning the indissolubility of marriage. The inner bond that joins the spouses to one another was forged by God himself. It designates a reality that comes from God and is therefore no longer at man's disposal.

Today some exegetes take the view that even in the apostolic era these dominical sayings were applied with a degree of flexibility, notably in the case of *porneia* or unchastity (cf. Mt 5:32; 19:9) and in the case of a separation between a Christian and a non-Christian spouse (cf. 1 Cor 7:12–15). The unchastity clauses have been the object of fierce debate among exegetes from the beginning. Many take the view that they refer not to exceptions to the indissolubility of marriage, but to invalid marital unions. Clearly, however, the Church cannot build her doctrine and practice on controversial exegetical hypotheses. She must adhere to the clear teaching of Christ.

Saint Paul presents the prohibition on divorce as the express will of Christ: "To the married I give charge, not I but the Lord, that the wife should not separate from her husband (but if she does, let her remain single or else be reconciled to her husband) and that the husband should not divorce his wife" (1 Cor 7:10–11). At the same time Saint Paul permits, on his own authority, that a non-Christian may separate from a spouse who has become Christian. In this case, the Christian is "not bound" to remain unmarried (1 Cor 7:12–16). On the basis of this passage, the Church has come to recognize that only a marriage between a baptized man and a baptized woman is a sacrament in the true sense, and only in this instance does unconditional indissolubility apply. The marriage of the unbaptized is indeed ordered to indissolubility, but it can under certain circumstances—for the sake of a higher good—be dissolved (*privilegium Paulinum*). Here, then, we are not dealing with an exception to our Lord's teaching. The indissolubility of sacramental marriage, that is to say, marriage that takes place within the mystery of Christ, remains assured.

Of greater significance for the biblical basis of the sacramental view of marriage is the Letter to the Ephesians, where we read: "Husbands, love your wives, as Christ loved the Church and gave himself up for her" (Eph 5:25). And shortly afterward, the apostle adds: "For this reason a man shall leave his father and mother and be joined to his wife, and the two shall become one flesh. This is a great mystery, and I mean in reference to Christ and the Church" (Eph 5:31–32). Christian marriage is an effective sign of the covenant between Christ and the Church. Because it designates and communicates the grace of this covenant, marriage between the baptized is a sacrament.

The Testimony of the Church's Tradition

The Church Fathers and Councils provide important testimony regarding the way the Church's position evolved. For the Fathers, the biblical precepts on the subject are binding. They reject the State's divorce laws as incompatible with the teaching of Jesus. The Church of the Fathers rejected divorce and remarriage and did so out of obedience to the gospel. On this question, the Fathers' testimony is unanimous.

In patristic times, divorced members of the faithful who had civilly remarried could not even be readmitted to the sacraments after a period of penance. Some patristic texts, however, seem to imply that abuses were not always rigorously corrected, and that from time to time pastoral solutions were sought for very rare borderline cases.

In many regions, greater compromises emerged later, particularly as a result of the increasing interdependence of Church and State. In the East this development continued to evolve, and especially after the separation from the See of Peter, it moved toward an increasingly liberal praxis. In the Orthodox Churches today, there are a great many grounds for divorce, which are mostly justified in terms of *oikonomia*, or pastoral leniency in difficult individual cases, and they open the path to a second or third marriage marked by a penitential character. This practice cannot be reconciled with God's will, as expressed unambiguously in Jesus' sayings about the indissolubility of marriage. But it represents an ecumenical problem that is not to be underestimated.

In the West, the Gregorian reform countered these liberalizing tendencies and gave fresh impetus to the original understanding of Scripture and the Fathers. The Catholic Church defended the absolute indissolubility of marriage even at the cost of great sacrifice and suffering. The schism of a "Church of England" detached from the successor of Peter came about not because of doctrinal differences, but because the Pope, out of obedience to the sayings of Jesus, could not accommodate the demands of King Henry VIII for the dissolution of his marriage.

The Council of Trent confirmed the doctrine of the indissolubility of sacramental marriage and explained that this corresponded to the teaching of the gospel.[2] Sometimes it is maintained that the Church de facto tolerated the Eastern practice. But this is not correct. The canonists constantly referred to it as an abuse. And there is evidence that groups of Orthodox Christians on becoming Catholic had to subscribe to an express acknowledgment of the impossibility of second or third marriages.

The Second Vatican Council, in the Pastoral Constitution on the Church in the Modern World, *Gaudium et spes*, presents a theologically and spiritually profound doctrine of marriage. It upholds the indissolubility of marriage clearly and distinctly. Marriage is understood as an all-embracing communion of life and love, body and spirit, between a man and a woman who mutually give themselves and receive one another as persons. Through the personally free act of their reciprocal consent, an enduring, divinely ordered institution is brought into being, which is directed to the good of the spouses and of their offspring and is no longer dependent on human caprice: "As a mutual gift of two persons, this intimate union and the good of the children impose total fidelity on the spouses and argue for an unbreakable oneness between them".[3] Through the sacrament God bestows a special grace upon the spouses:

[2] See Denzinger-Hünermann, *Enchiridion Symbolorum*, no. 1807.

For as God of old made himself present to his people through a covenant of love and fidelity, so now the Saviour of men and the Spouse of the Church comes into the lives of married Christians through the sacrament of matrimony. He abides with them thereafter so that just as he loved the Church and handed himself over on her behalf, the spouses may love each other with perpetual fidelity through mutual self-bestowal.[4]

Through the sacrament the indissolubility of marriage acquires a new and deeper sense: it becomes the image of God's enduring love for his people and of Christ's irrevocable fidelity to his Church.

Marriage can be understood and lived as a sacrament only in the context of the mystery of Christ. If marriage is secularized or regarded as a purely natural reality, its sacramental character is obscured. Sacramental marriage belongs to the order of grace; it is taken up into the definitive communion of love between Christ and his Church. Christians are called to live their marriages within the eschatological horizon of the coming of God's Kingdom in Jesus Christ, the incarnate Word of God.

The Testimony of the Magisterium in the Present Day[5]

The Apostolic Exhortation *Familiaris consortio*—issued by Saint John Paul II on November 22, 1981, in the wake of

---

[3] Second Vatican Council, Pastoral Constitution on the Church in the Modern World, *Gaudium et spes*, December 7, 1965, no. 48 (hereafter cited as *GS*).
[4] Ibid.
[5] See the collection of Magisterial texts at the back of this volume.

the Synod of Bishops on the Christian family in the modern world, and of fundamental importance ever since— emphatically confirms the Church's dogmatic teaching on marriage. But it shows pastoral concern for the civilly remarried faithful who are still bound by an ecclesially valid marriage. The Pope shows a high degree of concern and understanding. Paragraph number 84 on "divorced persons who have remarried" contains the following key statements: (1) Pastors are obliged, by love for the truth, "to exercise careful discernment of situations". Not everything and everyone are to be assessed in an identical way. (2) Pastors and parish communities are bound to stand by the faithful who find themselves in this situation, with "attentive love". They too belong to the Church; they are entitled to pastoral care, and they should take part in the Church's life. (3) And yet they cannot be admitted to the Eucharist. Two reasons are given for this: (a) "their state and condition of life objectively contradict that union of love between Christ and the Church which is signified and effected by the Eucharist", and (b) "if these people were admitted to the Eucharist, the faithful would be led into error and confusion regarding the Church's teaching about the indissolubility of marriage." Reconciliation through sacramental confession, which opens the way to reception of the Eucharist, can only be granted in the case of repentance over what has happened and a "readiness to undertake a way of life that is no longer in contradiction to the indissolubility of marriage". Concretely this means that if for serious reasons, such as the children's upbringing, the new union cannot be dissolved, then the two spouses must "bind themselves to live in complete continence". (4) Clergy are expressly forbidden, for intrinsically sacramental and theological reasons and not through legalistic pressures, to "perform ceremonies of any kind" for divorced people who remarry civilly, as long as the first sacramentally valid marriage still exists.

The Congregation for the Doctrine of the Faith's statement of September 14, 1994, on the reception of Holy Communion by divorced and remarried members of the faithful,[6] emphasizes that the Church's practice in this question "cannot be modified because of different situations" (no. 5). It also makes clear that the faithful concerned may not present themselves for Holy Communion on the basis of their own conscience: "Should they judge it possible to do so, pastors and confessors ... have the serious duty to admonish them that such a judgment of conscience openly contradicts the Church's teaching" (no. 6). If doubts remain over the validity of a failed marriage, these must be examined by the competent marriage tribunals (cf. no. 9). It remains of the utmost importance

> with solicitous charity to do everything that can be done to strengthen in the love of Christ and the Church those faithful in irregular marriage situations. Only thus will it be possible for them fully to receive the message of Christian marriage and endure in faith the distress of their situation. In pastoral action one must do everything possible to ensure that this is understood not to be a matter of discrimination but only of absolute fidelity to the will of Christ who has restored and entrusted to us anew the indissolubility of marriage as a gift of the Creator. (no. 10)

[6] Congregation for the Doctrine of the Faith, Letter to the Bishops of the Catholic Church Concerning the Reception of Holy Communion by the Divorced and Remarried Members of the Faithful, September 14, 1994, in *Acta Apostolicae Sedis* 86 (1994): 974–79.

In the Post-Synodal Apostolic Exhortation *Sacramentum caritatis*, of February 22, 2007, Benedict XVI summarizes the work of the Synod of Bishops on the theme of the Eucharist, and he develops it further. In paragraph number 29 he addresses the situation of the divorced and remarried faithful. For Benedict XVI too, this is a "complex and troubling pastoral problem". He confirms "the Church's practice, based on Sacred Scripture (cf. Mk 10:2–12), of not admitting the divorced and remarried to the sacraments", but he urges pastors, at the same time, to devote "special concern" to those affected, in the wish that they "live as fully as possible the Christian life through regular participation at Mass, albeit without receiving communion, listening to the word of God, eucharistic adoration, prayer, participation in the life of the community, honest dialogue with a priest or spiritual director, dedication to the life of charity, works of penance, and commitment to the education of their children". If there are doubts concerning the validity of the failed marriage, these are to be carefully examined by the competent marriage tribunals. Today's mentality is largely opposed to the Christian understanding of marriage, with regard to its indissolubility and its openness to children. Because many Christians are influenced by this, marriages nowadays are probably invalid more often than they were previously, because there is a lack of desire for marriage in accordance with Catholic teaching, and there is too little socialization within an environment of faith. Therefore assessment of the validity of marriage is important and can help to solve problems. Where nullity of marriage cannot be demonstrated, the requirement for absolution and reception of Communion, according to the Church's established and approved practice, is that the couple live "as friends, as brother and sister". Blessings of irregular unions are to be avoided, "lest confusion arise among the faithful concerning the value of marriage". A blessing (*bene-dictio*, divine sanctioning) of a relationship that contradicts the will of God is a contradiction in terms.

During his homily at the Seventh World Meeting of Families in Milan on June 3, 2012, Benedict XVI once again had occasion to speak of this painful problem:

> I should also like to address a word to the faithful who, even though they agree with the Church's teachings on the family, have had painful experiences of breakdown and separation. I want you to know that the Pope and the Church support you in your struggle. I encourage you to remain united to your communities, and I earnestly hope that your dioceses are developing suitable initiatives to welcome and accompany you.

The most recent Synod of Bishops, on the theme "New Evangelization for the Transmission of the Christian Faith" (October 7–28, 2012), addressed once again the situation of the faithful who after the failure of a marital relationship (not the failure of a marriage, which being a sacrament still remains) have entered a new union and live together without a sacramental marriage bond. In the concluding *Message to the People of God at the Conclusion of the 13th Ordinary General Assembly of the Synod of Bishops* (October 26, 2012), the Synod Fathers addressed those concerned as follows:

> To all of them we want to say that God's love does not abandon anyone, that the Church loves them, too, that the Church is a house that welcomes all, that they remain members of the Church even if they cannot receive sacramental absolution and the Eucharist. May our Catholic

communities welcome all who live in such situations and support those who are in the path of conversion and reconciliation. (no. 7)

Observations Based on Anthropology and Sacramental Theology

The doctrine of the indissolubility of marriage is often met with incomprehension in a secularized environment. Where the fundamental insights of Christian faith have been lost, church affiliation of a purely conventional kind can no longer sustain major life decisions or provide a firm foothold in the midst of marital crises—as well as crises in priestly and religious life. Many people ask, how can I bind myself to one woman or one man for an entire lifetime? Who can tell me what my marriage will be like in ten, twenty, thirty, or forty years? Is a definitive bond to one person possible at all? The many marital relationships that founder today reinforce the skepticism of young people regarding definitive life choices.

On the other hand, the ideal—built into the order of creation—of faithfulness between one man and one woman has lost none of its fascination, as is apparent from recent opinion surveys among young people. Most of them long for a stable, lasting relationship, in keeping with the spiritual and moral nature of the individual person. Moreover, one must not forget the anthropological value of indissoluble marriage: it withdraws the spouses from caprice and from the tyranny of feelings and moods. It helps them to survive personal difficulties and to overcome painful experiences. Above all, it protects the children, who have the most to suffer from marital breakdown.

Love is more than a feeling or an instinct. Of its nature it is self-giving. In marital love, two people say consciously and intentionally to one another, only you—and you for ever. The word of the Lord, "What therefore God has joined together" (Mk 10:9; Mt 19:6), corresponds to the promise of the spouses: "I take you as my husband.... I take you as my wife.... I will love, esteem, and honor you, as long as I live, till death us do part." The priest blesses the covenant that the spouses have sealed with one another before God. If anyone should doubt whether the marriage bond is ontological, let him learn from the word of God: "Have you not read that he who made them from the beginning made them male and female, and said, 'For this reason a man shall leave his father and mother and be joined to his wife, and the two shall become one'? So they are no longer two but one" (Mt 19:4–6; cf. Mk 10:5–9).

For Christians, the marriage of baptized persons incorporated into the Body of Christ has a sacramental character and therefore represents a supernatural reality. A serious pastoral problem arises from the fact that many people today judge Christian marriage exclusively by worldly and pragmatic criteria. Those who think according to the "spirit of the world" (1 Cor 2:12) cannot understand the sacramentality of marriage. The Church cannot respond to the growing incomprehension of the sanctity of marriage by pragmatically accommodating the supposedly inevitable, but only by trusting in "the Spirit which is from God, that we might understand the gifts bestowed on us by God" (1 Cor 2:12). Sacramental marriage is a testimony to the power of grace, which changes man and prepares the whole Church for the holy city, the new Jerusalem, the Church, which is prepared "as a bride adorned for her husband" (Rev 21:2). The gospel of the sanctity of marriage is to be proclaimed with prophetic candor. By adapting to the spirit of the age, a weary prophet seeks his own salvation but not the salvation of the world in Jesus Christ. Faithfulness to marital consent is a prophetic sign of the salvation that God bestows upon the world. "He who is able to receive this, let him receive it" (Mt 19:12). Through sacramental grace, married love is purified, strengthened, and ennobled. "Sealed by mutual faithfulness and hallowed above all by Christ's sacrament, this love remains steadfastly true in body and in mind, in bright days or dark. It will never be profaned by adultery or divorce."[7] In the strength of the sacrament of marriage, the spouses participate in God's definitive, irrevocable love. They can therefore be witnesses of God's faithful love, but they must nourish their love constantly through living by faith and love.

Admittedly there are situations—as every pastor knows—in which marital cohabitation becomes for all intents and purposes impossible for compelling reasons, such as physical or psychological violence. In such hard cases, the Church has always permitted the spouses to separate and no longer live together. It must be remembered, though, that the marriage bond of a valid union remains intact in the sight of God, and the individual parties are not free to contract a new marriage, as long as the spouse is alive. Pastors and Christian communities must therefore take pains to promote paths of reconciliation in these cases too, or, should that not be possible, to help the people concerned to confront their difficult situation in faith.

[7] GS 49.

162

Observations Based on Moral Theology

It is frequently suggested that remarried divorcées should be allowed to decide for themselves, according to their conscience, whether or not to present themselves for Holy Communion. This argument, based on a problematical concept of "conscience", was rejected by a document of the Congregation for the Doctrine of the Faith in 1994.[8] Naturally, the faithful must consider every time they attend Mass whether it is possible to receive Communion, and a grave unconfessed sin would always be an impediment. At the same time they have the duty to form their conscience and to align it with the truth. In so doing they listen also to the Church's Magisterium, which helps them "not to swerve from the truth about the good of man, but rather, especially in more difficult questions, to attain the truth with certainty and to abide in it"[9]. If remarried divorcées are subjectively convinced in their conscience that a previous marriage was invalid, this must be proven objectively by the competent marriage tribunals. Marriage is not simply about the relationship of two people to God; it is also a reality of the Church, a sacrament, and it is not for the individuals concerned to decide on its validity, but rather for the Church, into which the individuals are incorporated by faith and baptism. "If the prior marriage of two divorced and remarried members of the faithful was valid, under no circumstances can their new union be considered lawful, and therefore reception of the sacraments is intrinsically

[8] That is, the Congregation's Letter to the Bishops Concerning the Reception of Holy Communion by the Divorced and Remarried, discussed above.
[9] John Paul II, Encyclical Letter *Veritatis splendor*, August 6, 1993, no. 64.

impossible. The conscience of the individual is bound to this norm without exception"[10]

The teaching on *epikeia*, too—according to which a law may be generally valid, but does not always apply to concrete personal situations—may not be invoked here, because in the case of the indissolubility of sacramental marriage we are dealing with a divine norm that is not at the disposal of the Church. Nevertheless—as we see from the *privilegium Paulinum*—the Church does have the authority to clarify the conditions that must be fulfilled for an indissoluble marriage, as taught by Jesus, to come about. On this basis, the Church has established impediments to marriage, she has recognized grounds for annulment, and she has developed a detailed process for examining these.

A further case for the admission of remarried divorcées to the sacraments is argued in terms of mercy. Given that Jesus himself showed solidarity with the suffering and poured out his merciful love upon them, mercy is said to be a distinctive quality of true discipleship. This is correct, but it misses the mark when adopted as an argument in the field of sacramental theology. The entire sacramental economy is a work of divine mercy, and it cannot simply be swept aside by an appeal to the same. An objectively false appeal to mercy also runs the risk of trivializing the image of God, by implying that God cannot do other than forgive. The mystery of God includes not only his mercy but also his holiness and his justice. If one were to suppress these characteristics of God and refuse to take sin seriously, ultimately it would not even be possible to bring God's mercy to man.

[10]Joseph Cardinal Ratzinger, "The Pastoral Approach to Marriage Must Be Founded on Truth", *L'Osservatore Romano*, English Edition, December 7, 2011, p. 4.

Jesus encountered the adulteress with great compassion, but he said to her, "[G]o, and do not sin again" (Jn 8:11). God's mercy does not dispense us from following his commandments or the rules of the Church. Rather it supplies us with the grace and strength needed to fulfill them, to pick ourselves up after a fall, and to live life in its fullness according to the image of our heavenly Father.

Pastoral Care

Even if there is no possibility of admitting remarried divorcées to the sacraments, in view of their intrinsic nature, it is all the more imperative to show pastoral concern for these members of the faithful, so as to point them clearly toward what the theology of revelation and the Magisterium have to say. The path indicated by the Church is not easy for those concerned. Yet they should know and sense that the Church as a community of salvation accompanies them on their journey. Insofar as the parties make an effort to understand the Church's practice and to abstain from Communion, they provide their own testimony to the indissolubility of marriage.

Clearly, the care of remarried divorcées must not be reduced to the question of receiving the Eucharist. It involves a much more wide-ranging pastoral approach, which seeks to do justice to the different situations. It is important to realize that there are other ways, apart from sacramental Communion, of being in fellowship with God. One can draw close to God by turning to him in faith, hope, and charity, as well as in repentance and prayer. God can grant his closeness and his salvation to people on different paths, even if they find themselves in a contradictory life situation. As recent documents of the Magisterium have emphasized, pastors and Christian communities are called to welcome people in irregular situations openly and sincerely, to stand by them sympathetically and helpfully, and to make them aware of the love of the Good Shepherd. If pastoral care is rooted in truth and love, it will discover the right paths and approaches in constantly new ways.

7

Sacramental Ontology and the Indissolubility of Marriage

Carlo Cardinal Caffarra

Rediscovering the Method

The institution of marriage has undergone a "storm" the likes of which has never been seen in history. Applying the language of genetics, Pierpaolo Donati shows that this upheaval involves not only *morphogenetic mutations* (changes of the form), but the *genome* of matrimony itself is changing.[1]

The upcoming Synod, in October of 2014, will be unable to avoid taking a position when faced with this dilemma: Is the manner in which the institution of marriage and the family is evolving positive for people, for their relationships, and for society? Or does it instead constitute the downfall of the person, of relationships, and of society?

The Church cannot help but think that what is happening (young people who do not marry but live together;

---

[1] Pierpaolo Donati, *La famiglia. Il genoma che fa vivere la società* (Soveria Mannelli: Rubbettino, 2013).

the introduction of so-called homosexual marriage in the juridical order; divorces that are ever more easily legally obtained) involves historical processes that she must recognize, and to which she must substantially conform herself. Yet, it is fundamentally important for the Synod to discover and to choose the proper path in order to announce to the world the gospel (good news) regarding matrimony and the family. The decisive question here is one of method.

Even in Jesus' time the rabbinical schools discussed the "question of marriage". More precisely, they debated the causes that justified divorce. Jesus was asked which conditions he held as justifying divorce. The fact that he kept the company of both "rigorists" and the "lax" was not important; among Jews, the licitness of divorce as such was not questioned by anyone (cf. Mt 19:3–9). Jesus refused to take a casuistic approach to the question, but he did indicate in what direction one ought to look in order to understand what marriage and its indissolubility truly were in order to avoid the "tyranny" represented in the opinions of the various rabbinic schools. He referred to what we shall call the "first principle".

The turning point implied by Jesus' response to man's approach regarding the questions of marriage is a radical one. It requires a true and proper *conversion*. The catechesis of Saint John Paul II is there to show us this way of conversion.

Jesus' first principle is not to be thought of as the universally valid moral law of indissolubility.[2] That was

---

[2] See Gilfredo Marengo, "L'antropologia adeguata nelle catechesi sull'amore umano. Linee di riflessione", in *Amare l'amore umano. L'eredità di Giovanni Paolo II sul matrimonio e la famiglia*, eds. Livio Melina and Stanislaw Grygiel (Siena: Cantagalli, 2007), p. 158.

precisely the Pharisees' view: a law exists for which Moses had already allowed objections. The Pharisees asked Jesus what extension—in his opinion—Moses' exception to the law could have. The method here consisted in applying the universal (the law of indissolubility) to the particular (the marital situation).

But the first principle referenced by Jesus is the truth about marriage and its indissolubility that is inscribed in the *person-body* and in the *body-person* of man and of woman by the creative act of God. This is the first principle, and its authority is demonstrated by virtue of its being the factor that they themselves understand as the intrinsic truth of their person, as the root that nourishes their marital experience: "This at last is bone of my bones and flesh of my flesh" (Gen 2:23).

I spoke of a *methodological conversion*. If we look at the first principle, as Jesus asks of us, the man and woman who marry do not encounter the law of indissolubility first and then decide whether or not they can conform to it. No, they are confronted with Jesus' first principle, that is, with the most profound truth of their being man and woman, with the dimension of their reciprocal gift, the expression of which is their body in all the original and pristine truth of their masculinity and femininity.

To put it bluntly, the drama of the individual person does not consist in the possibility of becoming a "case" considered exceptional or not according to the law. It consists in the fact that freedom can affirm or negate the truth of the person through the choices that person makes. Hence, the method we should apply does not consist in learning to proceed from the universal (the law of indissolubility) to the particular (the marital situation), but in educating the person to be free, that is, to be subject to the truth about the Good.[3]

In order to see the first principle and free themselves from the tyranny of contrasting opinions, the faithful are gifted with the supernatural *sensus fidei* (sense of the faith), which does not consist solely or necessarily in the consensus of the faithful. Following Christ, the Church seeks the truth, which is not always the same as the majority opinion. She listens to conscience and not to power, and in this way she defends the poor and the downtrodden. The Church values sociological and statistical research when it proves helpful in understanding the historical context in which pastoral action has to be developed, and when it leads to a better understanding of the truth. Such research alone, however, is not to be considered in itself an expression of the sense of faith.[4]

The methodological indication provided in *Familiaris consortio* is particularly timely, even more so now than when it was promulgated. I say this in consideration of two factors. One is the force, the pervasiveness of the major means of communication—real force that creates a consensus. The other is the consideration—typical of postmodernity—of the truth as a useless notion, and what follows in its wake: the supremacy of "feeling" when compared with "understanding".[5] From this feeling an experience of reality is derived, understood to be always submitted and placed under our manufacture. The result

[3] See Augustine, *De libero arbitrio* 2.13.37.

[4] See John Paul II, Apostolic Exhortation *Familiaris consortio*, November 22, 1981, no. 5 (hereafter cited as *FC*).

[5] See Maurizio Ferraris, *Manifesto del nuovo realismo* (Rome: Laterza, 2012), p. xi.

is that, in the West, the individual couple is thought of in the context of a privatized form of affectivity, without any social relevance.

The responsibility of the upcoming Synod is to recall us to a "conversion of thought" in an "orthoptic" way, to look at marriage without reducing it to the couple as it is considered in postmodern Western thought.

The Sacramental Gift of Indissolubility

Jesus, in responding to the Pharisees, spoke of a "hardness of heart" (Mt 19:8), which impeded them from understanding the first principle. The New Covenant was foreseen by two great prophets, Jeremiah (see Jer 31:33–34) and Ezekiel (see Ezek 36:26–27), as the substitution of the "heart of stone" for a "heart of flesh" (Ezek 36:26). Jesus, by instituting the sacrament of the Eucharist, revealed that the shedding of his blood constituted the New and Eternal Covenant (Lk 22:20).

By means of Christ's sacrifice, ever present in the Church through the Eucharist, man and woman have been reintegrated into the dignity of the first principle, freed from their incapacity to give themselves reciprocally "till death do us part."

It is in this context that one understands the true nature of marriage's indissolubility. It is not principally a moral or juridical obligation. It is a gift that ontologically configures the person of the spouses, inasmuch as they become joined to one another with a bond, a conjoining, which is the real symbol of the Church belonging to Christ and of Christ belonging to the Church. This real symbol is not only a sign that simply recalls a certain reality (*sacramentum tantum*); rather, the real thing is present in the sign (*res et sacramentum*).

Every sacrament is an act of the Father, who by Christ's mediation accomplishes the salvation of the person. In matrimony this sacrament is a divine action that unites the two. This union pertains not only to the person in his spiritual dimension but also in his carnal dimension. The spouses are the two person-bodies or the two body-persons who are united by the action of the Father. The one is given to the other, and contemporaneously in this reciprocal belonging the mystery is inscribed: the union of Christ and his Church. The *ratio sacramenti* remains in the indissolubility of the bond, put into being by a divine act.

The great Doctors of the Church are unanimous in this regard, even given the diversity of their theological thought. I cite only one reference that is particularly suggestive. A text by Saint Bonaventure compares marriage to baptism. In baptism we have a permanent reality, called a character, and a transitory reality that consists in the washing. Analogously, in matrimony we have something that is permanent that is called the marital bond, and a transitory reality that consists in the consent. The true essence of marriage lies in the marital bond.[6] Since the sacramentality of marriage consists principally in the indissoluble bond,[7] the indissolubility does not come into being exclusively or principally by the mutual obligation that is undertaken

---

[6] See Bonaventure, *In IV Sent., Dist.* XXVII, a. 1, q. 1.

[7] See *In IV Sent., Dist.* XXVI, a. 1, q. 2, ad 4: "ex ratione illius indissolubilitatis praecipue matrimonium tenet rationem sacramenti et signi sacri."

with the consent of the two, but by the action of God, who inscribes the sacramental meaning and signification.[8] God never acts against, or by overlooking and ignoring, the freedom of the person. The consent only renders possible God's action.[9] So it stands in the thought of the Seraphic Doctor. The symbolic reality that defines the sacramentality of marriage coincides with its indissolubility: it is a sacrament (a sign of sacred reality) because it is indissoluble; it is indissoluble because it is a sacrament.

Thus by means of the marital consent, an event occurs that includes and transcends the two who contract marriage. Their consent roots them definitively in the mystery, and the "sum figure" of this enrooting is its indissolubility. That which God gives remains forever: he does not repent of his gifts—or is not sorry about them.

So that the sacramental significance may penetrate ever more profoundly into the person of the spouses, the Holy Spirit gives a conjugal charity to the spouses. This love has a double form. It is the perfection of the erotic love (not its negation or denial), and it is the healing of the incapacity of the man and of the woman to love each other forever.

From all that has been said heretofore, there turns out to be a singular relationship between marriage and the Eucharist. However, one can only understand this if he thinks of matrimony in its relationship to Christ and to the Church, and not just as a sacred sign—an image that

[8] See *In IV Sent.*, *Dist.* XXVII, a. 2, q. 1: "causa prima est divina institutio, causa proxima est humana pactio."

[9] See *In IV Sent.*, *Dist.* XXVIII, art. unic. q. 2: "consensus non facit matrimonium nisi eatenus, quatenus praesupponit divinam institutionem; divina autem institutio respicit congruam significationem."

is purely formal that represents a mystery, which remains exterior to it. The matrimony of two of the baptized, to the contrary, "is in in a real, essential, and intrinsic relationship with the mystery of the union of Christ with the Church, and therefore it participates in its nature ... and is produced by and imbued with the same."[10]

The Eucharist is the memorial of Christ's sacrifice, during which he betrothed to himself his Church; he unites her to his body and becomes "one flesh" with her.

> The Eucharist is the sacrament of our redemption. It is the sacrament of the spouse and bridegroom. The Eucharist renders present—and in a sacramental manner—makes real anew the act of our redemption by Christ, which itself "creates" the Church, His body. With this "body" Christ is united as the bridegroom is with the bride.... In the "great mystery" of Christ and of the Church, the perennial "unity of the two" was introduced, constituted from the very beginning by man and woman.[11]

Marriage is deeply seated and rooted, therefore, in the Eucharistic mystery. The reality that is being celebrated expresses this, whence matrimony springs. The intimately mystical nature of the sacramentality of the marital union then establishes the productive efficacy that is proper to conjugal sacramentality: marital love, the origins of which are found in the mystery that is Eucharistically present.

It is not difficult now to note the true, objective contradiction between that which the Eucharist celebrates, the

---

[10] Matthias Joseph Scheeben, *I misteri del cristianesimo: essenza, significato e sintesi* (Brescia: Editrice Morcelliana, 1960), p. 594. English edition: *The Mysteries of Christianity*, trans. Cyril O. Vollert (St. Louis: B. Herder, 1947).

[11] John Paul II, Apostolic Letter *Mulieris dignitatem*, August 15, 1988, no. 26.

Eucharistic mystery, and the state of life in which a person finds himself when such a one does violence to the marital bond, by living as a spouse with someone who is not one's actual spouse.

This is dealing with an objective contradiction—independent of their subjective conditions—between their state of life and the Christ-Church union, which is signified and actualized by the Eucharist.[12]

When the Sacrament Becomes a Drama

Postmodernity has hurled a mortal dare at the family, because it has designed to substantially modify the relational character of matrimony upon which the family is founded. The Church has only one response that is adequate to this challenge: to announce the gospel of matrimony.

In this final section I would like to respond to only one of the questions: Does the proclamation of the gospel of matrimony also include the admission of the divorced and civilly remarried to the Eucharist?

In order to reorganize my reflection from a conceptual point of view, I shall take into consideration exclusively the *objective* condition of those who are divorced and subsequently remarried, their state as it is characterized by two elements: the validity of the former marriage (a matrimony that is ratified [*ratum*] and consummated), and an attempted civil marriage and/or cohabitation *more uxorio* with someone other than the spouse.

The circumstances in which these two elements are realized are very different from case to case, and "pastors

[12] See Benedict XVI, Post-Synodal Apostolic Exhortation *Sacramentum caritatis*, February 22, 2007, no. 29.

[must know that] ... for the love of truth they are obliged to exercise careful discernment of situations".[13] Nevertheless, we must ask ourselves if the simple and plain fact of finding oneself in that condition precludes the person from approaching the Eucharist. My response is in the affirmative, for three reasons, fundamentally.

The first is the tradition of the Church, founded on the Scriptures (cf. 1 Cor 11:28), that communion with the Body and with the Blood of the Lord requires of those who participate therein that they not find themselves in contradiction with what they receive. Now, as I tried to explain at the end of the previous section, the *status* of the divorced and civilly remarried is in objective contradiction with that bond of love that unites Christ and the Church, which is signified and actualized by the Eucharist.

The reason is founded on sacramental "economy", which configures and transforms *ontologically* the individual person. The married person is *ontologically*, in his being, consecrated to Christ, conformed to him. The conjugal bond is put into being by God himself, by means of the consent of the two (spouses). In fact, it is only by a divine act that the mystery of the union of Christ and the Church can be inscribed in the bond.

The spouse remains integrated into such a mystery, even if the spouse, through a subsequent decision, attacks the sacramental bond by entering into a state of life that contradicts it. How could a person in this condition receive the Eucharist, the sacrament of that union of which the marital bond is a real symbol?

When the Church speaks of the indissolubility of a matrimony that is *ratum et consummatum*, she is speaking of a

[13] *FC* 84.

bond that is not primarily a moral bond (*pacta sunt servanda*), even if it is thought of as a promise made *coram Deo* (before God). It is the work of Christ in the Church and is thus unassailable, whether by the spouses themselves or by any and every civil and ecclesiastical authority. Admission to the Eucharist of the divorced and civilly remarried would become plausible only by reducing the sacramental economy to the moral order.

The second reason is consequent upon the first. If the Church were to admit the divorced and civilly remarried to the Eucharist, by that very fact she would recognize the moral legitimacy of living *more coniugali* with a person who is not the true spouse. Now this contradicts what the Church herself has always taught, basing herself on the sacred Scriptures, that the use and practice of sexuality is appropriate for the individual person only within marriage.

The moral law is not simply the imposition of a higher will, be it even that of God's will. It was the devastating nominalist crisis that introduced into Christian thought this vision of the moral law.

The essence of normative statements of morality is to be found in the *truth* about the good that is contained therein. The intrinsic evil of the adulterous act consists in the fact that the freedom of the adulterer negates the truth about sexuality.

The drama of man does not consist in the difficulty of living through a historical event or incident, something that is by definition circumscribed and unrepeatable, in conformity to a law with universal character. The drama of man lies in the possibility that is inscribed in personal freedom—inasmuch as it is created and also wounded by sin—of denying by means of personal choices the truth regarding the good of the person, a truth known by either reason or by divine revelation.

To appeal to prudence in this case is out of place. Prudence concerns itself with the realization of the good to which the moral virtues are ordered. That which is in itself, per se, and intrinsically illicit can never be the object of the prudential judgment. To summarize: a prudent adultery cannot exist and neither can an imprudent adultery. The fundamental meaning of Jesus calling us back to the first principle is a calling back to the *truth* of the relationship between man and woman, which does not exist by power of an imposition, but simply by the force of their being persons, a male person and a female person.

The reference to *epikeia* is equally without a foundation. The reason for *epikeia* consists in the fact that, because of the limitation of legislators, it is impossible to promulgate a law that takes into account all the possible cases.

However, if the lawgiver is God himself, to apply *epikeia* to the divine laws would signify attributing to God an incapacity that is proper to the human legislator. The virtue of *epikeia* is exercised only in the domain of human laws.[14]

The legitimation, on the Church's part, of a life that is being lived *more coniugali* with a person who is not the actual spouse calls into discussion not only sexual ethics but also the very anthropology of sexuality. Someone might object by saying, "Well then, adultery is an unpardonable sin. But that is surely contrary to the gospel."

---

[14] Saint Thomas Aquinas speaks about the power of human law and *epikeia* especially at *Summa theologica*, I–II, q. 96, a. 6, and II–II, q. 20, respectively.

Let me respond by saying that I am not speaking simply of adultery as an act, but of adultery as a *status* of life. I hold it to be the doctrine of the faith that both the one and the other are forgiven by God's mercy. Yet, the Church teaches a doctrine of the faith regarding divine forgiveness that is profoundly imbedded in the "symphony of the truth". God does not forgive the person who does not repent, because he desires to restore a relation of true friendship in liberty. The Council of Trent defines repentance in a precise manner: "sorrow of the soul and detestation for the sin committed, together with the resolution not to sin again", and this same teaching was taken up by the *Catechism of the Catholic Church*.[15]

The sin committed is to have made an attempt against the sacramental marriage bond, thus constituting a state of life that is objectively adulterous, in which all conjugal relations are objectively adulterous. This firm resolution to sin no more therefore implies the intention to live in a form of life that is no longer in contradiction with the indissolubility of marriage.[16]

To speak of a path of penance that does not require this decision is dramatically contradictory, as if to say that in following the way of penance it is licit for me to remain in the same state of life for which I am sorry and doing penance! To think that there are situations in which this "firm resolve to sin no more" is impossible would be to conclude that sin is stronger than the redemptive grace of Christ, stronger than the mercy of God. Saint Thomas defined the *proprium* (the thing proper to) the mercy of

---

[15] See Denzinger-Hünermann, *Enchiridion Symbolorum*, no. 1676: "animi dolor atque detestatio de peccato commisso, cum proposito non peccandi de caetero", and see *Catechism of the Catholic Church*, no. 1451.

[16] See FC 84.

God in the following manner: "to liberate from misery, intending by the word misery any sort of defect".[17]

The third reason has a consequential character. The admission of the divorced and civilly remarried to the Eucharist would persuade, not only the faithful, but also any attentive person of the idea that, at its heart, there exists no marriage that is absolutely indissoluble, that the "forever" to which every true love cannot but aspire is an illusion. There is no doubt that this conclusion contradicts Jesus' words regarding matrimony.

In the end, to speak of the "second marriage" as one that participates in an imperfect way in the *ratio coniugii* (the essence of what marriage is) is a serious offense against logic.

Conclusion

I would like to conclude with a marvelous excerpt from Karol Wojtyla (Saint John Paul II).

> There exists nothing that is more unknown and mysterious than love. Behold the route of the drama: the divergence between that which one finds on the surface and that which the mystery of love actually is. This is one of the greatest dramas of human existence.[18]

The Church has the mission of leading mankind, of educating people to overcome "the divergence between that

---

[17] *Summa theologica*, I, q. 21. See the wonderful text of St. Augustine, *Commentary on the Gospel of John* 12.13, regarding the link between the mercy of God and the "detestatio de peccato commisso".

[18] Karol Wojtyla, *Tutte le opere letterarie* (Milan: Bompiani, 2001), p. 821.

which one finds on the surface and that which the mystery of love actually is." She has the mission of announcing the gospel of marriage. She has the mission of announcing *even* the gospel—let me repeat: *the gospel*—of indissolubility, a true treasure that the Church guards in vessels of clay. This is the most urgent and inescapable priority.

8

The Divorced and Civilly Remarried and the Sacraments of the Eucharist and Penance

Velasio Cardinal De Paolis, C.S.

Introduction

This paper is about the divorced and civilly remarried in the Church, although these remarks basically apply to all those who live in irregular family situations. The clarification "remarried" means that the divorced as such are not excluded from the sacraments indicated in the title; they are excluded only because they have entered a new bond and live in an irregular marital situation. And it is precisely this permanent, irregular situation that determines the exclusion from the sacraments. In this case, two people living together under the same roof without being married are openly violating the law of God as presented by the Church. Church law clarifies the conditions to be admitted to the sacraments, the verification of which is the responsibility of the faithful themselves. At the same time, sacred ministers are instructed as to when they are obliged to exclude the faithful from the Eucharist on account of scandal. We will limit ourselves to describing the necessary conditions that the faithful must respect in order to be legitimately and fruitfully admitted to the sacraments.

Marriage and the family is the theme that the Holy Father has chosen for the Church's reflection, submitting it to a Synod of Bishops on two different occasions, one year apart from one another, October of 2014 and October of 2015. Previously, an in-depth questionnaire was administered in order to have an overview that was as realistic as possible. Unfortunately, the mass media have laid stress on the most marginal aspects of the theme and have treated it mainly, if not exclusively, as something new on all imaginable levels. The theme was somewhat anticipated in the Extraordinary Consistory of February 20–21, 2014, which focused on the family. According to the limited information provided by the spokesman of the Vatican Press Office, the Consistory covered a wide range of themes, but the main focus was on the remarried being admitted to the Eucharist, according to the impression attributed to Philippe Cardinal Barbarin.

It may be useful to reflect on the points underlying this topic. First of all, let us clarify who are the divorced and civilly remarried. Then we will focus on Church teachings regarding these people when it comes to the sacraments of the Church, indicating the general canonical provisions for all the faithful in this matter. Following this explanation, we will treat the issues raised, elaborating on the reasons that underlie the teaching and the discipline of the Church. Finally, we will consider a specific case proposed by Walter Cardinal Kasper.

The Divorced and Civilly Remarried

First of all, we would like to point out that when we say divorced and civilly remarried we refer to those who, after contracting a valid canonical marriage, that is, marriage under the laws of the Church, and after being unsuccessful in this marriage, are unable to celebrate a second canonical marriage given the existing bond, and therefore have undertaken a new, civil marriage. They are therefore bound by a religious bond (canonical marriage) and a civil bond (civil marriage). In a broader sense we have in mind all those who, because they live in irregular situations, are not in a state in which they are able to participate in the sacraments of penance and the Eucharist.

It should also be noted that it is one thing to say that certain faithful do not meet the necessary conditions to be admitted to the sacraments; it is another for ministers to refuse these persons the sacraments. Sacred ministers should keep such persons away from these sacraments also in order to avoid scandalizing the faithful who know the true situations of these individuals. In our presentation we will focus mainly on these required conditions, failing which the faithful cannot be admitted to the sacraments.

The Teaching of the Church

The teaching of the Church is consistent in her tradition especially with regard to the friendship of God, to repentance, and to the resolution not to sin again in order to be absolved from a grave sin in the sacrament of penance. Since the plight of the divorced and civilly remarried has become more common, along with efforts to move the Church to change her discipline, the teaching of the Church on this issue has been reaffirmed more insistently, especially during the long pontificate of Saint John Paul II and that of his successor, Benedict XVI. This teaching does not merely repeat the traditional discipline, but it provides reasons that do not permit changes, while it also indicates other ways to deal with this pastoral problem.

From the texts of the Magisterium, we may sum up the Church's teaching in the following points:

1. This teaching pertains first of all to those who were previously united in the bond of sacramental marriage and have then moved on to a new union, be it by simply living together, or through a union recognized by the civil law.

2. The situations among the divorced and civilly remarried can vary greatly, and priests are obliged to discern among them. There is a difference between those who have sincerely tried to save their first marriage and have been unjustly abandoned, and those who through their own grave fault have destroyed a canonically valid marriage. Finally, there are those who have contracted a second marriage for the sake of the children, and sometimes are subjectively certain in all conscience that their previous and irreparably destroyed marriage was never valid.

3. In regard to these various and different situations, the Church reaffirms her practice, based on Holy Scripture, of not admitting to the sacrament of reconciliation and to Eucharistic Communion divorced persons who have remarried.

4. The Church not only reiterates her discipline; she gives the reasons for it. The Church supports fidelity to

the words of Jesus (cf. Mk 10:11–12), according to which a new union cannot be recognized as valid until the previous marriage is declared invalid by the relevant authorities. Please note the words *"cannot be"*—the Church has no power to do so. Even assuming she wanted to do it, she does not have the power. As a result, if divorced persons have moved on to a new union living together as husband and wife, their new condition of life objectively contradicts the union of love between Christ and the Church, signified and effected by the Eucharist.

5. This truth lays the foundation for the provisions of canon 915, which requires the minister not to admit to the Eucharist those who persevere in a situation of objectively manifest, grave sin.

6. The grave sin must be objectively understood. "Obstinate persistence" refers to an objective situation of sin that endures over time and is not voluntarily terminated. The expression "manifest character" means that this situation is known to the community.

7. Nor can these persons approach the sacrament of penance. Sacramental absolution can be given only to those who have repented for violating the law of God and are sincerely ready to undertake a way of life that no longer contradicts the indissolubility of marriage. So, repentance and the resolution to make amends are necessary. This implies the will to leave behind a sinful living situation.

8. This teaching is not a punitive or discriminatory rule against the divorced and the civilly remarried, but rather expresses an objective situation that makes impossible admission to the Eucharistic Communion per se.

9. The Church cannot leave the divorced and civilly remarried to their own devices. Priests must help them

with attentive charity. They should not be considered as being separated from the Church (they are not excommunicated, nor are they subject to a canonical sanction). They continue to belong to the Church. Indeed, they are encouraged to listen to the word of God, attend the Sacrifice of the Mass, persevere in prayer, do works of mercy, educate their children in the Christian faith, and cultivate the spirit and the practice of penance.

10. The path for admission to the sacraments, however, is not completely closed. The divorced and civilly remarried, whose objective conditions make their cohabitation irreversible, will be admitted to the sacraments if they undertake to live in complete continence, that is, abstinence from the acts proper to married couples. They also need to avoid scandal, because whereas their condition as divorced and remarried is perhaps widely known in their communities, the fact that they do not live as husband and wife is not so clear.

11. Where there are doubts concerning the validity of the contracted sacramental marriage, the subjective certainty on the part of the spouses concerning the invalidity of the previous bond does not of itself legitimize the new union. In such a case, one must take the necessary measures under the law to verify the legitimacy of the doubt concerning the validity of the marriage. However, one must avoid setting pastoral care and Church law in opposition to each other. A common ground between law and pastoral care is love for the truth.

The discipline described above is not developed specifically for the divorced and civilly remarried. Rather, these regulations apply to the life of every Christian with regard to the sacraments of penance and the Eucharist. No Christian can approach the Eucharist without prior sacramental confession, if he is aware of being in a situation of grave sin. And no Christian can receive absolution from sin if he has not repented and is not willing to make amends.

Participation in the Sacraments: The Code of Canon Law and the Discipline of the Church

The Right of Every Christian to Receive the Sacraments: As regards the reception of the sacraments, in general the Code of Canon Law recognizes the right of every believer to receive from pastors the necessary spiritual means for salvation. Among these means, the sacraments are of particular importance. Canon 213 reads: "Christ's faithful have the right to be assisted by the pastors from the spiritual riches of the Church, especially by the word of God and the sacraments." Established by Christ and entrusted to the Church, they "are signs and means which express and strengthen the faith, render worship to God, and effect the sanctification of humanity and thus contribute in the greatest way to establish, strengthen, and manifest ecclesiastical communion" (can. 840).[1] For this reason, the ministers and the faithful, through the celebration of the sacraments, "must show the greatest veneration and necessary diligence" (can. 840). The sacraments are so important

---

[1] *Code of Canon Law Annotated*, prepared under the responsibility of the Instituto Martín de Azpilcueta, eds. Ernest Caparros, Michel Thériault, Jean Thorn, second edition revised and updated of the 6th Spanish language edition, eds. Ernest Caparros and Hélène Aubé (Montreal: Wilson & Lafleur Limitée, 2004), p. 173. This version of the Code is used for all quotations throughout this essay.

for salvation that the Code sets out for sacred ministers the obligation to administer them, and they may not deny the sacraments to those who seek them at appropriate times (can. 843, §1).

Required Conditions: While the legislator recognizes that every believer is entitled to receive the sacraments, the dignity of the sacraments and their correct administrations must also be taken into account in such a way that they contribute to the spiritual benefit of the faithful, and not for their condemnation. Therefore, after forbidding the ministers to deny the sacraments to those who request them, canon 843, § 1 lists the basic conditions for the faithful to be admitted to them. They must be "properly disposed and not prohibited by law from receiving them". These conditions for the faithful to access the sacraments are required particularly for the sacraments of the Eucharist and penance.[2]

Admission to the Eucharist: With regard to participation in the Eucharist, the sacrament of divine love, the Code of Canon Law, following along the lines of Saint Paul, requires that before approaching the sacraments the faithful should examine their conduct; otherwise they run the risk of receiving their condemnation: "Whoever, therefore, eats the bread or drinks the cup of the Lord in an

[2] Also in regard to the Anointing of the Sick, the provisions of canon 1007 should be recalled, according to which this sacrament is not to be conferred upon those who persevere obstinately in manifest grave sin. This canon is similar to canon 915, which requires ministers to refuse the Eucharist to those who "obstinately persevere in manifest grave sin". The faithful in such a state cannot fruitfully receive the sacraments whereby the Church entrusts the sick to the Lord to relieve and save them (can. 998).

unworthy manner will be guilty of profaning the body and blood of the Lord. Let a man examine himself, and so eat of the bread and drink of the cup. For any one who eats and drinks without discerning the body eats and drinks judgment upon himself" (1 Cor 11:27–29). Canon 916 reads, "A person who is conscious of grave sin is not to celebrate Mass or receive the body of the Lord without previous sacramental confession."

To approach the Eucharist, the Church requires the faithful to be in the state of grace, normally achieved through the sacrament of penance. Those in fact who are aware of having committed a grave sin must obtain God's forgiveness through confession in order to approach the Eucharist, unless there is an urgent need to receive and celebrate the Eucharist and no confessors are available. In any case, the sorrow for sins that is always necessary for forgiveness implies that, in addition to sorrow for having offended God (contrition), one undertakes and commits to go to confession with the firm resolution of not sinning again and avoiding the occasions of sin. These requirements are not met by the divorced and civilly remarried who practice cohabitation. These individuals cannot approach the Eucharist because they are in a permanent and objective state of grave sin, and they cannot obtain forgiveness because by definition they want to stay in a sinful situation and therefore do not demonstrate the true and necessary contrition to be admitted to the Eucharist. And if in spite of this they approach the Eucharist, the priest must refuse it to them whenever the conditions set out in canon 915 apply.

Impossibility of Receiving the Sacramental Absolution: The penitent may be absolved from sin only if well-disposed, meaning that he has repented of sin and promises not to sin again, along with the resolution to avoid the occasions of sin. Canon 987 is clear in this respect: "To receive the salvific remedy of the sacrament of penance, a member of the Christian faithful must be disposed in such a way that, rejecting sins committed and having a purpose of amendment, the person turns back to God." Only by meeting these provisions, the repudiation of sins and firm purpose of amendment, can the faithful receive the sacrament in a healthful way, that is, one that leads to salvation. Thus, the ban on access to the Eucharist and the impossibility of being absolved in the sacrament of penance are closely related.

The Duty to Reject Those Who Approach Communion—canon 915: If the status of serious opposition to the law of God and of the Church is known to the community, and an individual nevertheless dares to approach the Eucharist, he should not be admitted to Communion. Canon 915 reads: "Those upon whom the penalty of excommunication or interdict has been imposed or declared, and others who obstinately persist in manifest grave sin, are not to be admitted to holy communion." A statement of the Pontifical Council for Legislative Texts reaffirmed the validity of the prohibition contained in canon 915 in the face of claims by some that this rule does not apply in the case of the divorced and civilly remarried. The statement reads:

> In the concrete case of the admission to holy communion of the faithful who are divorced and remarried, the scandal, understood as an action that prompts others towards wrongdoing, affects at the same time both the sacrament

of the Eucharist and the indissolubility of marriage. That scandal exists even if such behaviour, unfortunately, no longer arouses surprise: in fact it is precisely with respect to the deformation of the conscience that it becomes more necessary for pastors to act, with as much patience as firmness, as a protection to the sanctity of the sacraments and a defence of Christian morality, and for the correct formation of the faithful.[3]

The situation of the divorced and civilly remarried is in conflict with ecclesiastical discipline in some essential points that concern divine law.

The Position of Cardinal Kasper

What about the question posed by Cardinal Kasper during the Extraordinary Consistory of February 20–21, 2014? Kasper asks whether such a path is feasible even for the divorced and civilly remarried. He suggests conditions to be considered as a way of penance for these individuals.

The question that confronts us is this: Is this the path beyond rigorism and laxity, the path of conversion, which issues forth in the sacrament of mercy—the sacrament of penance—also the path that we can follow in this matter? Certainly not in every case. But if a divorced and remarried person is truly sorry that he or she failed in the first marriage, if the commitments from the first marriage are clarified and a return is definitively out of the question,

[3] Pontifical Council for Legislative Texts, *Declaration Concerning the Admission to Holy Communion of Faithful Who Are Divorced and Remarried,* June 24, 2000, as published in *Communicationes* 32 (2000): 159–62.

if he or she cannot undo the commitments that were assumed in the second civil marriage without new guilt, if he or she strives to the best of his or her abilities to live out the second civil marriage on the basis of faith and to raise their children in faith, if he or she longs for the sacraments as a source of strength in his or her situation, do we then have to refuse or can we refuse him or her the sacrament of penance and communion, after a period of reorientation?[4]

Kasper observes, "The path in question would not be a general solution. It is not a broad path for the great masses, but a narrow path for the indeed smaller segment of divorced and remarried individuals who are honestly interested in the sacraments. Is it not necessary precisely here to prevent something worse [i.e., the loss of the children with the loss of a whole second generation]?"[5] He then clarifies, "A civil marriage as described with clear criteria must be distinguished from other forms of 'irregular' cohabitation, such as clandestine marriages, unmarried couples, and especially fornication and so-called 'serial marriages' (*matrimoni selvaggi*). Life is not just black and white. In fact, there are many nuances."[6]

Kasper seems inclined toward a positive reply to the question he poses; however, his answer depends on several precise preconditions. For this reason, as he says, the

---

[4] Walter Cardinal Kasper, *The Gospel of the Family* (Mahwah, N.J.: Paulist Press, 2014), p. 32.

[5] Ibid., pp. 32–33.

[6] This quotation is not to be found in the English version of Cardinal Kasper's address to the Extraordinary Consistory, published as *The Gospel of the Family* (cited above). Cardinal De Paolis is quoting here from an Italian version of the address, which was published as "Bibbia, Eros e famiglia", Vatican Exclusive, in *Il Foglio Quotidiano* 19, no. 51 (March 1, 2014): 3.—Ed.

positive answer would not be a general solution, but a path that can be pursued only by few, whose situations conform to certain conditions. These would be unusual cases that could not be categorized anywhere, but should be studied and examined one by one to avoid a greater evil. He further suggests that his solution finds some justification in the Church's penitential practice, particularly with respect to the lapsed (*lapsi*). It is known, in fact, that regarding the readmission of the lapsed to the Church and to the Eucharist, the solution was found in a *via media* between rigor and laxity, the way of repentance.[7]

Kasper does not set other conditions, at least not explicitly. But one can clearly infer them from the conditions he sets out, in particular, the following: "if the commitments from the first marriage are clarified and a return is definitively out of the question", and "if one cannot undo the commitments that were assumed in the second civil marriage without new guilt", and finally, "if one strives to the best of his or her abilities to live out the second civil marriage on the basis of faith and to raise their children in faith." These three conditions in fact demonstrate a conflict of rights and duties, which, by Kasper's reasoning, require the choice of a lesser evil.

I have tried to understand Kasper's reasons. Inasmuch as I have been able to understand them, I do not find any valid argument to give an affirmative response to the question whether a penitential *via media* between laxity and rigorism can be found that would enable the divorced and

[7] Cardinal De Paolis is referring here to those Christians in the early Church who denied the faith under threat of persecution. In his address to the Extraordinary Consistory, Cardinal Kasper referenced this episode in Church history. See Kasper, *Gospel*, pp. 30–31.—ED.

civilly remarried to receive the sacraments of penance and the Eucharist.

Kasper's starting point offers no point of reference. The laxity and rigor concerning the readmission of the lapsed has nothing in common with readmitting the divorced and civilly remarried to these sacraments. In regard to the lapsed, the issue concerned readmitting repentant individuals who undertook the commitment to live a Christian life in a consistent manner. Conversely, the question of the divorced and civilly remarried consists in readmitting to penance and to the Eucharist individuals who intend to persevere in irregular marital situations in violation of the divine law. The lapsed fulfill the requirements of the law of God for the sacraments; the divorced and the remarried do not. In the case of the divorced, we are not facing opposing rigorist and lax currents within the Church, but simply a grave and permanent rejection of the divine law concerning the sanctity of marriage. If such a condition persists, the way of the sacraments is precluded by divine law, because the conditions of the divine law for the reception of the sacraments do not exist in such cases, especially for the Eucharist and penance. A way that would legitimize the existing situation in which the divine law is violated cannot be called a way of penance and conversion. It would rather legitimate the existing situation, which is intrinsically evil, and therefore could not be made good or admissible under any circumstances.

As regards the conditions that Kasper poses for his hypothesis, one can certainly agree that they limit access to penance only to very few people. But this cannot justify an affirmative answer even if there were only one case involved.

We must therefore explore the issue of legitimacy itself. First of all, I do not see why the existence of a new civil bond between divorced persons should matter at all to Kasper's argument. Civil marriage does not create a marital bond that accords with the laws of the Church. In any case, the conditions described by Kasper may also occur in other situations involving irregular cohabitation. It is not clear why some of these circumstances may be considered legitimate while others are not.

The real and unsolvable problem is not so much the education of children. The obligation of parents to educate their children is always present, in spite of separation and divorce. The real problem is the conjugal relationship. Civil marriage does not and cannot turn two people into spouses; indeed, what the moral law of God will not permit is that two people who are not married should live as husband and wife. This is the real problem. Spouses can never be forced to remain together as husband and wife on the basis of some hypothetical situation involving a conflict of duties. No human law can impose this, and no one can accept such an imposition. It would cause the failure of the marital relationship and of the family; it would destroy its foundations as well as the whole moral law concerning sexuality.

Respect for the moral rule that prohibits marital life between people who are not married cannot admit exceptions. The difficulty one encounters in respecting the moral law does not then permit that person to turn around and violate the same moral law. Sadly, there are many cases in life in which the faithful, as individuals, as a family, or as a community, are faced with difficult situations, almost humanly impossible to tackle. But fidelity to the divine law is always binding and admits no exception.

Indeed, what seems humanly impossible becomes possible precisely because of the faith and grace of the Lord.

The word of God on the one hand warns: "[A]part from me you can do nothing" (Jn 15:5), while on the other hand it provides reassurance: "[W]ith God all things are possible" (Mt 19:26). But if it were accepted that in difficult situations, even in almost impossible ones, it is lawful to look for an escape, the moral life would dissolve quickly and the common good would be subject to the individual will, as history has shown us.

I would like to understand better Kasper's point when he seems to say that the case under consideration is particular and that it represents only a specific situation that cannot be regulated by the moral law, but that requires opting for the lesser evil. In fact there is no case that cannot and should not be governed by the moral law, because every human act is measured by the moral law, according to the principle *bonum faciendum, malum vitandum*. The encyclical *Veritatis splendor* quotes a beautiful text by Saint Gregory of Nyssa: "All things subject to change and to becoming never remain constant, but continually pass from one state to another, for better or worse.... Now, human life is always subject to change; it needs to be born ever anew.... But here birth does not come about by a foreign intervention, as is the case with bodily beings ...; it is the result of a free choice. Thus *we are* in a certain way *our own parents*, creating ourselves as we will, by our decisions."[8] Following this quotation, the encyclical continues:

> The *morality of acts* is defined by the relationship of man's freedom with the authentic good. This good is established,

---

[8] Saint Gregory of Nyssa, *De Vita Moysis*, 2.2–3, quoted in John Paul II, Encyclical Letter *Veritatis splendor*, August 6, 1993, no. 71 (all italics in quotations from *Veritatis splendor* are in the original).

as the eternal law, by divine wisdom which orders every being towards its end: this eternal law is known both by man's natural reason (hence it is "natural law"), and—in an integral and perfect way—by God's supernatural Revelation (hence it is called "divine law"). Acting is morally good when the choices of freedom are *in conformity with man's true good* and thus express the voluntary ordering of the person towards his ultimate end: God himself, the supreme good in whom man finds his full and perfect happiness. (no. 72)

If we were to say that there are cases where morality cannot be measured by the human law alone—because human law is limited in its expressive capabilities, and even in its obligation, since it does not oblige with grave inconvenience—or that it may be dispensed with, or that it may not be observed in accordance with the highest principles of morality, such as *equity* and *epikeia*, we would be saying something true and correct. But in the case introduced by Cardinal Kasper we are not faced with a human law, but with a divine law, to which there are no exceptions or dispensations, and there is no way to resort to other principles. The only possible explanation for that statement could be (but we believe that Kasper did not mean it this way) a situational ethic, condemned several times by the teaching of the Church.

The justification of a choice made because of the lesser evil clashes with the principle set out in the doctrine of the Church: the end does not justify the means; "non sunt facienda mala ut veniant bona" ("Let us not do evil that there may come good" [Rom 3:8]). Likewise, the morality of the action cannot be justified under the principle of proportionalism. Finally, we should also recall the doctrine of the intrinsically evil act, which can never be made good by the right intention or circumstances or by the principle of the lesser evil. What is intrinsically evil is never acceptable on any account. In *Veritatis splendor*, we read:

> Reason attests that there are objects of the human act which are by their nature "incapable of being ordered" to God, because they radically contradict the good of the person made in his image. These are the acts which, in the Church's moral tradition, have been termed "intrinsically evil" (*intrinsece malum*): they are such *always and per se*, in other words, on account of their very object, and quite apart from the ulterior intentions of the one acting and the circumstances. Consequently, without in the least denying the influence on morality exercised by circumstances and especially by intentions, the Church teaches that "there exist acts which per se and in themselves, independently of circumstances, are always seriously wrong by reason of their object." (no. 80)
>
> Consequently, circumstances or intentions can never transform an act intrinsically evil by virtue of its object into an act "subjectively" good or defensible as a choice. (no. 81)

It is useful to compare certain statements concerning the moral justification of acts, either explicit or implicit, with the teaching of the encyclical *Veritatis splendor*, particularly nos. 71–83. There is no human act that is not regulated by a moral law or subject to it.

> *Only the act in conformity with the good can be a path that leads to life*. The rational ordering of the human act to the good in its truth and the voluntary pursuit of that good, known by reason, constitute morality. Hence human activity

cannot be judged as morally good merely because it is a means for attaining one or another of its goals, or simply because the subject's intention is good. Activity is morally good when it attests to and expresses the voluntary ordering of the person to his ultimate end and the conformity of a concrete action with the human good as it is acknowledged in its truth by reason. If the object of the concrete action is not in harmony with the true good of the person, the choice of that action makes our will and ourselves morally evil, thus putting us in conflict with our ultimate end, the supreme good, God himself. (no. 72)

Theories that exclude the object itself as the primary and necessary source of moral judgment are contrary to Catholic moral teaching.

Certain ethical theories, called "teleological", claim to be concerned for the conformity of human acts with the ends pursued by the agent and with the values intended by him. The criteria for evaluating the moral rightness of an action are drawn from the weighing of the non-moral or pre-moral goods to be gained and the corresponding non-moral or pre-moral values to be respected. For some, concrete behaviour would be right or wrong according as whether or not it is capable of producing a better state of affairs for all concerned. Right conduct would be the one capable of "maximizing" goods and "minimizing" evils. (no. 74)

Indeed, there are acts whose object is intrinsically evil and can never be justified.

Consequently, as the *Catechism of the Catholic Church* (no. 1761) teaches, "there are certain specific kinds of behaviour that are always wrong to choose, because choosing them involves a disorder of the will, that is, a moral evil." And St. Thomas observes that, "it often happens that man acts with a good intention, but without spiritual gain, because he lacks a good will. Let us say that someone robs in order to feed the poor: in this case, even though the intention is good, the uprightness of the will is lacking. Consequently, no evil done with a good intention can be excused: 'There are those who say: And why not do evil that good may come? Their condemnation is just' (*Rom* 3:8)." (no. 78)[9]

Catholic teaching speaks of an intrinsic evil that can never be justified.

One must therefore reject the thesis, characteristic of teleological and proportionalist theories, *which holds that it is impossible to qualify as morally evil according to its species—its* "object"—*the deliberate choice of certain kinds of behaviour or specific acts, apart from a consideration of the intention for which the choice is made or the totality of the foreseeable consequences of that act for all persons concerned.* The primary and decisive element for moral judgment is the object of the human act, which establishes whether it is *capable of being ordered to the good and to the ultimate end, which is God.* This capability is grasped by reason in the very being of man, considered in his integral truth, and therefore in his natural inclinations, his motivations and his finalities, which always have a spiritual dimension as well. It is precisely these which are the contents of the natural law and hence that ordered complex of "personal goods" which

[9] Citing Saint Thomas Aquinas, *In duo praecepta caritatis et in decem legis praecepta. De dilectione Dei: Opuscula theologica,* II, no. 1168.

serve the "good of the person": the good which is the person himself and his perfection. These are the goods safeguarded by the commandments, which, according to St. Thomas, contain the whole natural law (cf. *Summa Theologiae*, I–II, q. 100, a. 1). (no. 79)

By way of conclusion, with regard to Cardinal Kasper's question, we can say that beyond good intentions, the question, in my opinion, cannot have a positive answer. Beyond the different situations in which the divorced and civilly remarried find themselves, the same problem arises in all situations: the illegitimacy of cohabitation between two people who live as husband and wife without a real marital bond uniting them. In the light of this situation, it is not clear how the divorced may receive sacramental absolution and approach the Eucharist.

The Misunderstandings of Pastoral Care

Pastoral care is often placed in opposition to doctrine, both moral and dogmatic, because the latter is thought to be abstract and not relevant to real life or spirituality, as if doctrine proposes an ideal of Christian life inaccessible to the faithful. Similarly it is commonly thought that because the moral law is universal and regulates life in general, it should be adapted to concrete cases, or not applied at all, because not all concrete cases can be covered by the law.

But this is an erroneous view of pastoral care, which is an art, the art with which the Church makes herself into the people of God in everyday life. It is an art based on dogmatics, morality, spirituality, and the right to act prudently in the specific case. There can be no pastoral care that is not in harmony with the truths of the Church and her morality. A pastoral care in contrast to the truth believed and lived by the Church easily becomes a harmful arbitrariness.

As to the laws, one must not lose sight of the distinction between God's laws and the laws of the human legislator. If the latter may in some cases be dispensed with, or not oblige in the case of grave inconvenience, the same cannot be said about the laws of God, both positive and natural, which do not admit exceptions. Moreover, if the prohibited acts are intrinsically evil, they cannot be legitimized under any circumstances. Thus, a sexual act with a person who is not one's spouse is never acceptable and can never be declared lawful on any account. The end can never justify the means. The moral teaching of the Church has been recently reaffirmed, particularly in *Veritatis splendor*. Situational ethics is not acceptable, nor is an ethics that is measured by the consequences, or by purposes, or by the negation of intrinsically evil acts.

The Misunderstandings of Mercy

"Mercy" is another word easily subject to misunderstandings, like the word "love", with which it is easily identified. Because of this identification, mercy is often contrasted with the law and with justice. However, as is well-known, there is no love without justice, without truth, and without the law, be it human or divine. Speaking against those who badly interpreted his words about the law and love, Saint Paul said, "[T]he whole law is fulfilled in one word, 'You shall love your neighbor as yourself'" (Gal 5:14).

But it must be said that although mercy is one beautiful aspect of love, one cannot identify it with love. Love, in fact, has many facets. The good always pursued by love is realized in different ways according to what love requires in a given situation. This can be seen very well in Saint Paul's Letter to the Galatians, where he speaks of "the fruit of the Spirit", which "is love" (Gal 5:22). These are the different facets of love, which expresses benevolence and generosity, as well as reproach, punishment, correction, the necessity of the norm, and so on. Christian faith proclaims, God is love! The face of the love of God is the face of the Incarnate Word. Jesus is the face of God's love: he is love when he forgives, heals, and cultivates friendships, as well as when he reproaches and condemns. Even condemnation is part of love. Mercy is an aspect of love, especially forgiving love. God always forgives, because he wants salvation for all of us. But God cannot forgive us if we have lost the way to salvation and persevere in it. In this case, the love of God is manifested in reproach and correction, acts of mercy but not of misunderstood "mercy": a legitimization of what is bad, leading to death or confirming it.[10]

Mercy is often presented in opposition to the law, even divine law. But setting God's mercy in opposition to his own law is an unacceptable contradiction.

---

[10] "As proof of this a person is said to be merciful [*misericors*], when he is, so to speak, sorrowful at heart [*miserum cor*], being affected with sorrow at the misery of another as though it were his own. Hence it follows that he endeavors to dispel the misery of this other, as if it were his; and this is the effect of mercy. To sorrow, therefore, over the misery of others belongs not to God; but it does most properly belong to Him to dispel that misery, whatever be the defect we call by that name" (St. Thomas Aquinas, *Summa theologica*, I, q. 21, a. 3).

Often, and rightly so, it is said that we are not called to condemn people; in fact, judgment belongs to God. But one thing is to condemn and another is to evaluate a situation from a moral perspective, to discriminate between what is good and what is bad—to consider whether it responds to God's plan for man. This evaluation is right and proper. Faced with different life situations, such as those of the divorced and civilly remarried, we can and must say that we should not condemn, but help; however, we cannot limit ourselves simply to refraining from condemnation. We are called to assess the situation in the light of faith and of God's plan for the good of the family, for the people involved. Otherwise, we run the risk of no longer being able to appreciate the law of God and of considering it almost as a bad thing. From a certain viewpoint, some may even argue that if the law of the indissolubility of marriage did not exist, we would be better off. These are aberrations which highlight the distortions in the way we think and reason.

The Culture

There is a strong tendency to try to blame everything today on the prevailing culture. It is undeniable that culture has its own weight. But it is also true that culture results from a mentality and an anthropological perspective, as well as from a philosophical view of reality. Culture cannot therefore be the ultimate explanation for everything. Not every culture or philosophical and anthropological perspective can be accepted uncritically and without some caution. Dogmatic and moral theology, which is also expressed in law, is based on a philosophical and anthropological perspective, without which faith cannot be expressed. We know that the Church has always claimed the power to interpret the truths of natural law, which are at the basis of revelation and without which revelation would have no foundation. Canon 747, § 2 reads: "The Church has the right always and everywhere to proclaim moral principles, even in respect of the social order, and to make judgments about any human matter in so far as this is required by fundamental human rights or the salvation of souls."

For this reason, the Church assigns a great role to Saint Thomas, who devoted to it not only a *Summa theologica*, but also a *Summa* of philosophy, in which the teaching of the Church offers a vision of reality.[11] The same formula of faith distinguishes clearly revealed truths and natural truths that the Church interprets and considers necessary and indispensable. In fact, in interpreting these truths, the Church is infallible when she declares them with a definitive act. This means that culture is not the ultimate criterion of truth, and that truth cannot be measured based on a common opinion, even if prevailing.

---

[11] "The reason is that the capital theses in the philosophy of Saint Thomas are not to be placed in the category of opinions capable of being debated one way or another, but are to be considered as the foundations upon which the whole science of natural and divine things is based; if such principles are once removed or in any way impaired, it must necessarily follow that students of the sacred sciences will ultimately fail to perceive so much as the meaning of the words in which the dogmas of divine revelation are proposed by the Magisterium of the Church" ("Nam quae in philosophia Sancti Thomae sunt capita, non ea haberi debent in opinionum genere, de quibus in utramque partem disputare licet, sed velut fundamenta in quibus omnis naturalium divinarumque rerum scientia consistit: quibus submotis aut quoquo modo depravatis, illud etiam necessario consequitur, ut sacrarum disciplinarum alumni ne ipsam quidem percipiant significationem verborum, quibus revelata divinitus dogmata ab Ecclesiae magisterio proponuntur") (Saint Pius X, *Doctoris Angelici*, June 29, 1914, *Acta Apostolicae Sedis* 6 [1914]: 336–41).

Doctrine and Discipline

A distinction is often made between doctrine and discipline in order to say that in the Church doctrine does not change, whereas the discipline does. Actually, when used in this way, both words are misinterpreted. Doctrine, in fact, consists of several levels, and within this gradual progress, a doctrinal change cannot be ruled out. The Church distinguishes three levels of truth in her *formula fidei*: the truth of the divine and Catholic faith, contained in revelation and permanently proposed by the Magisterium; the truths that the Church proposes with a definitive act and which are therefore infallible; and other truths that—though belonging to the kingdom of the faith—do not possess this definitive nature. In regard to "discipline", it cannot be taken as a merely human and changeable datum, but it has a much broader meaning. Discipline includes the divine law, such as the commandments, which are not subject to change although they are not directly of a doctrinal nature. The same can be said of all the rules of divine law. Discipline often includes everything to which the believer must feel committed in his life in order to be a faithful disciple of our Lord Jesus Christ. It may be useful to note what is stated in the document of the Italian episcopate, *Communion, Community and Ecclesial Discipline*:

> The word "discipline", coming from the word "disciple" which in the Christian world identifies the followers of Jesus, has a particularly noble meaning. The discipline of the Church consists in a body of concrete rules and structures that give a visible and systemic configuration to the Christian community, by adjusting the individual and social life of its members to be fully consistent with

the path of the people of God in history, as an expression of communion given by Christ to His Church. In
its broadest sense, it can also include moral rules, while
in a more restricted meaning it only designates legal and
pastoral rules.[12]

The New Evangelization

We have been talking about the new evangelization
for decades now. There is no denying the commitment
undertaken by the Church to produce documents on catechesis and books or to introduce several initiatives, particularly during the recent Year of Faith. The results are
rather scarce, though. To have an idea of the situation,
let us look at its impact on marriage and the family. The
urgent question we should ask ourselves is the following:
What is missing in our efforts to evangelize and proclaim
Christ? Which way should we go? It seems that God and
his Word continue to be absent!

The Strength and the Light of Grace

Finally, I want to draw attention to the most important
reality, especially at this time when one is more likely to
forget it or not to attach the necessary and crucial importance to it. The Church is a supernatural community in
her nature, purposes, and means. She depends crucially on
grace, according to the words spoken by God: "[A]part

---

[12] Italian Episcopal Conference, *Communion, Community and Ecclesial Discipline*, January 1, 1989, no. 3.

from me you can do nothing" (Jn 15:5). Everything is possible with God. The Church is aware of it. She is not a power that is sustained by human means. Moreover, she does not rely on a wisdom that is the fruit of human intelligence; her wisdom is in the Cross, hidden in the secret of God and kept hidden from human wisdom. Her truth cannot be easily accessed and accepted by a culture that is purely the product of human intelligence. These statements clash with the secularized scientistic and positivistic Enlightenment culture of today's world. In the commendable attempt to start a dialogue with modern culture, the Church runs the risk of putting aside her own realities, that is, the divine truth, and adapting to the world. Of course the Church would not do this by denying her truths, but instead by not proposing or by hesitating to propose ideals of life that are conceivable and practicable only in the light of faith and enforceable only through grace. The Church runs the risk of watering down her truer and deeper message for fear of being rejected by modern culture. Certainly the Church always needs to believe in what is humanly impossible, especially in difficult times. In this way, she sheds light on her divine nature and conveys her message of salvation to mankind.

The Church, while taking into account culture and changing times, cannot fail to proclaim that Christ is always "the same yesterday and today and for ever" (Heb 13:8). The reference to culture cannot be the main reference for the Church, let alone the only one, because Christ and his truth should be. We should not dwell on the fact that many Christians today tend to water down the message of the gospel to be accepted by contemporary culture. Jesus came to bring man back to God's plan.

Final Remarks on the Administration of the Sacraments to the Remarried

On the basis of the remarks above, it seems clear that in regard to the divorced and civilly remarried and their admission to the sacraments of penance and the Eucharist, there can be no solution as long as their irregular marital situation remains unchanged. This fact cannot be attributed to the severity and rigor of the law, because we are not dealing with human laws that could be changed or even repealed, but with divine laws that are good for man and mark the path of salvation indicated by God himself. The desire for sacramental absolution and the Eucharist on the part of the divorced and civilly remarried should be also interpreted in this context. If this desire were granted while the person remained in a state of sin, the sacraments would have no effect on spiritual growth. Conversely, such a situation might lead to a state of spiritual death. The desire for the sacraments cannot but be combined with the desire and the will to change something in one's life in order to enter into communion with God. One cannot simply legitimate the current state of life without doing anything to change it. In this perspective, perhaps one should have more courage to propose that where it does not seem possible to change the situation of cohabitation, the couple should undertake a commitment to live in grace, relying on God's help. In short, the problem of the administration of the sacraments to the divorced and civilly remarried can be overcome only in the context of a profound spiritual renewal of Christian life, in light of the mystery of Christ, with which all Christians are called to comply.

9

The Canonical Nullity of the Marriage Process as the Search for the Truth

Raymond Leo Cardinal Burke

Introduction

In its 2013 Preparatory Document, the Third Extraordinary General Assembly of the Synod of Bishops, dedicated to the treatment of "Pastoral Challenges to the Family in the Context of Evangelization", raises the following question: "Could a simplification of canonical practice in recognizing a declaration of nullity of the marriage bond provide a positive contribution to solving the problems of the persons involved? If yes, what form would it take?"[1] In fact,

---

[1] "Lo snellimento della prassi canonica in ordine al riconoscimento della dichiarazione di nullità del vincolo matrimoniale potrebbe offrire un reale contributo positivo alla soluzione delle problematiche delle persone coinvolte? Se sì, in quali forme?", in the Preparatory Document under "Questionario, Sulla pastorale per far fronte ad alcune situazioni matrimoniali difficili", http://www.vatican.va/roman_curia/synod/documents/rc_synod _doc_20131105_iii-assemblea-sinodo-vescovi_it.html. English translation in the Preparatory Document under "Questions, Pastoral Care in Certain Difficult Marital Situations", http://www.vatican.va/roman_curia/synod/documents /rc_synod_doc_20131105_iii-assemblea-sinodo-vescovi_en.html.

in the discussions surrounding the upcoming meeting of the Synod of Bishops, a fair amount of attention has been given to the suggestion of significant changes to the process for the declaration of nullity of marriage as a pastoral remedy for persons who are in an irregular union. Some even suggest the abandonment of the judicial process altogether.

Walter Cardinal Kasper, in his presentation to the Extraordinary Consistory of Cardinals on February 20, 2014, raised the question of the fittingness of the judicial process. Regarding the declaration of nullity of marriage, he observed:

> Because marriage as a sacrament has a public character, the decision about the validity of a marriage cannot simply be left to the subjective judgment of the parties concerned. However, one can ask whether the juridical path, which is in fact not *iure divino* [by divine law], but has developed in the course of history, can be the only path to the resolution of the problem, or whether other, more pastoral and spiritual procedures are conceivable. Alternatively, one might imagine that the bishop could entrust this task to a priest with spiritual and pastoral experience as a penitentiary or episcopal vicar.[2]

---

[2] "Da die Ehe als Sakrament einen öfflentlichen Charakter hat, kann die Entscheidung über die Gültigkeit einer Ehe nicht allein dem subjektiven Ermessen der Betroffenen überlassen sein. Doch man kann sich fragen, ob der gerichliche Weg, der ja nicht iure divino (göttlichen Rechts) ist, sondern sich geschichtlich entwickelt hat, der einzige zur Lösung des Problems sein kann, oder ob nicht auch andere mehr pastorale und geistliche Verfahren denkbar sind. Alternativ könnte man sich vorstellen, dass der Bischof einen geistlich und pastoral erfahrenen Priester als Pönitentiar oder Bischofsvikar mit dieser Aufgabe betraut." Walter Kardinal Kasper, *Das Evangelium von der Famailie. Die Rede vor dem Konsistorium* (Freiburg im Breisgau: Verlag Herder GmbH, 2014), p. 59. English translation: Walter Cardinal Kasper, *The Gospel of the Family*, trans. William Madges (Mahwah, N.J.: Paulist Press, 2014), p. 28.

He went on to make a caricature of the marriage nullity process in the second and third instance, asking the rhetorical question: "Therefore, can it really be that decisions are made about the weal and woe of people at a second and a third hearing only on the basis of records, that is, on the basis of paper, but without knowledge of the persons and their situation?"[3]

In the context of the service of the Supreme Tribunal of the Apostolic Signatura as the dicastery that "ensures that justice in the Church is correctly administered",[4] having in mind the practical experience of the Supreme Tribunal in dealing with diocesan and interdiocesan tribunals over the past forty-five years, I offer some considerations for a response to the question raised by the Synod of Bishops and to Cardinal Kasper's suggestion of "more pastoral and spiritual procedures". I first offer two general clarifications. Then I treat the nature of the process for the declaration of nullity of marriage. Finally, I address some particular questions regarding the process as it has developed in the history of the Church.

The Right to an Objective Judgment in Accord with the Truth

It must be clear from the start that the claim of nullity of a particular marriage involves, in most cases, a complex

[3] "Kann es darum wirklich sein, dass über Wohl und Wehe von Menschen in zweiter und dritter Instanz nur aufgrund von Akten, also aufgrund von Papier, ohne Kenntnis der Personen und ihrer Situation, entschieden wird." Ibid., p. 60. English translation: Ibid., p. 29.

[4] "consulit ut iustitia in Ecclesia recte administretur". Ioannes Paulus PP. II, Constitutio Apostolica *Pastor Bonus*, "De Curia Romana", Iunii 28, 1988, *Acta Apostolicae Sedis* [*AAS*] 80 (1988): 891, art. 121. English translation: *Code of*

situation about which the parties involved seek an objective judgment. Apart from the situation of a party who was simply not free to marry or who patently was incapable of consenting to marriage, most petitions of declaration of nullity of marriage involve complex acts of the intellect and will, which must be studied with requisite objectivity, lest a true marriage be falsely declared null. While it is true that the judicial process for the declaration of nullity of marriage is not itself of divine law, it is also true that it has developed in response to divine law, which demands an effective and appropriate means of arriving at a just judgment regarding a claim of nullity.

For that reason, it is important to consider the process that has developed along the Christian centuries in its integrity. The observance of the procedural rules guarantees the objectivity of the process and avoids unnecessary complications and disputes, and damaging confusion. One must remember that the individual elements of the process have been developed over the Christian centuries to ensure that the process reaches its proper end, the truth about the alleged nullity of the marriage. According to the "hermeneutic of reform" or of continuity, as opposed to the "hermeneutic of discontinuity and rupture",[5] the development of the process should not be the object of disdain but of study in the light of the continuous effort of the Church to teach the truth about holy matrimony

Canon Law: Latin-English Edition, New English Translation (Washington, D.C.: Canon Law Society of America, 1998), p. 720, art. 121.

[5] "Ermeneutica della discontinuità e della rottura ... ermeneutica della riforma". Benedictus PP. XVI, Allocutio "Ad Romanam Curiam ob omina natalicia", Decembris 22, 2005, *AAS* 98 (2006): 46. English translation: Benedict XVI, "Address of His Holiness Benedict XVI to the Roman Curia Offering Them His Christmas Greetings", December 22, 2005, *L'Osservatore Romano*, English Edition, January 4, 2006, p. 5.

and to safeguard the same truth by means of her canonical discipline.

I recall the image used by the professor of canonical processes at the Pontifical Gregorian University, Father Ignacio Gordon, S.J., during the years of my study. He observed that the canonical process with its various elements is like a key whose teeth must match the winding contours of the lock of human nature, and only when all the teeth are cut correctly can the key open the door to truth and justice.[6] It is particularly surprising that today, despite so many proclamations of the rights of the individual person, one finds a lack of attention to the carefully developed judicial procedures through which the rights of all parties, in a matter pertaining to their very salvation, are carefully safeguarded and promoted. I refer to the right to a judgment, in accord with the truth, about the alleged nullity of their marriage. In this regard, I am especially concerned that in such a delicate and important matter it is not infrequently suggested that the careful judicial process be replaced by a rapid administrative process.

Judicial Process and Pastoral Charity

Secondly, it should be clear that there is no contrast or contradiction between the judicial process and the pastoral or spiritual approach to the faithful who allege the nullity of their marriage. In fact, the truly pastoral and spiritual

---

[6]See Ignacio Gordon, S.J., *De iudiciis in genere, I: Introductio Generalis. Pars statica*, 2nd ed. (Rome: Pontificia Universitas Gregoriana, Facultas Iuris Canonici, 1979), p. 22.

approach that aims to show compassion and love to the faithful in question must, by its very nature, be founded upon the truth of their situation. A practice can never be pastorally or spiritually sound if it does not respect the truth of the juridical state of the faithful.

The faithful can also be badly served by the ecclesiastical tribunal itself, if it is not correct and clear in its explanation of the Church's teaching and the role of the tribunal, or if it does not actually live up to what it correctly explains its purpose to be, or if it, too, falls into a kind of pseudo-pastoral pragmatism. Saint John Paul II in his 1994 annual address to the Roman Rota warned precisely against the temptation to exploit the canonical process "in order to achieve what is perhaps a 'practical' goal, which might perhaps be considered 'pastoral,' but is to the detriment of truth and justice."[7]

The saintly pontiff referred to his 1990 annual address to the Roman Rota, in which he had noted that those who approach the tribunal in order to clarify their situation in the Church have a right to the truth, declaring:

> [Ecclesiastical authority] thus takes note, on the one hand, of the great difficulties facing persons and families involved in unhappy conjugal living situations and recognizes their right to be objects of special pastoral concern. But it does not forget, on the other hand, that

[7] "Per raggiungere un fine 'pratico' che forse viene considerato 'pastorale', con detrimento però della verità e della giustizia". Ioannes Paulus PP. II, Allocutio, "Ad Romanae Rotae iudices et administros coram admissos", Ianuarii 28, 1994, *AAS* 86 (1994): 950, no. 5. (Hereafter, Allocutio 1994.) English translation: William H. Woestman, O.M.I., ed., *Papal Allocutions to the Roman Rota 1939–2011* (Ottawa: Faculty of Canon Law, Saint Paul University, 2011), p. 229, no. 5.

these people also have the right not to be deceived by a sentence of nullity which is in contrast to the existence of a true marriage. Such an unjust declaration of nullity would find no legitimate support in appealing to love or mercy, for love and mercy cannot put aside the demands of truth. A valid marriage, even one marked by serious difficulties, could not be considered invalid without doing violence to the truth and undermining thereby the only solid foundation which can support personal, marital and social life. A judge, therefore, must always be on guard against the risk of misplaced compassion, which would degenerate into sentimentality, itself only pastoral in appearance. The roads leading away from justice and truth end up in serving to distance people from God, thus yielding the opposite result from that which was sought in good faith.[8]

---

[8] [L'Autorità ecclesiastica] perciò prende atto, da una parte, delle grandi difficoltà in cui si muovono persone e famiglie coinvolte in situazioni di infelice convivenza coniugale, e riconosce il loro diritto ad essere oggetto di una particolare sollecitudine pastorale. Non dimentica però, dall'altra, il diritto, che pure esse hanno, di non esere ingannate con una sentenza di nullità che sia in contrasto con l'esistenza di un vero matrimonio. Tale ingiusta dichiarazione di nullità matrimoniale non troverebbe alcun legittimo avallo nel ricorso alla carità o alla misericordia. Queste, infatti, non possono prescindere dalle esigenze della verità. Un matrimonio valido, anche se segnato da gravi difficoltà, non potrebbe esser considerato invalido, se non facendo violenza alla verità e minando, in tal modo, l'unico fondamento saldo su cui può reggersi la vita personale, coniugale e sociale. Il giudice pertanto deve sempre guardarsi dal rischio di una malintesa compassione che scadrebbe in sentimentalismo, solo apparentemente pastorale. Le vie che si discostano dalla giustizia e dalla verità finiscono col contribuire ad allontanare le persone da Dio, ottenendo il risultato opposto a quello che in buona fede si cercava.

Ioannes Paulus PP. II, Allocutio, "Ad Romanae Rotae Praelatos, auditores, officiales et advocatos anno iudiciali ineunte", Ianuarii 18, 1990, *AAS* 82 (1990): 875, no. 5. (Hereafter, Allocutio 1990.) English translation: Woestman, *Papal Allocutions*, p. 211, no. 5.

It must be clear to all that the judicial process, in fact, serves aptly and fully the ultimate goal, which is pastoral charity.

It must also be observed that other members of Christ's faithful, who clearly understand both the Church's teaching and the function of the tribunal, can be disedified and even scandalized by superficial or erroneous explanations and by an incorrect *modus operandi*. Such is not infrequently the case among parties in a marriage nullity process who perceive the tribunal to be less than evenhanded, whether in its explanations or in its *modus operandi*. If a tribunal gives the impression that its main purpose is to enable those in failed marriages to remarry in the Church, then a party who has doubts about the alleged nullity of the marriage can feel that the tribunal itself considers the person an obstacle to be overcome.

One of the hallmarks of any tribunal should be the objectivity or impartiality that necessarily marks the search for the truth. Such objectivity should be especially evident in the tribunals of the Church that must take particular care not only to be impartial but also to appear to be so. The correct observance of procedural norms is an important means of guaranteeing the actual and evident impartiality of the tribunal, which can be undermined in many ways, some more subtle than others.

The discipline of the judicial process is not only not hostile to a truly pastoral or spiritual approach to an alleged nullity of marriage, but it safeguards and promotes the fundamental and irreplaceable justice without which it is impossible to show pastoral charity. The words of Pope Benedict XVI to the Apostolic Tribunal of the Roman Rota on January 29, 2010, are most instructive. Addressing himself to all who are dedicated to the administration of justice in the matrimonial tribunals of the Church, he observed:

> It must be reiterated that every work of authentic charity includes an indispensible reference to justice, all the more so in our case. "Love—*caritas*—is an extraordinary force which leads people to opt for courageous and generous engagement in the field of justice and peace" (*Caritas in Veritate*, n. 1). "If we love others with charity, then first of all we are just towards them. Not only is justice not extraneous to charity, not only is it not an alternative or parallel path to charity: justice is 'inseparable from charity'; and intrinsic to it" (ibid., n.6). Charity without justice is not charity, but a counterfeit, because charity itself requires that objectivity which is typical of justice and which must not be confused with inhuman coldness. In this regard, as my Predecessor, Venerable Pope John Paul II, said in his Address on the relationship between pastoral care and the law: "The judge ... must always guard against the risk of misplaced compassion, which could degenerate into sentimentality, itself pastoral only in appearance" (18 Jan. 1990, in *AAS* 82 [1990], p. 875, n. 5; *ORE*, 29 January 1990, p. 5–6, n. 5).[9]

---

[9] Tuttavia occorre ribadire che ogni opera di autentica carità comprende il riferimento indispensabile alla giustizia, tanto più nel nostro caso. "L'amore—'caritas'—è una forza straordinaria, che spinge le persone a impegnarsi con coraggio e generosità nel campo della giustizia e della pace" (Enc. *Caritas in veritate*, n. 1). "Chi ama con carità gli altri è anzitutto giusto verso di loro. Non solo la giustizia non è estranea alla carità, non solo non è una via alternativa o parallela alla carità: la giustizia è 'inseparabile dalla carità', intrinseca ad essa" (ibid., n. 6). La carità senza giustizia non è tale, ma soltanto una contraffazione, perché la stessa carità richiede quella oggettività tipica della giustizia, che non va confusa con disumana freddezza. A tale riguardo, come ebbe ad affermare il mio

The canonical process of declaration of nullity of marriage by its respect for the right to a judgment in accord with the truth is, therefore, a necessary element of the pastoral charity to be shown to those who allege the nullity of marriage consent.

Nature of the Process for the Declaration of Nullity of Marriage

Having clarified some underlying and fundamental concepts of the process for the declaration of nullity of marriage, it is now necessary to explore the nature of the process. It must be clear that the process for the declaration of nullity of marriage is not merely a matter of procedure, but the process is essentially connected with the doctrinal truth enunciated in canon 1141 of the 1983 Code of Canon Law for the Latin Church (*Codex Iuris Canonici* [CIC]): "A marriage that is *ratum et consummatum* can be dissolved by no human power and by no cause, except death."[10] Canon 853 of the Code of Canons of the Eastern Churches (*Codex*

Predecessore, il venerabile Giovanni Paolo II, nell'allocuzione dedicata ai rapporti tra pastorale e diritto: "Il giudice ... deve sempre guardarsi dal rischio di una malintesa compassione che scadrebbe in sentimentalismo, solo apparentemente pastorale."

Benedictus PP. XVI, Allocutio, "Ad sodales Tribunalis Romanae Rotae", Ianuarii 29, 2010, *AAS* 102 (2010): 112. (Hereafter, Allocutio 2010.) English translation: Woestman, *Papal Allocutions*, p. 308.

[10]"Matrimonium ratum et consummatum nulla humana potestate nullaque causa, praeterquam morte, dissolvi potest." Can. 1141. English translation: Canon Law Society of America, *Code of Canon Law: Latin-English Translation*, New English Translation (Washington, D.C.: Canon Law Society of America, 1998).

Canonum Ecclesiarum Orientalium [CCEO]) reads similarly: "The sacramental bond of marriage, once the marriage has been consummated, cannot be dissolved by any human power nor by any cause other than death."[11] This theological datum specifies the judicial process as one which has as its object the declaration of a juridic fact.[12] The marriage accused of nullity is either valid or not.

1. *The Importance of Language regarding Marriage Nullity*

Here it must be noted that the common use of the ambiguous term "annulment" in referring to the process for the declaration of the nullity of marriage can be misleading, for it can have either a constitutive or a declarative meaning. In general parlance, the constitutive meaning prevails. In other words, the term conveys the cancellation of a reality, not a declaration that the apparent reality in fact did not exist. "Declaration of nullity" is the proper term to use.

In general, careful attention must be given to the use of language in explanations of the process of declaration of nullity of marriage. The Apostolic Signatura has received a number of observations from members of the faithful regarding the use of the term "former spouse" in reference to the other party in a marriage whose validity is contested. To them this expression indicates a prejudice against the validity of the marriage. Whatever the actual intentions of the person using such an expression, the observation is

---

[11] "Matrimonii vinculum sacramentale matrimonio consummato nulla humana potestate nullaque causa praeterquam morte dissolvi potest". Can. 853. English translation: Canon Law Society of America, *Code of Canons of the Eastern Churches: Latin-English Edition*, New English Translation (Washington, D.C.: Canon Law Society of America, 2001).

[12] See CIC, can. 1400, § 1, no. 1; CCEO, can. 1055, § 1.

not frivolous. The matrimonial tribunal, for example, in its general explanations, should be careful not to use such ambiguous expressions. In reference to a particular case of nullity of marriage, it is correct and more respectful to use the name of the person in question, rather than referring prejudicially to "the former spouse".

A similar difficulty arises when a tribunal, in an effort to explain the nature of the canonical process, tries to acknowledge the existential reality or putative nature of the marriage in question—which would not be erased by a decision in favor of the invalidity of the marriage—but uses ambiguous expressions in doing so. A clear distinction must be made between the existential experience and the validity of the marriage before the Church, and likewise between the validity of the union in civil law and its validity in canon law.

Such well-meaning efforts even lead to erroneous explanations, such as those which state that the tribunal is not judging the existence of the marriage but only whether or not it was a sacrament in accordance with Church teaching, and whether or not it was binding. Apart from the fact that the Church does not recognize the sacramental nature of a marriage involving at least one nonbaptized person, such explanations can reveal a more fundamental error—that of making too great a distinction between marriage as a natural reality created by God and a sacramental marriage. Saint John Paul II warned against this, for example, in his allocution to the Roman Rota in 2001, when he declared:

> When the Church teaches that marriage is a natural reality, she is proposing a truth evinced by reason for the good of the couple and of society, and confirmed by the revelation of Our Lord, who closely and explicitly relates the marital

union to the "beginning" (Mt 19:4–8) spoken of in the Book of Genesis: "male and female he created them" (Gn 1:27), and "the two shall become one flesh" (Gn 2:24). The fact, however, that the natural datum is authoritatively confirmed and raised by our Lord to a sacrament in no way justifies the tendency, unfortunately widespread today, to ideologize the idea of marriage—nature, essential properties and ends—by claiming a different valid conception for a believer or a non-believer, for a Catholic or a non-Catholic, as though the sacrament were a subsequent and extrinsic reality to the natural datum and not the natural datum itself evinced by reason, taken up and raised by Christ to a sign and means of salvation.[13]

2. Judgment as a Declaration regarding the Truth of a Claim of Marriage Nullity

The college of judges or the single judge has no power to dissolve a valid marriage, but only to search for the truth

---

[13] Quando la Chiesa insegna che il matrimonio è una realtà naturale, essa propone una verità evidenziata dalla ragione per il bene dei coniugi e della società e confermata dalla rivelazione di Nostro Signore, che mette esplicitamente in stretta connessione l'unione coniugale con il "principio", di cui parla il Libro di Genesi: "li creò maschio e femmina", e "due saranno una carne sola". Il fatto però che il dato naturale sia autoritativamente confermato ed elevato a sacramento da nostro Signore non giustifica affatto la tendenza, oggi purtroppo largamente presente, a ideologizzare la nozione del matrimonio natura, essenziali proprietà e finalità, rivendicando una diversa valida concezione da parte di un credente o di un non credente, di un cattolico o di un non cattolico, quasi che il sacramento fosse una realtà successiva ed estrinseca al dato naturale e non lo stesso dato naturale, evidenziato dalla ragione, assunto ed elevato da Cristo a segno e mezzo di salvezza.

Ioannes Paulus PP. II, Allocutio, "Ad Romanae Rotae tribunal", Februarii 1, 2001, *AAS* 93 (2001): 359–60, no. 4. English translation: Woestman, *Papal Allocutions*, p. 261, no. 4.

about a particular marriage and declare authoritatively either that, with moral certitude, the truth of the nullity of the marriage has been established or proven (*constat de nullitate*) or that such moral certitude has not been reached (*non constat de nullitate*). It should be noted that, since the bond of marriage rightly enjoys the favor of the law,[14] there is no need to prove the validity of a marriage; it is enough to declare that the alleged nullity has not been proven.

This understanding of the marriage nullity process is not a new reality in the juridical life of the Church, but it has received renewed emphasis in the past seventy years, especially in the annual addresses to the Roman Rota of Pope Pius XII in 1944;[15] of Saint John XXIII in 1961;[16] of Pope Paul VI in 1978;[17] of Saint John Paul II in 1980,[18] 1982,[19] 1994,[20] and 2005;[21] and of Pope Benedict XVI in 2006,[22]

[14] See can. 1060.

[15] See Pius PP. XII, Allocutio, "Ad Praelatos Auditores ceterosque officiales et administros Tribunalis S. Romanae Rotae necnon eiusdem Tribunalis advocatos et procuratores", Octobris 2, 1944, *AAS* 36 (1944): 281–90. (Hereafter, Allocutio 1944.)

[16] See Ioannes PP. XXIII, Allocutio, "Ad Praelatos Auditores ceterosque Officiales, Advocatos et Procuratores Tribunalis Sacrae Romanae Rotae", Decembris 13, 1961, *AAS* 53 (1961): 817–20.

[17] See Paulus PP. VI, Allocutio, "Ad Tribunalis Sacrae Romanae Rotae Decanum, Praelatos Auditores, Officiales et Advocatos, ineunte anno iudiciali", Ianuarii 28, 1978, *AAS* 70 (1978): 181–86.

[18] See Ioannes Paulus PP. II, Allocutio, "Ad Tribunalis Sacrae Romanae Rotae Decanum, Praelatos Auditores, Officiales et Advocatos, novo Litibus iudicandis ineunte anno: de veritate iustitiae matre", Februarii 4, 1980, *AAS* 72 (1980): 172–78. (Hereafter, Allocutio 1980.)

[19] See Ioannes Paulus PP. II, Allocutio, "Ad Sacrae Romanae Rotae Tribunalis Praelatos Auditores, Officiales et Advocatos coram admissos", Ianuarii 28, 1982, *AAS* 74 (1982): 449–54.

[20] See Allocutio 1994, pp. 947–52.

[21] See Ioannes Paulus PP. II, Allocutio, "Ad Tribunal Rotae Romanae iudiciali ineunte anno", Ianuarii 29, 2005, *AAS* 97 (2005): 164–66.

[22] See Benedictus PP. XVI, Allocutio, "Ad Tribunal Rotae Romanae", Ianuarii 28, 2006, *AAS* 98 (2006): 135–38.

2007,[23] and 2010.[24] I single out for particular attention the annual addresses given by Pope Pius XII in 1944 and by Saint John Paul II in 1980.

In the former address, Pope Pius XII reminds us that "in a matrimonial trial, the *one end* is a judgment in accordance with truth and law, which in a suit for the declaration of nullity, is concerned with the alleged nonexistence of the matrimonial bond",[25] and that all who participate in the canonical process have this unity of purpose, carried out according to the proper nature of their respective functions. He also reminds us that this unified judicial activity is fundamentally pastoral, that is, directed to the same end that unifies the action of the whole Church, namely, the salvation of souls.

Saint John Paul II, in the latter address, reminds us anew that "the immediate purpose of these trials is to ascertain whether or not the facts exist that by natural, divine or ecclesiastical law invalidate marriage, in order to be able to issue a true and just sentence concerning the alleged non-existence of the marriage bond."[26] Worthy of special study is also the allocution given in 1994,[27] following the promulgation of the Encyclical Letter *Veritatis splendor*.

[23] See Benedictus PP. XVI, Allocutio, "Ad Tribunal Rotae Romanae in inauguratione Anni Iudicialis", Ianuarii 27, 2007, *AAS* 99 (2007): 86–91.

[24] See Allocutio 2010, pp. 110–14.

[25] "Nel processo matrimoniale il *fine unico* è un giudizio conforme alla verità e al diritto, concernente nel processo di nullità la asserita non esistenza del vincolo coniugale ". Allocutio 1944, p. 282. English translation: Woestman, *Papal Allocutions*, p. 24.

[26] "Fine immediato di questi processi è di accertare l'esistenza o meno dei fatti che, per legge naturale, divina od ecclesiastica, invalidano il matrimonio, cosicché si possa giungere all'emanazione di una sentenza vera e giusta circa l'asserita non esistenza del vincolo coniugale." Allocutio 1980, p. 173. English translation: Woestman, *Papal Allocutions*, p. 160.

[27] See Allocutio 1994, pp. 947–52.

This more recent emphasis in the papal Magisterium has been in part a response to the tendency of the modern age to relativize truth or even to deny its existence, a tendency that has had a negative influence even within the Church and her tribunals. Regarding law, in general, there has developed the notion that the law has no relation to objective truth but is constituted by whatever man, usually the judge, decides.[28] Such a theory was proposed in my homeland, the United States of America, already in 1897 by Justice Oliver Wendell Holmes, Jr.[29]

While one cannot exclude the possibility that there are those who consciously and explicitly reject the Church's doctrine on marriage and yet accept and exercise an office in a tribunal in a manner that betrays their oath of office,[30] the more common difficulties found in this regard arise from an acritical acceptance of certain principles and practices that in effect betray or weaken what should be the common underlying purpose of all who participate in canonical trials, which is the search for the truth. Quite often such practices are based upon a mistaken idea of what it means to be "pastoral", which has its source in the pervasive relativism in our culture. Such ways of operating can have serious repercussions not only for the individual decisions that touch the very first cell of the life of the Church and of society, but also for the public perception of the work of the tribunal and indeed of the teaching of the Catholic Church regarding marriage. As experience

[28] See Raymond L. Burke, "The Natural Moral Law: Foundation of Legal Realism", *Die fragile Demokratie—The Fragility of Democracy*, ed. Anton Rauscher (Berlin: Duncker & Humblot, 2007), pp. 29–45.

[29] See Oliver Wendell Holmes, Jr., *The Path of Law and the Common Law* (New York: Kaplan Publishing, 2009), pp. 1–29.

[30] See CIC, can. 1454; CCEO, can. 1112.

teaches, the world at large is not especially eager to accept what the Church has to say, especially when it is not reflected in the way that the Church lives.

The process has been articulated along the Christian centuries in order to search out ever more perfectly the truth of a claimed juridic fact, that is, the alleged nullity of marriage. The process constitutes a dialectic by means of which one is able to arrive at the truth. Here I refer again to Pope Pius XII's magisterial allocution to the Roman Rota of October 2, 1944.[31] Sometimes one hears the slogan that the process has become encrusted with burdensome juridicism. In the Apostolic Signatura's experience, however, it is clear that, if the servants of justice know the process and follow it attentively, especially with the assistance of the Instruction *Dignitas connubii*, a vade mecum for tribunals issued on January 25, 2005, by the Pontifical Council for Legislative Texts,[32] the task of the tribunal, which is certainly burdensome in itself, becomes quite workable. One also hears statements characterizing the process as a means to reach a so-called merciful solution to the situation of the divorced, which will give to them a second chance. Here one must observe that the declaration of nullity of marriage could offer "a positive contribution", in the sense of the question posed by the Synod of Bishops' 2013 Preparatory Document, only in the case in which, in truth, the marriage consent was in fact null.

[31] See Allocutio 1944, pp. 281–90.

[32] See Pontificium Consilium de Legum Textibus, *Dignitas connubii. Instructio servanda a tribunalibus dioecesanis et interdioecesanis in pertractandis causis nullitatis matrimonii*, Ianuarii 25, 2005 (Città del Vaticano: Libreria Editrice Vaticana, 2005). (Hereafter, *DC*.) English translation: Pontifical Council for Legislative Texts, *Dignitas connubii: Instruction to Be Observed by Diocesan and Interdiocesan Tribunals in Handling Causes of Nullity of Marriage* (Official Latin Text with English Translation) (Vatican City: Libreria Editrice Vaticana, 2005).

3. The Judicial Debate as an Instrument for Finding the Truth

The canonical process seeks to arrive at the truth through a dialectic process, the *contradictorium*. The principle, *et audiatur altera pars* (and the other party is to be heard), is not just a recognition of the right of the other party to be heard and to respond, but it is also a critical means of arriving at the truth. For this reason, in matrimonial cases every effort must be made not just to respect the right of the respondent to participate but also to seek actively such participation when he might be reluctant to exercise this right. In regard to causes of the nullity of marriage, this dialectic process is guaranteed in a special way.

Confronting a situation of matrimonial tribunals granting declarations of nullity with great license, Pope Benedict XIV, by his Apostolic Constitution *Dei miseratione* of November 3, 1741, reformed the process for the treatment and decision of cases of nullity of marriage. He recognized that both the petitioner and the respondent could be in favor of the nullity of the marriage. He therefore instituted in the ecclesiastical tribunal the office of "defender of the bond" (*Defensor Matrimonii* or *Defensor Matrimoniorum*) who is to guarantee that another voice is heard. He also instituted the requirement of a double agreeing sentence affirming the nullity of a marriage before a person could enter a new union.[33]

Furthermore, one of the distinguishing notes of the canonical process is the active role of the judge, something that can be somewhat foreign to those used to a common-law legal tradition. In the canonical process, the judge can

[33] See Benedictus PP. XIV, Constitutio Apostolica *Dei miseratione*, Novembris 3, 1741, in *Codicis Iuris Canonici Fontes*, vol. 1, ed. Pietro Gasparri (Romae: Typis Polyglottis Vaticanis, 1926), pp. 695–701, no. 318.

take the initiative in seeking out proofs in order to arrive at more complete understanding of the truth. Thus canon 1452, § 1 (CCEO, can. 1110, § 1) provides that in causes involving the public good, the judge can and should act *ex officio*. The second paragraph of the canon in both Codes also gives the judge the power to make up for the negligence of the parties in offering evidence or exceptions, whenever this is required to avoid an unjust sentence.

In this context it is helpful to remember that respect for the proper distinction of roles in the canonical process helps to guarantee both the objectivity of the tribunal and the dialectic nature of the process. As Pope Pius XII explained clearly in his allocution of 1944, all are engaged in the search for the truth in the canonical process, but each according to his proper role. Each of the parties and their respective advocates present that evidence and those arguments which, without untruth or fraud, favor their relative position, as the defender of the bond does in regard to the bond of marriage. The judge, with the auditors under his direction, represents the impartiality of the tribunal itself in the search for the truth, as do the notary and the promoter of justice in accord with their respective functions. *Dignitas connubii* prohibits the same person from exercising habitually several of these functions in the same tribunal (with the exception of the defender of the bond and the promoter of justice) or even in two tribunals related to one another by reason of appeal,[34] but in a most emphatic way it forbids any minister of the tribunal to act as advocate or procurator, even through an intermediary, in his own tribunal or any tribunal related to it by reason

[34]See *DC*, art. 36, §§ 1–2.

of appeal.[35] The importance of this distinction for a true dialectic to arrive at the truth is evident.

A possible simplification of the process for the declaration of nullity of marriage must respect its finality, that is, the search of the truth of a claimed juridic fact. It is helpful to recall again the words of Saint John Paul II[36] and of Pope Benedict XVI[37] on false mercy, which is not concerned with the truth and therefore cannot serve charity, which has as its only goal the salvation of souls. Given the relationship among the various elements of the process, any simplification would have to be studied by a commission of experts. Such a commission would pay attention to the harmony and to the integrity of the individual offices in the service of the process, to the necessary objectivity and impartiality of the tribunal, to the judicial dialectic as the necessary instrument for arriving at the truth with moral certitude, to the particular role of the defender of the bond in the judicial dialectic, and, finally, to the role of the tribunal of appeal in what regards the requirement of a double conforming sentence.

Particular Questions

1. Singular Importance of the Preparation of the Ministers of the Tribunal

Given the nature of the process, it is clear that the principal means of guaranteeing a rightful simplification of the

---

[35] See DC, art. 36, § 3.
[36] See Allocutio 1990, pp. 872–77.
[37] See Allocutio 2010, pp. 110–14.

process is the sound preparation of the ministers of the tribunal and, at the same time, the adequate disposition of their time to accomplish their important judicial responsibilities with full attention. So many priests are ministers in ecclesiastical tribunals and cover, at the same time, other quite demanding pastoral responsibilities, with the result that they cannot give the needed time and attention to the work of the tribunal. From another perspective, just compensation for tribunal work must be provided to the ministers of the tribunal, so that they do not have to look for other paid work to make up for the inadequate compensation offered by the ecclesiastical tribunal.

It is above all important that the ministers think with the Church (*sentire cum Ecclesia*) and are, therefore, reliable. In other words, in the canonical process, to arrive at the truth of the alleged nullity of marriage it is indispensable to have reliable ministers who are adequately prepared. Reliable ministers—priests, consecrated persons, and lay faithful—are necessary for just processes. To arrive at the truth with moral certitude they need a proper preparation acquired by means of study and experience.

In what regards the simplification of the process, it is necessary to underline the importance of the ecclesiastical tribunal as the ordinary means through which the bishop, as judge by nature (*iudex natus*) in the diocese, exercises his judicial power.[38] The bishop has, in fact, all of the necessary means to assure that the process for the declaration of nullity of marriage is carried out in an adequate manner and a just length of time. I think, for example, of the shorter process after a first affirmative decision,[39]

---

[38] See CIC, can. 1419; CCEO, can. 1066.
[39] See CIC, can. 1682, § 2; CCEO, can. 1368, § 2.

of the possibility of the constitution of a single judge,[40] and of the insistence on the observance of the precise time limits established by the law.[41]

2. Assistance Provided to Parties by the Ecclesiastical Tribunal

Tribunals should provide information to the public about the nature, purpose, and procedures of the tribunal, as well as information about the possible grounds of nullity of marriage. They also should have the practice of welcoming those whose marriages have failed to approach the tribunal. *Dignitas connubii* recommends that the tribunal have an office or person responsible for providing information about the possibility of introducing a cause of nullity and the manner in which this is to be done.[42] This personal service can even include giving general information about the various grounds of nullity for those who are interested. It must be clear that at this level, it is a matter of a conversation about how the tribunal works. Even so, in order to safeguard the impartiality of the trial, any tribunal minister who provides such preliminary information to a party, thus establishing a certain rapport with the party, cannot then take part in the concrete cause as judge or defender of the bond.[43] On the other hand, if one of the tribunal advocates provides this service, he can then act as the petitioner's advocate.[44]

There are those who do not accept the Church's teaching on marriage. After a failed marriage and divorce, they

[40]See CIC, can. 1425, § 4; CCEO, can. 1084, § 3.
[41]See CIC, can. 1453; CCEO, can. 1111.
[42]See *DC*, art. 113, § 1.
[43]See *DC*, art. 113, § 2.
[44]See *DC*, art. 113, § 3.

feel that it is their right to remarry and seek happiness in a new union. But there are many faithful Catholics in the same situation who accept that they cannot enter a new marriage without the approval of the Church, and so, encouraged by their priests, deacons, or other members of the parish staff, or family members or friends, they approach the tribunal for a solution to their most serious difficulty. They entrust themselves to the Church in good faith, even if they do not have a very clear idea of what exactly it is that the tribunal does.

Clearly, they can be badly served by their own pastoral ministers who do not explain to them in a clear and unambiguous way what the Church teaches and what the tribunal does in accord with the Church's teaching. What is worse, they may encounter an allegedly pastoral but actually merely pragmatic attitude that in effect would make the search for the truth about a marriage a secondary consideration to the pursuit of making possible a new marriage in the Church. It even happens that tribunal personnel who are trying to carry out their responsibilities faithfully are unduly pressured by such pastoral ministers who seem interested only in immediate results.

3. The Role of the Defender of the Bond

The participation of the defender of the bond in the process for the declaration of nullity of marriage is of such importance that the acts are null without it.[45] But this is just the minimum requirement for the integrity of the process. The search for the truth is impeded when the defender of

[45] See CIC, can. 1433; CCEO, can. 1111.

the bond is present but, through negligence and passivity, deprives, in effect, the process of an important voice in the judicial debate. Pope Pius XII noted that "it would be inconsistent with the importance of his office and the careful and conscientious fulfillment of his duty were he to content himself with a perfunctory review of the acts and a few superficial remarks."[46] *Dignitas connubii* makes it clear that the defender is to participate from the beginning of the process,[47] possibly even before the acceptance of the libellus.[48] Furthermore, such participation is not to be limited to presenting arguments against nullity but rather to propose any kind of proofs, responses, and exceptions that, without prejudice to the truth of the matter, contribute to the protection of the bond.[49] It is true that the defender has the right, as Pope Pius XII also noted, "to declare that after a careful, thorough, and conscientious examination of the acts, he has found no reasonable objection to propose against the petition of the plaintiff",[50] but this would remain an exception. In any event, the defender can never act in any way in favor of the nullity of marriage.[51]

Sadly, the Apostolic Signatura has seen many examples of negligence in this area. Even in the present day,

[46] "Non sarebbe compatibile con l'importanza della sua carica e con l'adempimento solerte e fedele del suo dovere, se egli si contentasse di una sommaria visione degli atti e di alcune superficiali osservazioni". Allocutio 1944, p. 284, no. 2b. English translation: Woestman, *Papal Allocutions*, p. 25, no. 2b.

[47] See *DC*, art. 56, § 2.

[48] See *DC*, art. 119, § 2.

[49] See *DC*, art. 56, § 3.

[50] "Di dichiarare: che dopo un diligente, accurate e coscienzioso esame degli atti, non ha rinvenuta alcuna ragionevole obiezione da muovere contro la domanda dell'attore o del supplicante." Allocutio 1944, p. 284, no. 2b. English translation: Woestman, *Papal Allocutions*, p. 26, no. 2b.

[51] See *DC*, art. 56, § 5.

there are tribunals in which the defender regularly does not participate in the process until the discussion phase, thus losing the opportunity to participate in the instruction of the cause. Likewise, in all too many cases the defender offers little in defense of the bond, even when it is clear from even a cursory study of the acts that there was much that could and should have been argued against the alleged nullity of the marriage. One still finds in use so-called ani-madversions of the defender of the bond that consist of a standardized brief form or a boilerplate text, with little or no concrete information about the specifics of the case in question. Such a form is simply a way for the defender of the bond to "sign off" on a marriage nullity cause. Some of these prepared forms even have the defender stating in advance that he would not appeal an affirmative decision.

Even worse than this effective abandonment of the defense of the bond is the practice of some defenders who offer arguments in favor of the nullity of the mar-riage, positively declaring in some cases that there is no bond to defend! It is clear that such abandonment or out-right betrayal of office by a defender in effect destroys the whole dialectic of the process, especially when the respondent is absent or in favor of nullity, and it puts the whole burden on the judges, who, as Pope Pius XII pointed out, "should find in the careful work of the defender of the bond an aid and complement to their own activity".[52] He further observed that "it is not to be supposed that [the judges] must do all his work."[53] Any

---

[52] "Nell'accurata opera di lui un aiuto e un complemento della propria atti-vità,". Allocutio 1944, p. 284, no. 2b. English translation: Woestman, *Papal Allocutions*, p. 25, no. 2b.

[53] "Nè è da pretendere che essi rifacciano sempre tutto il lavoro". Ibid.

discussion regarding the process of nullity of marriage within the context of the Church's pastoral care of the family should include a new appreciation of the role of the defender of the bond.

The last Plenary Session of the Supreme Tribunal of the Apostolic Signatura, celebrated November 6–8, 2013, was devoted to the importance of the service of the defender of the bond in the marriage nullity process. In his address to the members of the Supreme Tribunal, at the conclusion of their plenary session, Pope Francis underlined the important, indeed obligatory, service of the defender of the bond in the process for the declaration of nullity of marriage, recalling the duty of the defender "to propose any kind of proofs, responses and exceptions that, without prejudice to the truth of the matter, contribute to the protection of the bond".[54] Referring to the work of the Apostolic Signatura in assisting bishops to administer rightly justice to the faithful in their pastoral care by preparing well the ministers for their tribunals, he declared: "It is necessary, in fact, that [the defender of the bond] be able to carry out his role effectively, in order to facilitate the attainment of the truth in the final verdict, for the pastoral good of the parties involved in the cause."[55]

---

[54] "Proporre ogni genere di prove, di eccezioni, ricorsi ed appelli che, nel rispetto della verità, favoriscano la difesa del vincolo." Franciscus PP., Allocutio, "Ad Sessionem Plenariam Supremi Tribunalis Signaturae Apostolicae", Novembris 8, 2013, *AAS* 105 (2013), p. 1153. English translation: "Address of Pope Francis to Participants in the Plenary Assembly of the Supreme Tribunal of the Apostolic Signatura", November 8, 2013, *L'Osservatore Romano*, Weekly Edition in English, November 15, 2013, p. 8.

[55] "È necessario, infatti, che [il Difensore del vincolo] possa compiere la propria parte con efficacia, per facilitare il raggiungimento della verità nella sentenza definitiva, a favore del bene pastorale delle parti in causa." Ibid., p. 1152. English translation: Ibid., p. 8.

4. *The Requirement of the Double Conforming Sentence*

In the discussions surrounding the upcoming session of the Synod of Bishops, a frequently raised question pertains to the necessity of a double conforming decision for the execution of a declaration of nullity of marriage, that is, a second decision on the merits of the case. There is a sense among some in the Church that the decision has already been taken to eliminate the obligation of a double conforming decision as one of the elements of the so-called burdensome juridicism in the current process of nullity of marriage. Many have asserted that, if the process is done well in the first instance, there is no need of an obligatory review in the second instance.

First of all, I observe that, if the process is done well in the first instance, the process to arrive at a double agreeing decision, with the decree of ratification, will not take too long. By done well I mean that the case was well instructed and discussed, the acts are complete and well-ordered, and the sentence demonstrates the objective basis for the decision, indicating in a clear but prudent manner by what path the judge or judges, on the basis of the law and the facts of the case, reached moral certitude that the nullity of the marriage had been proven.[56] What is more, good judges, conscious of the fundamental importance of the marriage union for the life of the Church and of society in general, and of the normal challenges in reaching a just decision in a cause of nullity of marriage, are grateful that their judgment will be examined by other judges in a second instance.

[56] See *DC*, art. 254, §§1–2.

From the practical point of view, the fact of the oblig-atory review in the second instance is an incentive to do one's best. Without the second instance, there is a risk of carelessness in the treatment of causes. This was tragically evident during the period in which the so-called American Procedural Norms were in effect for the ecclesiastical tribunals in the United States of America. From July 1971 to November 1983, the obligatory double conforming sentence was in reality eliminated in the United States of America by means of a faculty given to the conference of bishops to dispense from the same in "those excep-tional cases where in the judgment of the defender of the bond and his Ordinary appeal against an affirmative deci-sion would clearly be superfluous".[57] By all accounts, in practice the only exceptional cases were those in which an appeal was *not* considered superfluous. Furthermore, I have never come across any indication that the conference of bishops ever denied a single request for dispensation out of the hundreds of thousands received.

In the course of those twelve years, when the Apostolic Signatura had occasion to review some of those same cases, it could not understand how the defender of the bond and his Ordinary could have considered an appeal super-fluous, much less how the conference of bishops could have granted the requested dispensation.[58] In the common

[57] Sacred Council for the Public Affairs of the Church, "Provisional Norms for Marriage Annulment Cases in United States", April 28, 1970, *The Canon Law Digest*, ed. James I. O'Connor (Chicago: Canon Law Digest, 1975), vol. 7, p. 964, Norm 23, II. (Hereafter, "Provisional Norms".)

[58] The "official published commentary" on Norm 23 of the "Provisional Norms" provided by the National Conference of Catholic Bishops discour-aged individual bishops from an attentive study of the cases before requesting a dispensation: "The judgment of the defender, therefore, should depend ...

and popular perception, and not without reason, the process began to be called "Catholic divorce". Even after this extraordinary situation was finally ended when the 1983 Code of Canon Law took effect, the poor quality of many first instance sentences examined by the Signatura, together with the evident lack of any serious review on the part of some appellate tribunals, demonstrated the grave damage done to the process of declaration of nullity of marriage by the effective omission of the second instance during those years.

on whether or not the truth has already been served in the process of first instance and whether, therefore, an appeal would be superfluous to the cause of truth. The norm also requires the Ordinary to make the same judgment. Obviously, this does not require the Ordinary to study thoroughly every case which receives an affirmative decision in his court. It would surely be sufficient for an Ordinary to select his defenders well, place confidence in their judgments and, generally, to ratify those judgments" ("Provisional Norms", p. 965).

In 1978, after the Provisional Norms had been in effect for a number of years, one diocesan bishop wrote the following to the Apostolic Signatura to express his concerns about the way Norm 23 was being applied: "Dispensations from the necessity of appeal are being sought in practically every instance. The Officialis of our Court of Appeals has made the statement that I am the only Ordinary in the entire Province who appeals cases. The dispensations are granted automatically by the office in Washington, and I know of no instance in which the dispensation was not granted. I know of one instance when the dispensation was granted even though the Ordinary had some misgivings about the validity of his own petition.... These dispensations are granted so automatically that the Officialis of our Metropolitan Tribunal advised a petitioner that by the time the letter was received by the petitioner the dispensation would have been granted in Washington, and the petitioner would be free to enter another marriage" (Supreme Tribunal of the Apostolic Signatura, Prot. N. 1020 SAT).

In this context, it is enlightening to read the observations made by the then Rotal Judge Monsignor Edward M. Egan during the 1981 Annual Convention of the Canon Law Society of America: Edward M. Egan, "Appeal in Marriage Nullity Cases: Two Centuries of Experiment and Reform", Canon Law Society of America, *Proceedings of the Forty-Third Annual Convention, Chicago, Illinois—October 12–15, 1981* (Washington, D.C.: Canon Law Society of America, 1982), pp. 132–144, esp. p. 144.

From the rich experience of the Apostolic Signatura, which obviously is not limited to that of the United States of America, the necessity of the double conforming decision for an adequate process for the declaration of nullity of marriage is shown without any shadow of a doubt. By means of the study of the annual reports of the tribunals and the examination of definitive sentences of tribunals of first instance, the wisdom and the importance of the requirement of the double conforming sentence is more than evident.

The experience of the Apostolic Signatura is the singular font of knowledge of how the administration of justice is carried out in the universal Church as it is incarnated in the particular Churches. If there is to be any simplification of the process of nullity of marriage, it will necessarily be studied in the light of the service of the Apostolic Signatura to the individual Churches.

Conclusion

The judicial process for the declaration of nullity of marriage is essential to the discovery of the truth regarding the claim that what appeared to be true marriage consent was, in fact, null. Given the complexity of human nature and its reflection in most cases of marriage nullity, the only way in which to know, with moral certitude, the truth about such a claim is the dialectic that the judicial process provides and that has been carefully articulated and developed in the history of the Church's discipline.

The Third Extraordinary General Assembly of the Synod of Bishops must address a wide spectrum of issues that constitute the "Pastoral Challenges to the Family in the Context of Evangelization", the subject of its discussions. One of those challenges, but certainly not among the principal challenges, is the situation of the faithful who are in irregular matrimonial unions. Among those faithful, there are a certain number who claim the nullity of their marriage that has ended in separation or divorce, and who rightly ask that the Church give a judgment, in accord with the truth, regarding their claim. In order to encounter them with true pastoral charity, it is important to understand the nature of the judicial process by which their claim is judged and to provide it for them in its integrity, so that the Church respects fully their right to a decision regarding their claim that respects fully the truth and, therefore, charity.

In conclusion, the response to the question about the canonical process for the declaration of nullity of marriage, raised in the Preparatory Document of the Third Extraordinary General Assembly of the Synod of Bishops, can only be found through full respect for the nature of the claim of nullity of marriage and the nature of the process by which the truth of the claim is decided. It is my hope that the celebration of the coming Extraordinary General Assembly of the Synod of Bishops will lead to a new appreciation of the canonical process for the declaration of marriage, and a new commitment to provide the process for the faithful who request it in its integrity, for the sake of their eternal salvation. I conclude by recalling to mind again the words of Saint John Paul II regarding the pastoral charity that the Church must exercise on behalf of those who claim the nullity of their marriage:

A valid marriage, even one marked by serious difficulties, could not be considered invalid without doing violence to the truth and undermining thereby the only solid foundation which can support personal, marital and social life. A judge, therefore, must always be on guard against the risk of misplaced compassion, which would degenerate into sentimentality, itself only pastoral in appearance. The roads leading away from justice and truth end up in serving to distance people from God, thus yielding the opposite result from that which was sought in good faith.[59]

May God grant that the coming meeting of the Synod of Bishops lead to a new commitment to "justice and truth" that is the indispensable foundation of a deeper love of God and of one's neighbor in the family and, from the family, in the whole Church.

[59] "Un matrimonio valido, anche se segnato da gravi difficoltà, non potrebbe esser considerato invalido, se non facendo violenza alla verità e minando, in tal modo, l'unico fondamento saldo su cui può reggersi la vita personale, coniugale e sociale. Il giudice pertanto deve sempre guardarsi dal rischio di una malintesa compassione che scadrebbe in sentimentalismo, solo apparentemente pastorale. Le vie che si discostano dalla giustizia e dalla verità finiscono col contribuire ad allontanare le persone da Dio, ottenendo il risultato opposto a quello che in buona fede si cercava." Allocutio 1990, p. 875, no. 5. English translation: Woestman, *Papal Allocutions*, p. 211, no. 5.

APPENDIX

Excerpts from Select Documents
of the Magisterium

Magisterial Texts concerning Marriage and Divorce

Concilium Vaticanum II, Constitutio Pastoralis de Ecclesia in mundo huius temporis «Gaudium et spes»—*die VII mensis decembris anno MCMLXV*.

47. De matrimonio et familia in mundo hodierno.

Salus personae et societatis humanae ac christianae arcte cum fausta condicione communitatis coniugalis et familiaris connectitur. Ideo christiani, una cum omnibus qui eandem communitatem magni aestimant, sincere gaudent de variis subsidiis quibus homines, in hac communitate amoris fovenda et in vita colenda, hodie progrediuntur, et coniuges atque parentes in praecellenti suo munere adiuvantur; meliora insuper exinde beneficia exspectant atque promovere student.

Non ubique vero huius institutionis dignitas eadem claritate illucescit, siquidem polygamia, divortii lue, amore sic dicto libero, aliisve deformationibus obscuratur; insuper amor nuptialis saepius egoismo, hedonismo et illicitis usibus contra generationem profanatur. Praeterea hodiernae condiciones oeconomicae, socio-psychologicae et civiles non leves in familiam perturbationes inducunt. In certis denique orbis partibus non absque sollicitudine problemata ex incremento demographico exorta observantur. Quibus omnibus conscientiae anguntur. Verumtamen matrimonialis familiarisque instituti vis et robur ex eo quoque apparent, quod profundae immutationes societatis hodiernae, non obstantibus difficultatibus inde prorumpentibus, saepe saepius veram eiusdem instituti indolem vario modo manifestant.

Magisterial Texts concerning Marriage and Divorce

Second Vatican Council, Pastoral Constitution on the Church in the Modern World, *Gaudium et spes*, December 7, 1965

47. The well-being of the individual person and of human and Christian society is intimately linked with the healthy condition of that community produced by marriage and family. Hence Christians and all men who hold this community in high esteem sincerely rejoice in the various ways by which men today find help in fostering this community of love and perfecting its life, and by which parents are assisted in their lofty calling. Those who rejoice in such aids look for additional benefits from them and labor to bring them about.

Yet the excellence of this institution is not everywhere reflected with equal brilliance, since polygamy, the plague of divorce, so-called free love and other disfigurements have an obscuring effect. In addition, married love is too often profaned by excessive self-love, the worship of pleasure and illicit practices against human generation. Moreover, serious disturbances are caused in families by modern economic conditions, by influences at once social and psychological, and by the demands of civil society. Finally, in certain parts of the world problems resulting from population growth are generating concern.

All these situations have produced anxiety of consciences. Yet, the power and strength of the institution of marriage and family can also be seen in the fact that time

Quapropter Concilium, quaedam doctrinae Ecclesiae capita in clariorem lucem ponendo, christianos hominesque universos illuminare et confortare intendit, qui nativam status matrimonialis dignitatem eiusque eximium valorem sacrum tueri et promovere conantur.

48. De sanctitate matrimonii et familiae.

Intima communitas vitae et amoris coniugalis, a Creatore condita suisque legibus instructa, foedere coniugii seu irrevocabili consensu personali instauratur. Ita actu humano, quo coniuges sese mutuo tradunt atque accipiunt, institutum ordinatione divina firmum oritur, etiam coram societate; hoc vinculum sacrum intuitu boni, tum coniugum et prolis tum societatis, non ex humano arbitrio pendet. Ipse vero Deus est auctor matrimonii, variis bonis ac finibus praediti; quae omnia pro generis humani continuatione, pro singulorum familiae membrorum profectu personali ac sorte aeterna, pro dignitate, stabilitate, pace et prosperitate ipsius familiae totiusque humanae societatis maximi sunt momenti. Indole autem sua naturali, ipsum institutum matrimonii amorque coniugalis ad procreationem et educationem prolis ordinantur iisque veluti suo fastigio coronantur. Vir itaque et mulier, qui foedere coniugali "iam non sunt duo, sed una caro" (Mt 19,6), intima personarum atque operum coniunctione mutuum sibi adiutorium et servitium praestant, sensumque suae unitatis experiuntur et plenius in dies adipiscuntur. Quae intima unio, utpote mutua duarum

and again, despite the difficulties produced, the profound changes in modern society reveal the true character of this institution in one way or another.

Therefore, by presenting certain key points of Church doctrine in a clearer light, this sacred synod wishes to offer guidance and support to those Christians and other men who are trying to preserve the holiness and to foster the natural dignity of the married state and its superlative value.

48. The intimate partnership of married life and love has been established by the Creator and qualified by His laws, and is rooted in the conjugal covenant of irrevocable personal consent. Hence by that human act whereby spouses mutually bestow and accept each other a relationship arises which by divine will and in the eyes of society too is a lasting one. For the good of the spouses and their off-springs as well as of society, the existence of the sacred bond no longer depends on human decisions alone. For, God Himself is the author of matrimony, endowed as it is with various benefits and purposes. All of these have a very decisive bearing on the continuation of the human race, on the personal development and eternal destiny of the individual members of a family, and on the dignity, stability, peace and prosperity of the family itself and of human society as a whole. By their very nature, the institution of matrimony itself and conjugal love are ordained for the procreation and education of children, and find in them their ultimate crown. Thus a man and a woman, who by their compact of conjugal love "are no longer two, but one flesh" (Matt 19:6), render mutual help and service to each other through an intimate union of their persons and of their actions. Through this union they experience the meaning of their oneness

personarum donatio, sicut et bonum liberorum, plenam coniugum fidem exigunt atque indissolubilem eorum unitatem urgent.

Christus Dominus huic multiformi dilectioni, e divino caritatis fonte exortae et ad exemplar suae cum Ecclesia unionis constitutae, abundanter benedixit. Sicut enim Deus olim foedere dilectionis et fidelitatis populo suo occurrit, ita nunc hominum Salvator Ecclesiaeque Sponsus, per sacramentum matrimonii christifidelibus coniugibus obviam venit. Manet porro cum eis, ut quemadmodum Ipse dilexit Ecclesiam et Semetipsum pro ea tradidit, ita et coniuges, mutua deditione, se invicem perpetua fidelitate diligant. Germanus amor coniugalis in divinum amorem assumitur atque virtute redemptiva Christi et salvifica actione Ecclesiae regitur ac ditatur, ut coniuges efficaciter ad Deum ducantur atque in sublimi munere patris et matris adiuventur et confortentur. Quapropter coniuges christiani ad sui status officia et dignitatem peculiari sacramento roborantur et veluti consecrantur; cuius virtute munus suum coniugale et familiare explentes, spiritu Christi imbuti, quo tota eorum vita, fide, spe et caritate pervaditur, magis ac magis ad propriam suam perfectionem mutuamque sanctificationem, ideoque communiter ad Dei glorificationem accedunt.

Unde, ipsis parentibus exemplo et oratione familiari praegredientibus, filii, immo et omnes in familiae convictu degentes, humanitatis, salutis atque sanctitatis viam facilius

and attain to it with growing perfection day by day. As a mutual gift of two persons, this intimate union and the good of the children impose total fidelity on the spouses and argue for an unbreakable oneness between them.

Christ the Lord abundantly blessed this many-faceted love, welling up as it does from the fountain of divine love and structured as it is on the model of His union with His Church. For as God of old made Himself present to His people through a covenant of love and fidelity, so now the Savior of men and the Spouse of the Church comes into the lives of married Christians through the sacrament of matrimony. He abides with them thereafter so that just as He loved the Church and handed Himself over on her behalf, the spouses may love each other with perpetual fidelity through mutual self-bestowal.

Authentic married love is caught up into divine love and is governed and enriched by Christ's redeeming power and the saving activity of the Church, so that this love may lead the spouses to God with powerful effect and may aid and strengthen them in sublime office of being a father or a mother. For this reason Christian spouses have a special sacrament by which they are fortified and receive a kind of consecration in the duties and dignity of their state. By virtue of this sacrament, as spouses fulfil their conjugal and family obligation, they are penetrated with the spirit of Christ, which suffuses their whole lives with faith, hope and charity. Thus they increasingly advance the perfection of their own personalities, as well as their mutual sanctification, and hence contribute jointly to the glory of God.

As a result, with their parents leading the way by example and family prayer, children and indeed everyone gathered around the family hearth will find a readier path to

invenient. Coniuges autem, dignitate ac munere paterni-
tatis et maternitatis ornati, officium educationis praesertim religiosae, quod ad ipsos imprimis spectat, diligenter
adimplebunt.

Liberi, ut viva familiae membra, ad sanctificationem
parentum suo modo conferunt. Gratae enim mentis
affectu, pietate atque fiducia beneficiis parentum respon-
debunt ipsisque in rebus adversis necnon in senectutis
solitudine filiorum more assistent. Viduitas, in continui-
tate vocationis coniugalis forti animo assumpta, ab omnibus honorabitur. Familia suas divitias spirituales cum aliis
quoque familiis generose communicabit. Proinde familia
christiana, cum e matrimonio, quod est imago et parti-
cipatio foederis dilectionis Christi et Ecclesiae, exoriatur,
vivam Salvatoris in mundo praesentiam atque germanam
Ecclesiae naturam omnibus patefaciet, tum coniugum
amore, generosa fecunditate, unitate atque fidelitate, tum
amabili omnium membrorum cooperatione.

49. De amore coniugali.

Pluries verbo divino sponsi atque coniuges invitantur, ut
casto amore sponsalia et indivisa dilectione coniugium
nutriant atque foveant. Plures quoque nostrae aetatis
homines verum amorem inter maritum et uxorem variis
rationibus secundum honestos populorum et temporum
mores manifestatum magni faciunt. Ille autem amor, utpote
eminenter humanus, cum a persona in personam volunta-
tis affectu dirigatur, totius personae bonum complectitur

human maturity, salvation and holiness. Graced with the dignity and office of fatherhood and motherhood, parents will energetically acquit themselves of a duty which devolves primarily on them, namely education and especially religious education.

As living members of the family, children contribute in their own way to making their parents holy. For they will respond to the kindness of their parents with sentiments of gratitude, with love and trust. They will stand by them as children should when hardships overtake their parents and old age brings its loneliness. Widowhood, accepted bravely as a continuation of the marriage vocation, should be esteemed by all. Families too will share their spiritual riches generously with other families. Thus the Christian family, which springs from marriage as a reflection of the loving covenant uniting Christ with the Church, and as a participation in that covenant, will manifest to all men Christ's living presence in the world, and the genuine nature of the Church. This the family will do by the mutual love of the spouses, by their generous fruitfulness, their solidarity and faithfulness, and by the loving way in which all members of the family assist one another.

49. The biblical Word of God several times urges the betrothed and the married to nourish and develop their wedlock by pure conjugal love and undivided affection. Many men of our own age also highly regard true love between husband and wife as it manifests itself in a variety of ways depending on the worthy customs of various peoples and times.

This love is an eminently human one since it is directed from one person to another through an affection of the will; it involves the good of the whole person, and

ideoque corporis animique expressiones peculiari dignitate ditare easque tamquam elementa ac signa specialia coniugalis amicitiae nobilitare valet. Hunc amorem Dominus, speciali gratiae et caritatis dono, sanare, perficere et elevare dignatus est. Talis amor, humana simul et divina consocians, coniuges ad liberum et mutuum sui ipsius donum, tenero affectu et opere probatum, conducit totamque vitam eorum pervadit; immo ipse generosa sua operositate perficitur et crescit. Longe igitur exsuperat meram eroticam inclinationem, quae, egoistice exculta, citius et misere evanescit.

Haec dilectio proprio matrimonii opere singulariter exprimitur et perficitur. Actus proinde, quibus coniuges intime et caste inter se uniuntur, honesti ac digni sunt et, modo vere humano exerciti, donationem mutuam significant et fovent, qua sese invicem laeto gratoque animo locupletant. Amor ille mutua fide ratus, et potissimum sacramento Christi sancitus, inter prospera et adversa corpore ac mente indissolubiliter fidelis est, et proinde ab omni adulterio et divortio alienus remanet. Aequali etiam dignitate personali cum mulieris tum viri agnoscenda in mutua atque plena dilectione, unitas matrimonii a Domino confirmata luculenter apparet. Ad officia autem huius vocationis christianae constanter exsequenda virtus insignis requiritur: quapropter coniuges, gratia ad vitam sanctam roborati, firmitatem amoris, magnitudinem animi et spiritum sacrificii assidue colent et oratione impetrabunt.

Germanus autem amor coniugalis altius aestimabitur atque sana circa eum opinio publica efformabitur, si

therefore can enrich the expressions of body and mind with a unique dignity, ennobling these expressions as special ingredients and signs of the friendship distinctive of marriage. This love God has judged worthy of special gifts, healing, perfecting and exalting gifts of grace and of charity. Such love, merging the human with the divine, leads the spouses to a free and mutual gift of themselves, a gift providing itself by gentle affection and by deed, such love pervades the whole of their lives: indeed by its busy generosity it grows better and grows greater. Therefore it far excels mere erotic inclination, which, selfishly pursued, soon enough fades wretchedly away.

This love is uniquely expressed and perfected through the appropriate enterprise of matrimony. The actions within marriage by which the couple are united intimately and chastely are noble and worthy ones. Expressed in a manner which is truly human, these actions promote that mutual self-giving by which spouses enrich each other with a joyful and a ready will. Sealed by mutual faithfulness and hallowed above all by Christ's sacrament, this love remains steadfastly true in body and in mind, in bright days or dark. It will never be profaned by adultery or divorce. Firmly established by the Lord, the unity of marriage will radiate from the equal personal dignity of wife and husband, a dignity acknowledged by mutual and total love. The constant fulfillment of the duties of this Christian vocation demands notable virtue. For this reason, strengthened by grace for holiness of life, the couple will painstakingly cultivate and pray for steadiness of love, large heartedness and the spirit of sacrifice.

Authentic conjugal love will be more highly prized, and wholesome public opinion created about it if Christian

coniuges christiani testimonio fidelitatis et harmoniae in eodem amore necnon sollicitudine in filiis educandis, eminent atque in necessaria renovatione culturali, psychologica et sociali in favorem matrimonii et familiae partes suas agunt. Iuvenes de amoris coniugalis dignitate, munere et opere, potissimum in sinu ipsius familiae, apte et tempestive instruendi sunt, ut, castitatis cultu instituti, convenienti aetate ab honestis sponsalibus ad nuptias transire possint.

Adhortatio Apostolica Familiaris consortio Ioannis Pauli PP. II Summi Pontificis ad Episcopos, Sacerdotes et Christifideles totius Ecclesiae Catholicae de familiae christianae muneribus in mundo huius temporis.
—*die XXII mensis Novembris anno MCMLXXXI*

84. Cotidianum rerum experimentum pro dolor docet eum qui divortium fecerit, plerumque animo intendere novam transire ad convivendi societatem, sine ritu religioso catholicorum, ut patet. Cum de malo agatur, quod, sicut et alia, latius usque inficiat etiam greges catholicos, haec difficultas est cum cura et sine ulla mora omnino aggredienda. Synodi Patres eam data opera investigaverunt. Nam Ecclesia, idcirco instituta ut ad salutem omnes homines imprimisque baptizatos perduceret, non potest sibimet ipsis illos derelinquere, qui—iam sacramentali vinculo matrimonii coniuncti—transire conati sunt ad nuptias novas. Nitetur propterea neque umquam defessa curabit Ecclesia ut iis praesto sint salutis instrumenta.

Noverint pastores ex veritatis amore se bene distinguere debere inter vadas rei condiciones. Etenim aliquid interest inter eos qui sincero animo contenderunt primum

couples give outstanding witness to faithfulness and harmony in their love, and to their concern for educating their children also, if they do their part in bringing about the needed cultural, psychological and social renewal on behalf of marriage and the family. Especially in the heart of their own families, young people should be aptly and seasonably instructed in the dignity, duty and work of married love. Trained thus in the cultivation of chastity, they will be able at a suitable age to enter a marriage of their own after an honorable courtship.

Saint John Paul II, Apostolic Exhortation *Familiaris consortio*, November 22, 1981

84. Daily experience unfortunately shows that people who have obtained a divorce usually intend to enter into a new union, obviously not with a Catholic religious ceremony. Since this is an evil that like the others is affecting more and more Catholics as well, the problem must be faced with resolution and without delay. The synod fathers studied it expressly. The church, which was set up to lead to salvation all people and especially the baptized, cannot abandon to their own devices those who have been previously bound by sacramental marriage and who have attempted a second marriage. The church will therefore make untiring efforts to put at their disposal her means of salvation.

Pastors must know that for the sake of truth they are obliged to exercise careful discernment of situations. There is, in fact, a difference between those who have sincerely

matrimonium servare quique prorsus iniuste sunt deserti, atque eos qui sua gravi culpa matrimonium canonice validum everterunt. Sunt denique alii, qui novam inierunt convivendi societatem educationis filiorum gratia atque interdum certi sua in intima conscientia sunt superius matrimonium iam irreparabiliter disruptum numquam validum fuisse.

Una cum Synodo vehementer cohortamur pastores totamque fidelium communitatem ut divortio digressos adiuvent, caventes sollicita cum caritate ne illos ab Ecclesia seiunctos arbitrentur, quoniam iidem possunt, immo debent ut baptizati vitam ipsius participare. Hortandi praeterea sunt ut verbum Dei exaudiant, sacrificio Missae intersint, preces fundere perseverent, opera caritatis necnon incepta communitatis pro iustitia adiuvent, filios in christiana fide instituant, spiritum et opera paenitentiae colant ut cotidie sic Dei gratiam implorent. Pro illis Ecclesia precetur, eos confirmet, matrem se exhibeat iis misericordem itaque in fide eos speque sustineat.

Nihilominus Ecclesia inculcat consuetudinem suam, in Sacris ipsis Litteris innixam, non admittendi ad eucharisticam communionem fideles, qui post divortium factum novas nuptias inierunt. Ipsi namque impediunt ne admittantur, cum status eorum et condicio vitae obiective dissideant ab illa amoris coniunctione inter Christum et Ecclesiam, quae Eucharistia significatur atque peragitur. Restat praeterea alia peculiaris ratio pastoralis: si homines illi ad Eucharistiam admitterentur, in errorem turbationemque inducerentur fideles de Ecclesiae doctrina super indissolubilitate matrimonii.

tried to save their first marriage and have been unjustly abandoned and those who, through their own grave fault, have destroyed a canonically valid marriage.

Finally, there are those who have entered into a second union for the sake of the children's upbringing and who are sometimes subjectively certain in conscience that their previous and irreparably destroyed marriage had never been valid.

Together with the synod, I earnestly call upon pastors and the whole community of the faithful to help the divorced and with solicitous care to make sure that they do not consider themselves as separated from the church, for as baptized persons they can and indeed must share in her life. They should be encouraged to listen to the word of God, to attend the sacrifice of the Mass, to persevere in prayer, to contribute to works of charity and to community efforts in favor of justice, to bring up their children in the Christian faith, to cultivate the spirit and practice of penance and thus implore, day by day, God's grace. Let the church pray for them, encourage them and show herself a merciful mother and thus sustain them in faith and hope.

However, the church reaffirms her practice, which is based upon sacred scripture, of not admitting to eucharistic communion divorced persons who have remarried. They are unable to be admitted thereto from the fact that their state and condition of life objectively contradict that union of love between Christ and the church which is signified and effected by the Eucharist. Besides this there is another special pastoral reason: If these people were admitted to the Eucharist the faithful would be led into error and confusion regarding the church's teaching about the indissolubility of marriage.

Porro reconciliatio in sacramento paenitentiae—quae ad Eucharistiae sacramentum aperit viam—illis unis concedi potest, qui dolentes quod signum violaverint Foederis et fidelitatis Christi, sincere parati sunt vitae formam iam non amplius adversam matrimonii indissolubitati suscipere. Hoc poscit revera ut, quoties vir ac mulier gravibus de causis—verbi gratia, ob liberorum educationem—non valeant necessitati separationis satisfacere, officium in se suscipiant omnino continenter vivendi, scilicet se abstinendi ab aetibus, qui solis coniugibus competunt.

Observantia similiter erga matrimonii sacramentum, tum etiam erga coniuges eorumque familiares necnon erga ipsam fidelium communitatem, vetat quemlibet pastorem ullam propter causam vel praetextum etiam pastoralem ne pro divortio digressis, qui novas nuptias inierunt, ritus cuiusvis generis faciant; hi enim ostenderent novas nuptias sacramentales validas celebrari ac proinde errorem inicerent de indissolubilitate prioris matrimonii valide contracti.

Hoc quidem pacto agens, Ecclesia profitetur fidelitatem suam in Christum eiusque veritatem; simul vero materno affectu se gerit erga hos filios suos, potissimum eos qui nulla propria intercedente culpa a proprio derelicti sunt legitimo coniuge.

Firma insuper cum fiducia Ecclesia credit quotquot a mandato Domini recesserint in eoque etiamnunc statu vivant, a Deo gratiam conversionis ac salutis assequi posse, si in precatione, paenitentia, caritate perseveraverint.

Reconciliation in the sacrament of penance, which would open the way to the Eucharist, can only be granted to those who, repenting of having broken the sign of the convenant and of fidelity to Christ, are sincerely ready to undertake a way of life that is no longer in contradiction to the indissolubility of marriage.

This means, in practice, that when, for serious reasons such as, for example, the children's upbringing, a man and a woman cannot satisfy the obligation to separate, they "take on themselves the duty to live in complete continence, that is, by abstinence from the acts proper to married couples."

Similarly, the respect due to the sacrament of matrimony, to the couples themselves and their families, and also to the community of the faithful forbids any pastor for whatever reason or pretext, even of a pastoral nature, to perform ceremonies of any kind for divorced people who remarry. Such ceremonies would give the impression of the celebration of a new, sacramentally valid marriage and would thus lead people into error concerning the indissolubility of a validly contracted marriage.

By acting in this way the church professes her own fidelity to Christ and to his truth. At the same time she shows motherly concern for these children of hers, especially those who, through no fault of their own, have been abandoned by their legitimate partner.

With firm confidence she believes that those who have rejected the Lord's command and are still living in this state will be able to obtain from God the grace of conversion and salvation, provided that they have persevered in prayer, penance and charity.

Catechismus Catholicae Ecclesiae (1992; 1997)

1644. Coniugum amor, sua ipsa natura, unitatem et indissolubilitatem exigit eorum communitatis personalis quae
totam eorum amplectitur vitam: «Quod ergo Deus coni-
unxit, homo non separet» (Mt 19,6). Coniuges adiguntur
ad crescendum continenter in communione sua per coti-
dianam fidelitatem erga matrimoniale promissum mutuae
plenae donationis. Haec humana communio confirmatur,
purificatur et perficitur communione in Iesu Christo, a
Matrimonii sacramento donata. Ipsa per fidei communis
vitam et per Eucharistiam in communi receptam profun-
dior fit.

1645. Aequali etiam dignitate personali cum mulieris
tum viri agnoscenda in mutua atque plena dilectione, unitas Matrimonii a Domino confirmata luculenter apparet.
Polygamia huic aequali dignitati est contraria atque coniugali amori qui unicus est et exclusivus.

1646. Amor coniugalis, sua ipsa natura, inviolabilem
a coniugibus exigit fidelitatem. Hoc ex eorum ipsorum
consequitur dono quod sibi mutuo impertiunt coniuges.
Amor definitivus esse vult. Ipse "usque ad novam decisionem" esse non potest. Haec intima unio, utpote mutua
duarum personarum donatio, sicut et bonum liberorum,
plenam coniugum fidem exigunt atque indissolubilem
eorum unitatem urgent.

1647. Profundissimum motivum in fidelitate Dei ad
Eius Foedus invenitur, Christi ad Ecclesiam. Per Matrimonii sacramentum, coniuges apti fiunt qui hanc reprae-
sentent fidelitatem eamque testentur. Per sacramentum,
indissolubilitas Matrimonii novum et profundiorem accipit
sensum.

Catechism of the Catholic Church (1992; 1997)

1644. The love of the spouses requires, of its very nature, the unity and indissolubility of the spouses' community of persons, which embraces their entire life: "so they are no longer two, but one flesh" (*Mt* 19:6; cf. *Gen* 2:24). They "are called to grow continually in their communion through day-to-day fidelity to their marriage promise of total mutual self-giving" (*FC* 19). This human communion is confirmed, purified, and completed by communion in Jesus Christ, given through the sacrament of matrimony. It is deepened by lives of the common faith and by the Eucharist received together.

1645. "The unity of marriage, distinctly recognized by our Lord, is made clear in the equal personal dignity which must be accorded to man and wife in mutual and unreserved affection" (*GS* 49 § 2). Polygamy is contrary to conjugal love which is undivided and exclusive.

1646. By its very nature conjugal love requires the inviolable fidelity of the spouses. This is the consequence of the gift of themselves which they make to each other. Love seeks to be definitive; it cannot be an arrangement "until further notice". The "intimate union of marriage, as a mutual giving of two persons, and the good of the children, demand total fidelity from the spouses and require an unbreakable union between them" (*GS* 48 § 1).

1647. The deepest reason is found in the fidelity of God to his covenant, in that of Christ to his Church. Through the sacrament of matrimony the spouses are enabled to represent this fidelity and witness to it. Through the sacrament, the indissolubility of marriage receives a new and deeper meaning.

1648. Videri potest difficile, immo impossibile, se pro tota vita personae ligare humanae. Eo ipso maximi est momenti Bonum Nuntium proclamare: Deum nos amore definitivo amare et irrevocabili, coniuges hunc participare amorem qui eos ducit et sustinet, eosque per suam fidelitatem testes esse posse Dei fidelis amoris. Coniuges qui, cum Dei gratia, hoc dant testimonium, saepe in valde difficilibus condicionibus, gratitudinem communitatis ecclesialis merentur et fulcimentum.

1649. Condiciones tamen exstant in quibus matrimonialis cohabitatio, valde diversis e causis, practice impossibilis fit. In talibus casibus, Ecclesia physicam coniugum admittit separationem et finem cohabitationis. Coniuges maritus et uxor coram Deo esse non desinunt; liberi non sunt ad novam contrahendam unionem. In tali difficili condicione, reconciliatio, si possibilis sit, optima esset solutio. Communitas christiana vocatur ad has personas adiuvandas ut in sua condicione christiane vivant, in fidelitate ad sui matrimonii vinculum quod indissolubile permanet.

1650. Plures sunt catholici, in non paucis regionibus, qui, secundum leges civiles, ad divortium recurrunt et novam civilem contrahunt unionem. Ecclesia, propter fidelitatem ad Iesu Christi verbum: «Quicumque dimiserit uxorem suam et aliam duxerit, adulterium committit in eam; et si ipsa dimiserit virum suum et alii nupserit, moechatur» (Mc 10,11–12), tenet se non posse hanc novam unionem ut validam agnoscere, si primum matrimonium validum erat. Si divortio seiuncti novas civiliter inierunt nuptias, in condicione inveniuntur quae obiective Dei Legem transgreditur. Exinde ad eucharisticam Communionem accedere non possunt, dum haec condicio permaneat. Eadem

1648. It can seem difficult, even impossible, to bind oneself for life to another human being. This makes it all the more important to proclaim the Good News that God loves us with a definitive and irrevocable love, that married couples share in this love, that it supports and sustains them, and that by their own faithfulness they can be witnesses to God's faithful love. Spouses who with God's grace give this witness, often in very difficult conditions, deserve the gratitude and support of the ecclesial community.

1649. Yet there are some situations in which living together becomes practically impossible for a variety of reasons. In such cases the Church permits the physical separation of the couple and their living apart. The spouses do not cease to be husband and wife before God and so are not free to contract a new union. In this difficult situation, the best solution would be, if possible, reconciliation. The Christian community is called to help these persons live out their situation in a Christian manner and in fidelity to their marriage bond which remains indissoluble.

1650. Today there are numerous Catholics in many countries who have recourse to civil divorce and contract new civil unions. In fidelity to the words of Jesus Christ: "Whoever divorces his wife and marries another, commits adultery against her; and if she divorces her husband and marries another, she commits adultery" (*Mk* 10:11–12). The Church maintains that a new union cannot be recognized as valid, if the first marriage was. If the divorced are remarried civilly, they find themselves in a situation that objectively contravenes God's law. Consequently, they cannot receive Eucharistic communion as long as this situation persists. For the same reason, they cannot exercise

ex causa, quasdam responsabilitates ecclesiales non possunt exercere. Reconciliatio per Poenitentiae sacramentum nonnisi illis concedi potest, quos poenitet, se Foederis signum et fidelitatis erga Christum esse transgressos, et se ad vivendum in completa continentia obligant.

1651. Relate ad christianos qui in hac condicione vivunt et qui saepe fidem servant et suos filios christiane exoptant educare, sacerdotes et tota communitas attentam ostendere debent sollicitudinem, ne illi se tamquam separatos ab Ecclesia considerent, cuius vitam ut baptizati possunt et debent participare. Hortandi praeterea sunt ut Verbum Dei exaudiant, Sacrificio Missae intersint, preces fundere perseverent, opera caritatis necnon incepta communitatis pro iustitia adiuvent, filios in christiana fide instituant, spiritum et opera paenitentiae colant ut cotidie sic Dei gratiam implorent.

Congregatio pro Doctrina Fidei, Epistula ad Catholicae Ecclesiae Episcopos de receptione Communionis Eucharisticae a fidelibus qui post divortiumm novas inierunt nuptias—*die 14 Septembris 1994*

Excellentia Reverendissima,

1. Annus Internationalis Familiae peculiaris momenti occasionem praebet, ut testificationes denuo retegantur caritatis curaeque Ecclesiae in familiam, et simul rursus proponantur inaestimabiles divitiae matrimonii christiani, quod familiae fundamentum constituit.

certain ecclesial responsibilities. Reconciliation through the sacrament of penance can be granted only to those who have repented for having violated the sign of the covenant and of fidelity to Christ, and who are committed to living in complete continence.

1651. Toward Christians who live in this situation, and who often keep the faith and desire to bring up their children in a Christian manner, priests and the whole community must manifest an attentive solicitude, so that they do not consider themselves separated from the Church, in whose life they can and must participate as baptized persons: "They should be encouraged to listen to the Word of God, to attend the sacrifice of the Mass, to persevere in prayer, to contribute to works of charity and to community efforts for justice, to bring up their children in the Christian faith, to cultivate the spirit and practice of penance and thus implore, day by day, God's grace" (FC 84).

Congregation for the Doctrine of the Faith, Letter to the Bishops of the Catholic Church concerning the Reception of Holy Communion by the Divorced and Remarried Members of the Faithful, September 14, 1994

Your Excellency,
1. The International Year of the Family is a particularly important occasion to discover anew the many signs of the Church's love and concern for the family and, at the same time, to present once more the priceless riches of Christian marriage, which is the basis of the family.

2. In praesentibus rerum adiunctis specialem animi attentionem postulant difficultates et angores eorum fidelium, qui in abnormibus matrimonii condicionibus versantur. Pastores efficere debent, ut Christi caritas et proxima Ecclesiae maternitas animadvertantur; illos ergo cum amore excipiant atque hortentur ut in Dei misericordia fiduciam reponant, prudenterque et cum respectu eis suggerentes concreta itinera conversionis et participationis vitae in communitate ecclesiali.

3. Cum vero conscii sint veram comprehensionem germanamque misericordiam numquam seiungi a veritate, pastores officio obstringuntur hos fideles commonendi de Ecclesiae doctrina quae ad sacramentorum celebrationem, peculiarique modo ad Eucharistiae receptionem attinet. Hac in re, postremis his in annis, in variis regionibus diversae solutiones pastorales propositae sunt, secundum quas fideles, qui post divortium novas nuptias inierunt, quamvis generali ratione profecto ad Communionem Eucharisticam admittendi non sunt, ad ipsam tamen accedere queunt quibusdam in casibus, cum scilicet secundum iudicium suae ipsorum conscientiae putent se hoc facere posse. Quod quidem evenire potest, verbi gratia, cum prorsus iniuste deserti fuerint, quamvis prius matrimonium salvum facere sincere conati sint, vel cum persuasi sint de nullitate prioris matrimonii, quae tamen probari non possit in foro externo, vel cum iam longum reflexionis et paenitentiae iter emensi sint, vel etiam cum ob rationes moraliter validas iidem separationis obligationi satisfacere non possint.

Iuxta quasdam opiniones, ad veram suam condicionem obiective examinandam, divortio digressis, qui novas inierunt nuptias, colloquium ineundum esset cum

2. In this context the difficulties and sufferings of those faithful in irregular marriage situations merit special attention. Pastors are called to help them experience the charity of Christ and the maternal closeness of the Church, receiving them with love, exhorting them to trust in God's mercy and suggesting, with prudence and respect, concrete ways of conversion and sharing in the life of the community of the Church.

3. Aware however that authentic understanding and genuine mercy are never separated from the truth, pastors have the duty to remind these faithful of the Church's doctrine concerning the celebration of the sacraments, in particular, the reception of the holy communion. In recent years, in various regions, different pastoral solutions in this area have been suggested according to which, to be sure, a general admission of divorced and remarried to Eucharistic communion would not be possible, but the divorced and remarried members of the faithful could approach holy communion in specific cases when they consider themselves authorised according to a judgement of conscience to do so. This would be the case, for example, when they had been abandoned completely unjustly, although they sincerely tried to save the previous marriage, or when they are convinced of the nullity of their previous marriage, although unable to demonstrate it in the external forum or when they have gone through a long period of reflexion and penance, or also when for morally valid reasons they cannot satisfy the obligation to separate.

In some places, it has also been proposed that in order objectively to examine their actual situation, the divorced and remarried would have to consult a prudent and expert

presbytero prudenti ac experto. Idem sacerdos tamen observet oportet eorum adventiciam decisionem conscientiae accedendi ad Eucharistiam, quin hoc significet admissionem ex parte auctoritatis.

His et similibus in casibus ageretur de toleranti ac benevola solutione pastorali, ut ratio inducatur diversarum condicionum divortio digressorum, qui novas nuptias inierunt.

4. Etsi notum sit similes solutiones pastorales a quibusdam Ecclesiae Patribus propositas easdemque etiam in praxim deductas fuisse, hae tamen numquam consensum Patrum obtinuerunt nulloque modo doctrinam communem Ecclesiae constituerunt nec eius disciplinam determina runt. Spectat ad ipsius Magisterium universale, fidelitate servata erga S. Scripturam et Traditionem, docere et authentice interpretari *depositum fidei.*

Quare haec Congregatio, prae oculis habens novas superius memoratas propositiones pastorales, suum officium esse ducit in memoriam revocare doctrinam et disciplinam Ecclesiae hac in re. Ipsa enim, propter fidelitatem erga Iesu Christi verbum, affirmat se non posse validum agnoscere novum coniugium, si prius matrimonium validum fuit. Divortio digressi, si ad alias nuptias civiliter transierunt, in condicione versantur obiective legi Dei contraria. Idcirco, quoad haec durat condicio, ad Eucharisticam Communionem accedere iis non licet.

Quae norma minime habet indolem poenalem vel utcumque discriminantem erga eos de quibus agimus, sed potius obiectivam condicionem exprimit, quae suapte natura impedit accessionem ad Communionem Eucharisticam. "Ipsi namque impediunt ne admittantur, cum status eorum et condicio vitae obiective dissideant ab illa amoris

priest. This priest, however, would have to respect their eventual decision to approach holy communion, without this implying an official authorisation.

In these and similar cases it would be a matter of a tolerant and benevolent pastoral solution in order to do justice to the different situations of the divorced and remarried.

4. Even if analogous pastoral solutions have been proposed by a few Fathers of the Church and in some measure were practiced, nevertheless these never attained the consensus of the Fathers and in no way came to constitute the common doctrine of the Church nor to determine her discipline. It falls to the universal Magisterium, in fidelity to Sacred Scripture and Tradition, to teach and to interpret authentically the *depositum fidei*.

With respect to the aforementioned new pastoral proposals, this Congregation deems itself obliged therefore to recall the doctrine and discipline of the Church in this matter. In fidelity to the words of Jesus Christ, the Church affirms that a new union cannot be recognised as valid if the preceding marriage was valid. If the divorced are remarried civilly, they find themselves in a situation that objectively contravenes God's law. Consequently, they cannot receive holy communion as long as this situation persists.

This norm is not at all a punishment or a discrimination against the divorced and remarried, but rather expresses an objective situation that of itself renders impossible the reception of holy communion: "They are unable to be admitted thereto from the fact that their state and condition of life objectively contradict that union of love between

coniunctione inter Christum et Ecclesiam, quae Eucharistia significatur et peragitur. Restat praeterea alia peculiaris ratio pastoralis: si homines illi ad Eucharistiam admitterentur, in errorem turbationemque inducerentur fideles de Ecclesiae doctrina super indissolubilitate matrimonii".

Fidelibus, qui in tali condicione matrimoniali versantur, accessio ad Communionem Eucharisticam patet unice per absolutionem sacramentalem, quae dari potest "tantum illis qui, dolentes quod signum violaverint Foederis et fidelitatis Christi, sincere parati sunt vitae formam iam non amplius adversam indissolubilitati suscipere. Hoc poscit revera ut, quoties vir ac mulier gravibus de causis—verbi gratia, ob liberorum educationem—non valeant necessitati separationis satisfacere, 'officium in se suscipiant omnino continenter vivendi, scilicet se abstinendi ab actibus, qui solis coniugibus competunt'". Tunc ad Communionem Eucharisticam accedere possunt, salva tamen obligatione vitandi scandalum.

5. Ecclesiae doctrina et disciplina hac de re fuse expositae sunt, tempore post Concilium, in Adhortatione Apostolica *Familiaris consortio*. Adhortatio, praeter alia, in memoriam revocat pastores, ob amorem veritatis, officio adstringi recte distinguendi varias condiciones, atque eos hortatur ut animum addant iis qui post divortium novas nuptias inierunt ut varia vitae Ecclesiae momenta participent. Simul confirmat consuetudinem constantem et universalem "in Sacris ipsis Litteris innixam, non admittendi ad Eucharisticam Communionem fideles qui post divortium novas nuptias inierunt", atque huius rei rationes

Christ and his Church which is signified and effected by the Eucharist. Besides this, there is another special pastoral reason: if these people were admitted to the Eucharist, the faithful would be led into error and confusion regarding the Church's teaching about the indissolubility of marriage" (Apostolic Exhortation *Familiaris consortio*, n. 84: AAS 74 [1982] 185–186).

The faithful who persist in such a situation may receive holy communion only after obtaining sacramental absolution, which may be given only "to those who, repenting of having broken the sign of the covenant and of fidelity to Christ, are sincerely ready to undertake a way of life that is no longer in contradiction to the indissolubility of marriage. This means, in practice, that when for serious reasons, for example, for the children's upbringing, a man and a woman cannot satisfy the obligation to separate, they 'take on themselves the duty to live in complete continence, that is, by abstinence from the acts proper to married couples'" (*Ibid.*, n. 84: AAS 74 [1982] 186). In such a case they may receive holy communion as long as they respect the obligation to avoid giving scandal.

5. The doctrine and discipline of the Church in this matter, are amply presented in the post-conciliar period in the Apostolic Exhortation *Familiaris consortio*. The Exhortation, among other things, reminds pastors that out of love for the truth they are obliged to discern carefully the different situations and exhorts them to encourage the participation of the divorced and remarried in the various events in the life of the Church. At the same time it confirms and indicates the reasons for the constant and universal practice, "founded on Sacred Scripture, of not admitting the divorced and remarried to holy communion" (Apostolic

adducit. Structura textus Adhortationis et ipsa verba clare demonstrant huiusmodi consuetudinem, quae exhibetur obligandi vi praedita, immutari non posse ob differentes condiciones.

6. Fidelis qui ex consuetudine convivit «more uxorio» cum persona quae neque legitima est uxor neque legitimus vir, non potest accedere ad Communionem Eucharisticam. Quod si ille hoc fieri posse existimet, tunc pastores et confessores, propter gravitatem materiae nec non ob exigentias boni spiritualis personae et boni communis Ecclesiae, gravi obstringuntur officio eundem commonendi huiusmodi conscientiae iudicium aperte contradicere doctrinae Ecclesiae. Debent insuper memoriam facere huius doctrinae, cum omnes fideles sibi commissos instituunt.

Hoc non significat Ecclesiae cordi non esse condicionem horum fidelium, qui, ceterum, minime excluduntur a communione ecclesiali. Ipsa sollicitudine ducitur eos pastorali actione prosequendi eosque invitandi ad vitam ecclesialem participandam, quantum fieri potest, salvis praescriptis iuris divini, a quibus Ecclesia nullam habet dispensandi potestatem. Necesse alioquin est illuminare fideles, quorum interest, ne censeant suam vitae Ecclesiae participationem exclusive reduci ad quaestionem de Eucharistiae receptione. Fideles adiuventur oportet, ut magis magisque comprehendant valorem participandi sacrificium Christi in Missa, communionis spiritualis, orationis, meditationis verbi divini, operum caritatis et iustitiae.

7. Errata persuasio, vi cuius aliquis post divortium et novas initas nuptias putat se posse accedere ad Communionem Eucharisticam, plerumque supponit conscientiae

Exhortation *Familiaris consortio,* n. 84: AAS 74 [1982] 185).
The structure of the Exhortation and the tenor of its
words give clearly to understand that this practice, which
is presented as binding, cannot be modified because of
different situations.

6. Members of the faithful who live together as husband
and wife with persons other than their legitimate spouses
may not receive Holy Communion. Should they judge it
possible to do so, pastors and confessors, given the gravity
of the matter and the spiritual good of these persons as
well as the common good of the Church, have the serious duty to admonish them that such a judgment of conscience openly contradicts the Church's teaching. Pastors
in their teaching must also remind the faithful entrusted to
their care of this doctrine.

This does not mean that the Church does not take to
heart the situation of these faithful, who moreover are not
excluded from ecclesial communion. She is concerned to
accompany them pastorally and invite them to share in the
life of the Church in the measure that is compatible with
the dispositions of divine law, from which the Church has
no power to dispense. On the other hand, it is necessary
to instruct these faithful so that they do not think their
participation in the life of the Church is reduced exclusively to the question of the reception of the Eucharist.
The faithful are to be helped to deepen their understanding of the value of sharing in the sacrifice of Christ in the
Mass, of spiritual communion, of prayer, of meditation on
the Word of God, and of works of charity and justice.

7. The mistaken conviction of a divorced and remarried
person that he may receive holy communion normally
presupposes that personal conscience is considered in the

personali tribui facultatem ultimatim decidendi—ratione habita propriae persuasionis—de existentia vel minus prioris matrimonii deque alterius unionis valore. At talis attributio admitti nollo modo potest. Matrimonium enim, quatenus imago unionis sponsalis inter Christum et eius Ecclesiam atque nucleus primarius et elementum magni momenti in vita societatis civilis, est sua ipsius natura realitas publica.

8. Verum quidem est iudicium de propriis dispositionibus pro accessione ad Eucharistiam a conscientia morali recte formata procedere debere. At verum pariter est consensum, quo matri monium constituitur, non esse decisionem mere privatam, quia tum unicuique coniugi tum utrique statum gignit specifice ecclesialem et socialem. Quare iudicium conscientiae de proprio statu matrimoniali non respicit dumtaxat relationem immediatam inter hominem et Deum, quasi necessaria non sit ecclesialis illa mediatio quae etiam leges canonicas conscientiam obligantes includit. Non agnoscere hunc essentialem aspectum idem est ac negare revera matrimonium existere veluti Ecclesiae realitatem, hoc est veluti sacramentum.

9. Ceterum Adhortatio *Familiaris consortio*, cum pastores invitat ad bene distinguendas varias condiciones eorum qui post divortium novam inierunt unionem, mentionem etiam facit condicionis eorum qui certi sua in intima conscientia sunt superius matrimonium iam irreparabiliter disruptum numquam validum fuisse. Discernendum utique est, num per viam fori externi ab Ecclesia statutam huiusmodi matrimonii nullitas obiective existat. Disciplina Ecclesiae, dum in examine de validitate matrimoniorum catholicorum confirmat competentiam exclusivam tribunalium ecclesiasticorum vias etiam novas ad probandam

final analysis to be able, on the basis of one's own convictions, to come to a decision about the existence or absence of a previous marriage and the value of the new union. However, such a position is inadmissable. Marriage, in fact, because it is both the image of the spousal relationship between Christ and his Church as well as the fundamental core and an important factor in the life of civil society, is essentially a public reality.

8. It is certainly true that a judgment about one's own dispositions for the reception of holy communion must be made by a properly formed moral conscience. But it is equally true that the consent that is the foundation of marriage is not simply a private decision since it creates a specifically ecclesial and social situation for the spouses, both individually and as a couple. Thus the judgment of conscience of one's own marital situation does not regard only the immediate relationship between man and God, as if one could prescind from the Church's mediation, that also includes canonical laws binding in conscience. Not to recognise this essential aspect would mean in fact to deny that marriage is a reality of the Church, that is to say, a sacrament.

9. In inviting pastors to distinguish carefully the various situations of the divorced and remarried, the Exhortation *Familiaris consortio* recalls the case of those who are subjectively certain in conscience that their previous marriage, irreparably broken, had never been valid. It must be discerned with certainty by means of the external forum established by the Church whether there is objectively such a nullity of marriage. The discipline of the Church, while it confirms the exclusive competence of ecclesiastical tribunals with respect to the examination of the validity of the marriage of Catholics, also offers new ways to

nullitatem unionis praecedentis offert hac mente, ut omne discrimen—inquantum fieri potest—inter veritatem in processu accessibilem et veritatem obiectivam, a recta conscientia cognitam, excludatur.

Adhaerere utcumque Ecclesiae iudicio et observare vigentem disciplinam circa obligationem formae canonicae utpote necessariae pro validitate matrimoniorum catholicorum, est quod vere prodest spirituali bono fidelium quorum causa agitur. Ecclesia enim est Corpus Christi atque vivere in communione ecclesiali est vivere in Corpore Christi et pasci eius Corpore. In Eucharistiae sacramento recipiendo communio cum Christo capite nullo modo a communione cum eius membris, i.e. cum eius Ecclesia separari potest. Qua de causa sacramentum nostrae cum Christo unionis etiam sacramentum unitatis Ecclesiae est. Sumere Communionem Eucharisticam, dispositionibus communionis ecclesialis non servatis, est ergo res in se repugnans. Communio sacramentalis cum Christo implicat et supponit observantiam, interdum quidem difficilem, ordinis communionis ecclesialis, nec fieri potest recte et fructuose per modum agendi quo fidelis desiderans immediate accedere ad Christum, hunc ordinem non servat.

10. Secundum ea quae hucusque exposita sunt, plene est amplectendum votum a Synodo Episcoporum expressum, proprium a Beatissimo Patre Ioanne Paulo II factum, et ad rem deductum studio laudabilibusque inceptis ab Episcopis, sacerdotibus, religiosis et fidelibus laicis: hoc est, sollicita cum caritate summopere adniti ut fideles, qui in condicione matrimoniali abnormi versantur, in Christi et Ecclesiae caritate roborentur. Hoc tantum modo eis licebit plene recipere matrimonii christiani nuntium atque

demonstrate the nullity of a previous marriage, in order to exclude as far as possible every divergence between the truth verifiable in the judicial process and the objective truth known by a correct conscience.

Adherence to the Church's judgment and observance of the existing discipline concerning the obligation of canonical form necessary for the validity of the marriage of Catholics are what truly contribute to the spiritual welfare of the faithful concerned. The Church is in fact the body of Christ and to live in ecclesial communion is to live in the body of Christ and to nourish oneself with the body of Christ. With the reception of the sacrament of the Eucharist, communion with Christ the Head can never be separated from communion with his members, that is, with his Church. For this reason, the sacrament of our union with Christ is also the sacrament of the unity of the Church. Receiving Eucharistic communion contrary to ecclesial communion is therefore in itself a contradiction. Sacramental communion with Christ includes and presupposes the observance, even if at times difficult, of the order of ecclesial communion, and it cannot be right and fruitful if a member of the faithful, wishing to approach Christ directly, does not respect this order.

10. In keeping with what has been said above, the desire expressed by the synod of bishops, adopted by the Holy Father John Paul II as his own and put into practice with dedication and with praiseworthy initiatives by bishops, priests, religious and lay faithful is yet to be fully realized, namely, with solicitous charity to do everything that can be done to strengthen in the love of Christ and the Church those faithful in irregular marriage situations. Only thus will it be possible for them fully to receive the message

sustinere in fide angores condicionis suae. In actione pastorali omni ope adnitendum est, ut recte intellegatur non agi hic de discrimine, sed solummodo de fidelitate absoluta erga Christi voluntatem, qui rursus nobis dedit et noviter concredidit matrimonii indissolubilitatem veluti Creatoris donum. Necesse erit ut pastores atque communitas fidelium patiantur atque diligant una simul cum iis ad quos pertinet, ut conspicere valeant etiam in onere oboedientiae iugum suave atque onus leve Iesu. Eorum onus non est dulce et leve quatenus parvum vel inane, sed fit leve quia Dominus—atque cum eo omnis Ecclesia—id participat. Proprium est pastoralis navitatis integra deditione exercendae praebere eiusmodi auxilium, veritate simulque amore innixum.

Tecum coniunctus in munere collegiali ut Iesu Christi veritas in Ecclesiae vita et consuetudine splendescat, me profiteri gaudeo Excellentiae Tuae Reverendissimae in Domino

Joseph Card. Ratzinger
Praefectus

+ Albertus Bovone
Archiepiscopus Tit. Caesariensis in Numidia
Secretarius

Hanc Epistulam in sessione ordinaria huius Congregationis deliberatam, Summus Pontifex Ioannes Paulus II, in Audientia Cardinali Praefecto concessa, adprobavit et publici iuris fieri iussit.

of Christian marriage and endure in faith the distress of their situation. In pastoral action one must do everything possible to ensure that this is understood not to be a matter of discrimination but only of absolute fidelity to the will of Christ who has restored and entrusted to us anew the indissolubility of marriage as a gift of the Creator. It will be necessary for pastors and the community of the faithful to suffer and to love in solidarity with the persons concerned so that they may recognise in their burden the sweet yoke and the light burden of Jesus. Their burden is not sweet and light in the sense of being small or insignificant, but becomes light because the Lord—and with him the whole Church—shares it. It is the task of pastoral action, which has to be carried out with total dedication, to offer this help, founded in truth and in love together.

United with you in dedication to the collegial task of making the truth of Jesus Christ shine in the life and activity of the Church, I remain,

Yours devotedly in the Lord,

Joseph Card. Ratzinger
Prefect

+ Alberto Bovone
Titular Archbishop of Caesarea in Numidia
Secretary

During an audience granted to the Cardinal Prefect, the Supreme Pontiff, John Paul II, gave his approval to this letter, drawn up in the ordinary session of this Congregation, and ordered its publication.

Pontifical Council for Legislative Texts, Declaration concerning the Admission to Holy Communion of Faithful Who Are Divorced and Remarried, June 24, 2000

The Code of Canon Law establishes that "Those upon whom the penalty of excommunication or interdict has been imposed or declared, and others who obstinately persist in manifest grave sin, are not to be admitted to holy communion" (can. 915). In recent years some authors have sustained, using a variety of arguments, that this canon would not be applicable to faithful who are divorced and remarried. It is acknowledged that paragraph 84 of the Apostolic Exhortation *Familiaris consortio*, issued in 1981, had reiterated that prohibition in unequivocal terms and that it has been expressly reaffirmed many times, especially in paragraph 1650 of the *Catechism of the Catholic Church*, published in 1992, and in the Letter written in 1994 by the Congregation for the Doctrine of the Faith, *Annus internationalis Familiae*. That notwithstanding, the aforementioned authors offer various interpretations of the above-cited canon that exclude from its application the situation of those who are divorced and remarried. For example, since the text speaks of "grave sin", it would be necessary to establish the presence of all the conditions required for the existence of mortal sin, including those which are subjective, necessitating a judgment of a type that a minister of communion could not make *ab externo*; moreover, given that the text speaks of those who "obstinately" persist in that sin, it would be necessary to verify an attitude of defiance on the part of an individual who had received a legitimate warning from the pastor. Given this alleged contrast between the discipline of the 1983 Code and the constant teachings of the Church in this area, this Pontifical Council, in agreement with the Congregation for the Doctrine of the Faith and with the Congregation for Divine Worship and the Discipline of the Sacraments declares the following:

1. The prohibition found in the cited canon, by its nature, is derived from divine law and transcends the domain of positive ecclesiastical laws: the latter cannot introduce legislative changes which would oppose the doctrine of the Church. The scriptural text on which the ecclesial tradition has always relied is that of St. Paul: "This means that whoever eats the bread or drinks the cup of the Lord unworthily sins against the body and blood of the Lord. A man should examine himself first only then should he eat of the bread and drink of the cup. He who eats and drinks without recognizing the body eats and drinks a judgment on himself " (1 Cor 11:27–29).

This text concerns in the first place the individual faithful and their moral conscience, a reality that is expressed as well by the Code in can. 916. But the unworthiness that comes from being in a state of sin also poses a serious juridical problem in the Church: indeed the canon of the Code of Canons of the Eastern Churches that is parallel to can. 915 of Code of Canon Law of the Latin Church makes reference to the term "unworthy": "Those who are publicly unworthy are forbidden from receiving the divine Eucharist" (can. 712). In effect, the reception of the body of Christ when one is publicly unworthy constitutes an objective harm to the ecclesial communion: it is a behavior that affects the rights of the Church and of all the faithful to live in accord with the exigencies of that communion. In the concrete case of the admission to holy communion of faithful who are divorced and remarried, the scandal, understood as an action that prompts others towards wrongdoing, affects at the same time both the sacrament of the Eucharist and the indissolubility of marriage. That scandal exists even if such behavior, unfortunately, no longer arouses surprise: in fact it is precisely with respect to the deformation of the conscience that it becomes more necessary for pastors to act, with as much patience as firmness, as a protection to the sanctity of the sacraments and a defense of Christian morality, and for the correct formation of the faithful.

2. Any interpretation of can. 915 that would set itself against the canon's substantial content, as declared uninterruptedly by the Magisterium and by the discipline of the Church throughout the centuries, is clearly misleading. One cannot confuse respect for the wording of the law (cfr. can. 17) with the improper use of the very same wording as an instrument for relativizing the precepts or emptying them of their substance.

The phrase "and others who obstinately persist in manifest grave sin" is clear and must be understood in a manner that does not distort its sense so as to render the norm inapplicable. The three required conditions are:

a) grave sin, understood objectively, being that the minister of communion would not be able to judge from subjective imputability;

b) obstinate persistence, which means the existence of an objective situation of sin that endures in time and which the will of the individual member of the faithful does not bring to an end, no other requirements (attitude of defiance, prior warning, etc.) being necessary to establish the fundamental gravity of the situation in the Church.

c) the manifest character of the situation of grave habitual sin.

Those faithful who are divorced and remarried would not be considered to be within the situation of serious habitual sin who would not be able, for serious motives—such as, for example, the upbringing of the children—"to satisfy the obligation of separation, assuming the task of living in full continence, that is, abstaining from the acts proper to spouses" (*Familiaris consortio*, n. 84), and who on the basis of that intention have received the sacrament of penance. Given that the fact that these faithful are not living *more uxorio* is per se occult, while their condition as persons who are divorced and remarried is per se manifest, they will be able to receive Eucharistic communion only *remoto scandalo*.

3. Naturally, pastoral prudence would strongly suggest the avoidance of instances of public denial of holy communion. Pastors must strive to explain to the concerned faithful the true ecclesial sense of the norm, in such a way that they would be able to understand it or at least respect it. In those situations, however, in which these precautionary measures have not had their effect or in which they were not possible, the minister of communion must refuse to distribute it to those who are publicly unworthy. They are to do this with extreme charity, and are to look for the opportune moment to explain the reasons that required the refusal. They must, however, do this with firmness, conscious of the value that such signs of strength have for the good of the Church and of souls.

The discernment of cases in which the faithful who find themselves in the described condition are to be excluded from Eucharistic communion is the responsibility of the priest who is responsible for the community. They are to give precise instructions to the deacon or to any extraordinary minister regarding the mode of acting in concrete situations.

4. Bearing in mind the nature of the above-cited norm (cfr. n. 1), no ecclesiastical authority may dispense the minister of holy communion from this obligation in any case, nor may he emanate directives that contradict it.

5. The Church reaffirms her maternal solicitude for the faithful who find themselves in this or other analogous situations that impede them from being admitted to the Eucharistic table. What is presented in this *Declaration* is not in contradiction with the great desire to encourage the participation of these children in the life of the Church, in the many forms compatible with their situation that are already possible for them. Moreover, the obligation of reiterating this impossibility of admission to the Eucharist is required for genuine pastoral care and for an authentic concern for the well-being of these faithful and of the whole Church, being that it indicates the conditions necessary for the fullness of that conversion to which all are always invited by the Lord, particularly during this Holy Year of the Great Jubilee.

Benedicti PP. XVI Summi Pontificis Adhortatio
Apostolica Postsynodalis *Sacramentum Caritatis* ad
Episcopos Sacerdotes Consecratos Consecratasque
necnon Christifideles Laicos de Eucharistia vitae
missionisque Ecclesiae fonte et culmine—*die XXII
mensis Februarii anno MMVII*

Eucharistia, sacramentum sponsale.

27. Eucharistia, caritatis sacramentum, peculiarem demon-
strat necessitudinem cum amore inter hominem et feminam,
matrimonio coniunctos. Penitus hunc nexum cognoscere
nostrae omnino est aetatis. Ioannes Paulus II Pontifex Ma-
ximus pluries occasione usus est ut sponsalem adfirmaret
indolem Eucharistiae eiusque peculiarem necessitudinem
cum sacramento Matrimonii: «Nostrae sacramentum est
Eucharistia redemptionis. Sponsi sacramentum est Spon-
saeque». Ceterum «tota vita christiana signum amoris sponsalis fert Christi et Ecclesiae. Iam Baptismus, in populum
Dei ingressus, mysterium est nuptiale: est quasi nuptiarum
lavacrum quod nuptiarum praecedit convivium, Eucharistiam». Eucharistia ratione inexhausta unitatem amoremque
indissolubiles cuiusque Matrimonii christiani corroborat.
In eo, vi sacramenti, vinculum coniugale intrinsece cum
unitate conectitur eucharistica inter Christum sponsum et
Ecclesiam sponsam (cfr *Eph* 5,31–32). Mutuus consensus
quem maritus et uxor inter se in Christo commutant, et
qui ex iis communitatem vitae amorisque constituit, indolem etiam habet eucharisticam. Revera, in Pauli theologia,
amor sponsalis signum est sacramentale amoris Christi erga
Ecclesiam eius, amoris qui tamquam in summum evadit ad
Crucem, documentum eius cum humanitate nuptiarum

Pope Benedict XVI, Post-Synodal Apostolic
Exhortation *Sacramentum caritatis*, February 22, 2007

The Eucharist, a nuptial sacrament.

27. The Eucharist, as the sacrament of charity, has a
particular relationship with the love of man and woman
united in marriage. A deeper understanding of this
relationship is needed at the present time. Pope John
Paul II frequently spoke of the nuptial character of the
Eucharist and its special relationship with the sacrament
of Matrimony: "The Eucharist is the sacrament of our
redemption. It is the sacrament of the Bridegroom and
of the Bride" (Apostolic Letter *Mulieris dignitatem*, 26).
Moreover, "the entire Christian life bears the mark
of the spousal love of Christ and the Church. Already
Baptism, the entry into the People of God, is a nuptial mystery; it is so to speak the nuptial bath which
precedes the wedding feast, the Eucharist" (*Catechism
of the Catholic Church*, 1617). The Eucharist inexhaust-
ibly strengthens the indissoluble unity and love of every
Christian marriage. By the power of the sacrament,
the marriage bond is intrinsically linked to the eucharistic unity of Christ, the bridegroom, and his bride,
the Church (cf. Eph 5:31–32). The mutual consent that
husband and wife exchange in Christ, which establishes
them as a community of life and love, also has a Eucharistic dimension. Indeed, in the theology of Saint Paul,

et, eodem tempore, origo et culmen Eucharistiae. Hanc
ob rem Ecclesia peculiarem manifestat spiritalem necessitudinem cum omnibus qui suas familias in matrimonii
sacramento fundaverunt. Familia—ecclesia domestica—
ambitus est primarius vitae Ecclesiae, praesertim ob necessarium munus filios christiana disciplina educandi. Hoc in
rerum contextu Synodus ut agnosceretur peculiaris mulieris
in familia societateque missio monuit, quae missio defen-
denda est, servanda atque promovenda. Eo quod sponsa est
et mater, id rem efficit inexstinguibilem, quae numquam
suam vim amittere debet.

Eucharistia et matrimonii unitas.

28. Hac revera sub luce istius interioris necessitudinis inter
matrimonium, familiam et Eucharistiam considerari possunt quaedam pastorales quaestiones. Fidele vinculum,
indissolubile et exclusivum quod Christum coniungit
cum Ecclesia, quodque notionem invenit sacramentalem
in Eucharistia, cum pristino congreditur anthropologico
elemento, ex quo definitum in modum vir coniungatur
oportet una cum femina et vicissim (cfr *Gn* 2,24; Mt 19,5).
Hoc in cogitationum prospectu, Synodus Episcoporum
argumentum tractavit pastoralis consuetudinis erga illum
qui nuntium experitur Evangelii quique ex cultura prove-
nit in qua polygamia exsistit. Ii, qui in eiusmodi versantur
condicione atque se ad fidem aperiunt christianam, oportet adiuventur ut consilium suum humanum in praecipua

conjugal love is a sacramental sign of Christ's love for his Church, a love culminating in the Cross, the expression of his "marriage" with humanity and at the same time the origin and heart of the Eucharist. For this reason the Church manifests her particular spiritual closeness to all those who have built their family on the sacrament of matrimony. The family—the domestic Church—is a primary sphere of the Church's life, especially because of its decisive role in the Christian education of children. In this context, the Synod also called for an acknowledgment of the unique mission of women in the family and in society, a mission that needs to be defended, protected and promoted. Marriage and motherhood represent essential realities which must never be denigrated.

The Eucharist and the unicity of marriage.

28. In the light of this intrinsic relationship between marriage, the family and the Eucharist, we can turn to several pastoral problems. The indissoluble, exclusive and faithful bond uniting Christ and the Church, which finds sacramental expression in the Eucharist, corresponds to the basic anthropological fact that man is meant to be definitively united to one woman and vice versa (cf. Gen 2:24, Matt 19:5). With this in mind, the synod of bishops addressed the question of pastoral practice regarding people who come to the Gospel from cultures in which polygamy is practised. Those living in this situation who open themselves to Christian faith need to be helped to integrate their life-plan into the radical newness of Christ. During the catechumenate, Christ encounters them in

integrent novitate Christi. In catechumenorum curriculo, Christus eos attingit in eorum peculiari condicione eosque ad plenam vocat veritatem amoris per abnegationes transeuntes necessarias, perfectam prospicientes communionem ecclesialem. Ecclesia illos comitatur per pastoralem actionem, dulcedine simul et firmitate plenam, demonstrans eis lucem praesertim quae ex mysteriis christianis in naturam repercutitur et humanos affectus.

Eucharistia et matrimonii indissolubilitas.

29. Si Eucharistia irreversibilitatem exprimit amoris Dei in Christo pro eius Ecclesia, intellegitur cur ea postulet, pro Matrimonii sacramento, hanc indissolubilitatem, ad quam omnis verus amor haud tendere non potest. Omnino iusta videtur pastoralis cura quam Synodus ad acerbas condiciones destinavit, in quibus non pauci versantur fideles qui, sacramento Matrimonii celebrato, divortium fecerunt atque novas inierunt nuptias. Agitur de quaestione pastorali ardua et complicata, vera quadam plaga hodierni contextus socialis, quae ipsas provincias catholicas crescente transgreditur modo. Pastores, propter amorem veritatis, ad recte discernendas tenentur rerum condiciones, ut implicatos fideles aptis modis spiritaliter adiuvent. Synodus Episcoporum Ecclesiae usum confirmavit, Sacris Scripturis innixum (cfr *Mc* 10,2–12), non ammittendi ad Sacramenta divortiatos iterum matrimonio iunctos, quia eorum status eorumque vitae condicio obiective unioni contradicunt amoris inter Christum et Ecclesiam, quae in Eucharistia significatur et efficitur. Divortio seiuncti et iterum matrimonio coniuncti, tamen, praeter hunc statum, ad Ecclesiam pergunt pertinere, quae eos peculiari cura

their specific circumstances and calls them to embrace the full truth of love, making whatever sacrifices are necessary in order to arrive at perfect ecclesial communion. The Church accompanies them with a pastoral care that is gentle yet firm, above all by showing them the light shed by the Christian mysteries on nature and on human affections.

The Eucharist and the indissolubility of marriage.

29. If the Eucharist expresses the irrevocable nature of God's love in Christ for his Church, we can then understand why it implies, with regard to the sacrament of matrimony, that indissolubility to which all true love necessarily aspires. There was good reason for the pastoral attention that the synod gave to the painful situations experienced by some of the faithful who, having celebrated the sacrament of matrimony, then divorced and remarried. This represents a complex and troubling pastoral problem, a real scourge for contemporary society, and one which increasingly affects the Catholic community as well. The Church's pastors, out of love for the truth, are obliged to discern different situations carefully, in order to be able to offer appropriate spiritual guidance to the faithful involved. The synod of bishops confirmed the Church's practice, based on Sacred Scripture (cf. Mark 10:2–12), of not admitting the divorced and remarried to the sacraments, since their state and their condition of life objectively contradict the loving union of Christ and the Church signified and made present in the Eucharist. Yet the divorced and remarried continue to belong to the Church, which accompanies them with special

prosequitur, desiderans ut illi, quantum fieri potest, christianum colant vivendi modum per sanctam Missam participandam, licet Communionem non recipiant, divini Verbi auscultationem, eucharisticam Adorationem, orationem, vitae communitatis participationem, dialogum fidentem cum sacerdote vel spiritali moderatore, deditionem actae caritati, paenitentiae opera, munus educationis erga filios.

Ubi dubia de Matrimonii sacramentalis contracti validitate legitime oriuntur, id suscipiendum est quod ad probandam coniugii validitatem est necessarium. Oportet praeterea curetur ut, iure canonico prorsus servato, in territorio tribunalia ecclesiastica adsint, videlicet eorum pastoralis indoles eorumque recta promptaque operositas. Necesse est ut in unaquaque dioecesi numerus sit sufficiens personarum ad sollicitam tribunalium ecclesiasticorum actuositatem paratarum. Recordamur « munus grave esse istud opus institutionale reddendi Ecclesiae apud tribunalia ecclesiastica semper ad fideles propius». Opus est tamen vitare ne illa pastoralis opera contraria iuri habeatur. Ab hac potius condicione sumendum est initium: ius et opus pastorale in *veritatis amorem* convenire debent. Haec revera numquam a rebus abstrahitur, sed cum humano consociatur et christiano cuiusque fidelis itinere. Postremo ubi nullitas vinculi matrimonialis non agnoscitur atque condiciones dantur obiectivae quae convictum reddunt irreversibilem, Ecclesia illos adhortatur fideles ut se implicent ad suam vivendam necessitudinem secundum legis Dei postulata, veluti amici, veluti frater et soror; hoc modo ad mensam eucharisticam accedere possunt, cum regulis significatis a comprobato usu ecclesiali. Eiusmodi iter, ut possibile efficiatur atque fructus adferat, sustineri debet pastorum adiumento atque aptis inceptis ecclesialibus;

concern and encourages them to live as fully as possible the Christian life through regular participation at Mass, albeit without receiving communion, listening to the Word of God, Eucharistic adoration, prayer, participation in the life of the community, honest dialogue with a priest or spiritual director, dedication to the life of charity, works of penance, and commitment to the education of their children.

When legitimate doubts exist about the validity of the prior sacramental marriage, the necessary investigation must be carried out to establish if these are well-founded. Consequently there is a need to ensure, in full respect for canon law, the presence of local ecclesiastical tribunals, their pastoral character, and their correct and prompt functioning. Each Diocese should have a sufficient number of persons with the necessary preparation, so that the ecclesiastical tribunals can operate in an expeditious manner. I repeat that it is a grave obligation to bring the Church's institutional activity in her tribunals ever closer to the faithful. At the same time, pastoral care must not be understood as if it were somehow in conflict with the law. Rather, one should begin by assuming that the fundamental point of encounter between the law and pastoral care is *love for the truth*: truth is never something purely abstract, but a real part of the human and Christian journey of every member of the faithful. Finally, where the nullity of the marriage bond is not declared and objective circumstances make it impossible to cease cohabitation, the Church encourages these members of the faithful to commit themselves to living their relationship in fidelity to the demands of God's law, as friends, as brother and sister; in this way they will be able to return to the table of the Eucharist, taking care to observe the Church's established and approved practice

vitetur tamen benedictio harum relationum, ne confusio de Matrimonii aestimatione oriatur inter fideles.

Cum implicatus sit culturalis contextus in quo Ecclesia versatur in multis Nationibus, Synodus maximam porro inculcavit sollicitudinem pastoralem in formandis nuptias inituris atque in praevia probatione eorum opinationum de oneribus omnino tenendis ad validitatem sacramenti Matrimonii. Solida quaedam discretio de hac re vitare poterit ne emotionum impulsus vel leves rationes duos iuvenes inducant ad assumendam responsalitatem, quam deinde servare non valeant. Maius est bonum, quod Ecclesia atque tota societas a matrimonio exspectant familiaque in eo fundata, quam ut in hoc peculiari ambitu pastorali quis non laboret. Matrimonium et familia sunt instituta quae promoveri defendique debent, omnibus ambiguitatibus de ipsarum veritate amotis, quandoquidem omnis iniuria illis illata vulnus est quod hominum convictui ut tali affertur.

Francisci Summi Pontificis Litterae Encyclicae *Lumen fidei* Episcopis Presbyteris ac Diaconis Viris et Mulieribus Consecratis Omnibusque Christifidelibus Laicis de fide—*die undetricesimo mensis Iunii anno Domini bis millesimo tertio decimo*

Fides et familia.

52. De Abraham itinere ad futuram civitatem, Epistula ad Hebraeos breviter attingit benedictionem quae a

in this regard. This path, if it is to be possible and fruitful, must be supported by pastors and by adequate ecclesial initiatives, nor can it ever involve the blessing of these relations, lest confusion arise among the faithful concerning the value of marriage.

Given the complex cultural context which the Church today encounters in many countries, the Synod also recommended devoting maximum pastoral attention to training couples preparing for marriage and to ascertaining beforehand their convictions regarding the obligations required for the validity of the sacrament of Matrimony. Serious discernment in this matter will help to avoid situations where impulsive decisions or superficial reasons lead two young people to take on responsibilities that they are then incapable of honouring. The good that the Church and society as a whole expect from marriage and from the family founded upon marriage is so great as to call for full pastoral commitment to this particular area. Marriage and the family are institutions that must be promoted and defended from every possible misrepresentation of their true nature, since whatever is injurious to them is injurious to society itself.

Pope Francis, Encyclical Letter *Lumen fidei*, June 29, 2013

52. In Abraham's journey towards the future city, the Letter to the Hebrews mentions the blessing which was passed

parentibus in filios transmittitur (cfr *Heb* 11,20–21). Primus ambitus in quo fides illuminat hominum civitatem invenitur in familia. Cogitamus praesertim stabilem viri mulierisque consortionem in matrimonio. Ipsa oritur ex eorum amore, signo praesentiaque Dei amoris, ex cognitione et acceptatione bonitatis in differentia sexuali, cuius vi coniuges iungi possunt in una carne (cfr *Gen* 2,24) atque sunt capaces novam vitam generandi, manifestationem bonitatis Creatoris, eius sapientiae eiusque consilii amoris. Hoc amore constituti, vir et mulier mutuum amorem spondere possunt gestu quodam qui totam vitam complectitur et tot fidei signa memorat. Spondere amorem qui in perpetuum observetur dari potest cum inceptum detegitur maius propriis propositis, quod nos sustinet nosque sinit integrum futurum personae dilectae tradere. Fides porro opem fert ut filiorum generatio tota in sua altitudine divitiisque percipiatur, quoniam efficit ut in ea agnoscatur creans amor, qui tradit et committit nobis novae personae mysterium. Itaque suam per fidem Sara mater facta est, in Dei fidelitate eiusque repromissione confidens (cfr *Heb* 11,11).

on from fathers to sons (cf. Heb 11:20–21). The first setting in which faith enlightens the human city is the family.
I think first and foremost of the stable union of man and
woman in marriage. This union is born of their love, as a
sign and presence of God's own love, and of the acknowledgment and acceptance of the goodness of sexual differentiation, whereby spouses can become one flesh (cf. Gen
2:24) and are enabled to give birth to a new life, a manifestation of the Creator's goodness, wisdom and loving plan.
Grounded in this love, a man and a woman can promise
each other mutual love in a gesture which engages their
entire lives and mirrors many features of faith. Promising
love for ever is possible when we perceive a plan bigger
than our own ideas and undertakings, a plan which sustains
us and enables us to surrender our future entirely to the
one we love. Faith also helps us to grasp in all its depth
and richness the begetting of children, as a sign of the love
of the Creator who entrusts us with the mystery of a new
person. So it was that Sarah, by faith, became a mother, for
she trusted in God's fidelity to his promise (cf. Heb 11:11).

Pope Francis, Apostolic Exhortation *Evangelii
gaudium*, November 24, 2013

66. The family is experiencing a profound cultural crisis,
as are all communities and social bonds. In the case of the
family, the weakening of these bonds is particularly serious because the family is the fundamental cell of society,
where we learn to live with others despite our differences
and to belong to one another; it is also the place where
parents pass on the faith to their children. Marriage now

tends to be viewed as a form of mere emotional satisfaction that can be constructed in any way or modified at will. But the indispensible contribution of marriage to society transcends the feelings and momentary needs of the couple. As the French bishops have taught, it is not born "of loving sentiment, ephemeral by definition, but from the depth of the obligation assumed by the spouses who accept to enter a total communion of life" (Conférence Des Évêques De France, Conseil Famille et Société, *Élargir le mariage aux personnes de même sexe? Ouvrons le débat!* [28 September 2012]).

Pope Francis, General Audience Address, April 2, 2014

Today we conclude the series of catecheses on the sacraments by speaking about matrimony. This sacrament leads us to the heart of God's design, which is a plan for a covenant with his people, with us all, a plan for communion. At the beginning of the Book of Genesis, the first book of the Bible, at the culmination of the creation account it says: "God created man in his own image, in the image of God he created him; male and female he created them.... Therefore a man leaves his father and his mother and cleaves to his wife, and they become one flesh" (Gen 1:27; 2:24). The image of God is the married couple: the man and the woman; not only the man, not only the woman, but both of them together. This is the image of God: love, God's covenant with us is represented in that covenant between man and woman. And this is very beautiful! We are created in order to love, as a reflection of God and his love. And in the marital union man and woman fulfil this vocation through their mutual reciprocity and their full and definitive communion of life.

When a man and woman celebrate the Sacrament of Matrimony God as it were "is mirrored" in them; he impresses in them his own features and the indelible character of his love. Marriage is the icon of God's love for us. Indeed, God is communion too: the three Persons of the Father, the Son and the Holy Spirit live eternally in perfect unity. And this is precisely the mystery of matrimony: God makes of the two spouses one single life. The Bible uses a powerful expression and says "one flesh", so intimate is the union between man and woman in marriage. And this is precisely the mystery of marriage: the love of God which is reflected in the couple that decides to live together. Therefore a man leaves his home, the home of his parents, and goes to live with his wife and unites himself so strongly to her that the two become—the Bible says—one flesh.

St. Paul, in the Letter to the Ephesians, emphasizes that a great mystery is reflected in Christian spouses: the relationship established by Christ with the Church, a nuptial relationship (cf. Eph 5:21–33). The Church is the bride of Christ. This is their relationship. This means that matrimony responds to a specific vocation and must be considered as a consecration (cf. *Gaudium et Spes*, n. 48; *Familiaris consortio*, n. 56). It is a consecration: the man and woman are consecrated in their love. The spouses, in fact, in virtue of the sacrament, are invested with a true and proper mission, so that starting with the simple ordinary things of life they may make visible the love with which Christ loves his Church, by continuing to give his life for her in fidelity and service.

Pope Francis, Address to the Bishops of the
Episcopal Conferences of Botswana, South Africa,
and Swaziland on the Occasion of Their "Ad
Limina" Visit, April 25, 2014

You have spoken to me of some of the serious pastoral
challenges facing your communities. Catholic families have
fewer children, with repercussions on the number of voca-
tions to the priesthood and religious life. Some Catholics
turn away from the Church to other groups who seem to
promise something better. Abortion compounds the grief
of many women who now carry with them deep physical
and spiritual wounds after succumbing to the pressures of a
secular culture which devalues God's gift of sexuality and
the right to life of the unborn. In addition, the rate of separation and divorce is high, even in many Christian families,
and children frequently do not grow up in a stable home
environment. We also observe with great concern, and can
only deplore, an increase in violence against women and
children. All these realities threaten the sanctity of marriage, the stability of life in the home and consequently
the life of society as a whole. In this sea of difficulties, we
bishops and priests must give a consistent witness to the
moral teaching of the Gospel. I am confident that you will
not weaken in your resolve to teach the truth "in season
and out of season" (2 Tim 4:2), sustained by prayer and
discernment, and always with great compassion....

The holiness and indissolubility of Christian matrimony,
often disintegrating under tremendous pressure from the
secular world, must be deepened by clear doctrine and
supported by the witness of committed married couples.
Christian matrimony is a lifelong covenant of love between

one man and one woman; it entails real sacrifices in order to turn away from illusory notions of sexual freedom and in order to foster conjugal fidelity. Your programmes of preparation for the sacrament of matrimony, enriched by Pope John Paul's teaching on marriage and the family, are proving to be promising and indeed indispensable means of communicating the liberating truth about Christian marriage and are inspiring young people with new hope for themselves and for their future as husbands and wives, fathers and mothers.

Magisterial Texts concerning *Sensus fidei*

Concilium Vaticanum II, Constitutio Dogmatica de Ecclesia «*Lumen gentium*»—*die XXI mensis Novembris anno MCMLXIV*

12. Populus Dei sanctus de munere quoque prophetico Christi participat, vivum Eius testimonium maxime per vitam fidei ac caritatis diffundendo, et Deo hostiam laudis offerendo, fructum labiorum confitentium nomini Eius. Universitas fidelium, qui unctionem habent a Sancto, in credendo falli nequit, atque hanc suam peculiarem proprietatem mediante supernaturali sensu fidei totius populi manifestat, cum "ab Episcopis usque ad extremos laicos fideles" (Augustinus, *De Praed. Sanct.* 14,27: PL 44,980) universalem suum consensum de rebus fidei et morum exhibet. Illo enim sensu fidei, qui a Spiritu veritatis excitatur et sustentatur, Populus Dei sub ductu sacri magisterii, cui fideliter obsequens, iam non verbum hominum, sed vere accipit verbum Dei, semel traditae sanctis fidei, indefectibiliter adhaeret, recto iudicio in eam profundius penetrat eamque in vita plenius applicat.

35. Christus, Propheta magnus, qui et testimonio vitae et verbi virtute Regnum proclamavit Patris, usque ad plenam manifestationem gloriae suum munus propheticum adimplet, non solum per Hierarchiam, quae nomine et potestate Eius docet, sed etiam per laicos, quos ideo et testes constituit et sensu fidei et gratia verbi instruit, ut

Magisterial Texts concerning *Sensus fidei*

Second Vatican Council, Dogmatic Constitution on the Church *Lumen gentium*, November 21, 1964

12. The holy people of God shares also in Christ's prophetic office; it spreads abroad a living witness to Him, especially by means of a life of faith and charity and by offering to God a sacrifice of praise, the tribute of lips which give praise to His name. The entire body of the faithful, anointed as they are by the Holy One, cannot err in matters of belief. They manifest this special property by means of the whole peoples' supernatural discernment in matters of faith when "from the bishops down to the last of the lay faithful" (Augustine, *De Praed. Sanct.* 14.27: PL 44.980) they show universal agreement in matters of faith and morals. That discernment in matters of faith is aroused and sustained by the Spirit of truth. It is exercised under the guidance of the sacred teaching authority, in faithful and respectful obedience to which the people of God accepts that which is not just the word of men but truly the word of God. Through it, the people of God adheres unwaveringly to the faith given once and for all to the saints, penetrates it more deeply with right thinking, and applies it more fully in its life.

35. Christ, the great Prophet, who proclaimed the Kingdom of His Father both by the testimony of His life and the power of His words, continually fulfills His prophetic office until the complete manifestation of glory. He does this not only through the hierarchy who teach in His name and with His authority, but also through the laity whom

virtus Evangelii in vita quotidiana, familiari et sociali eluceat. Ipsi se praebent ut filios repromissionis, si fortes in
fide et spe praesens momentum redimunt et futuram glo-
riam per patientiam exspectant. Hanc autem spem non in
animi interioritate abscondant sed conversione continua et
colluctatione adversus mundi rectores tenebrarum harum,
contra spiritualia nequitiae etiam per vitae saecularis struc-
turas exprimant.

Adhortatio Apostolica Familiaris consortio Ioannis
Pauli PP. II Summi Pontificis ad Episcopos,
Sacerdotes et Christifideles totius Ecclesiae Catholicae
de familiae christianae muneribus in mundo
huius temporis.—*die XXII mensis Novembris anno
MCMLXXXI*

5. Hoc rectum iudicium ab Ecclesia factum evadit direc-
tio, quae proponitur, ad servandam et efficiendam totam
veritatem ac plenam dignitatem matrimonii et familiae.

Idem iudicium fit sensu fidei, qui est donum a Spiritu omnibus fidelibus imperiium, estque igitur opus totius
Ecclesiae secundum varietatem multiplicium donorum et
charismatum, quae, una cum cuiusque munere et officio et
secundum ea, ad altiorem intellectum et effectionem verbi
Dei cooperantur. Ecclesia ergo proprium iudicium evan-
gelicum non solum per Pastores facit, qui nomine et potestate Christi docent, sed etiam per laicos: "quos (Christus)
ideo et testes constituit et sensu fidei et gratia verbi instruit
(cfr. *Act* 2,17–18; *Apoc* 19,10), ut virtus Evangelii in vita
quotidiana, familiari et sociali eluceat". Quin etiam laici

He made His witnesses and to whom He gave understanding of the faith (*sensus fidei*) and an attractiveness in speech so that the power of the Gospel might shine forth in their daily social and family life. They conduct themselves as children of the promise, and thus strong in faith and in hope they make the most of the present, and with patience await the glory that is to come. Let them not, then, hide this hope in the depths of their hearts, but even in the program of their secular life let them express it by a continual conversion and by wrestling against the world rulers of this darkness, against the spiritual forces of wickedness.

Saint John Paul II, Apostolic Exhortation *Familiaris consortio*, November 22, 1981

5. The discernment effected by the church becomes the offering of an orientation in order that the entire truth and the full dignity of marriage and the family may be preserved and realized.

This discernment is accomplished through the sense of faith, which is a gift that the Spirit gives to all the faithful, and is therefore the work of the whole Church according to the diversity of the various gifts and charisms that, together with and according to the responsibility proper to each one, work together for a more profound understanding and activation of the word of God. The Church, therefore, does not accomplish this discernment only through the pastors, who teach in the name and with the power of Christ, but also through the laity: Christ "made them his witnesses and gave them understanding of the

propter peculiarem suam vocationem singulari obstringuntur munere interpretandi, luce Christi affulgente, huius
mundi historiam, quatenus vocantur ad illuminanda et
ordinanda secundum consilium Dei Creatoris et Redemp-
toris ea quae sunt temporalia.

Verumtamen "supernaturalis sensus fidei" non solum
nec necessario in consensione fidelium est positus. Ecclesia enim Christum sequendo veritatem exquirit, quae non
semper cum opinione maioris hominum congruit partis.
Ea conscientiae praebet aures, non potestatibus, et hac in
re pauperes et despectos defendit. Ecclesia potest quidem
magni aestimare investigationes sociologicas et rationalis
doctrinae proprias, si utiles sunt ad perspiciendas historicas
rerum temporumque condiciones, in quibus actio pastoralis debet impleri, et ut veritatem melius cognoscat; tales
vero investigationes solae non haberi possunt ilico signifi-
cationes sensus fidei nuntiae.

Quoniam munus est ministerii apostolici curare ut
Ecclesia in veritate Christi persistat et ut in eam usque
altius penetret, Pastores sensum fidei in cunctis fidelibus
debent promovere, cum auctoritate expendere et iudicare
germanam indolem modorum, quibus ille exprimitur, cre-
dentes ad maturiorem usque intellectum veritatis evange-
licae adducere.

faith and the grace of speech (cf. Acts 2:17–18; Rev 19:10), so that the power of the Gospel might shine forth in their daily social and family life" (*Lumen gentium*, 35). The laity, moreover, by reason of their particular vocation have the specific role of interpreting the history of the world in the light of Christ, inasmuch as they are called to illuminate and organize temporal realities according to the plan of God, creator and redeemer.

The "supernatural sense of faith," however, does not consist solely or necessarily in the consensus of the faithful. Following Christ, the Church seeks the truth, which is not always the same as the majority opinion. She listens to conscience and not to power, and in this way she defends the poor and the downtrodden. The Church values sociological and statistical research when it proves helpful in understanding the historical context in which pastoral action has to be developed and when it leads to a better understanding of the truth. Such research alone, however, is not to be considered in itself an expression of the sense of faith.

Because it is the task of the apostolic ministry to ensure that the Church remains in the truth of Christ and to lead her ever more deeply into that truth, the pastors must promote the sense of faith in all the faithful, examine and authoritatively judge the genuineness of its expressions and educate the faithful in an ever more mature evangelical discernment.

Congregatio pro Doctrina Fidei, Instructio de
Ecclesiali theologici vocatione «Donum veritatis»,
die 24 Maii 1990

35. [...] Revera opiniones christifidelium ad "sensum fidei"
simpliciter redigi non possunt. Hic est proprietas ipsius fidei
theologalis quae, cum sit Dei donum quod efficit ut veritati
unusquisque singillatim adhaereat, falli nequit. Porro haec
fides uniuscuiusque, simul etiam Ecclesiae fides est, quandoquidem Deus Ecclesiae concredidit custodiam Verbi, proin-
deque quod Ecclesia credit, credit et christifidelis. Itaque natura
sua "sensus fidei" infert secum intimum spiritus cordisque
consensum cum Ecclesia, id est illud "sentire cum Ecclesia".

Si ergo theologalis fides qua talis falli non potest, nihilominus fidelis fovere intus erratas opiniones potest,
quoniam non universae eius cogitationes ex fide progrediuntur. Cogitata non omnia, quae intra Dei Populum cir-
cumferuntur, cum fide ipsa concinunt, eoque magis quod
facile subire possunt impulsum alicuius publicae opinionis,
quae recentioribus communicationis instrumentis pervehi-
tur. Non sine causa Concilium Vaticanum II necessariam
coniunctionem in luce ponit inter "sensum fidei" et re-
gimen Populi Dei, quod magisterio Pastorum concreditur:
nam duae res sunt, quarum altera ab altera separari non
potest.

Congregation for the Doctrine of the Faith,
Instruction *Donum veritatis*, On the Ecclesial
Vocation of the Theologian, May 24, 1990

35. [...] Actually, the opinions of the faithful cannot be purely and simply identified with the *"sensus fidei"*. The sense of the faith is a property of theological faith; and, as God's gift which enables one to adhere personally to the Truth, it cannot err. This personal faith is also the faith of the Church since God has given guardianship of the Word to the Church. Consequently, what the believer believes is what the Church believes. The *"sensus fidei"* implies then by its nature a profound agreement of spirit and heart with the Church, *"sentire cum Ecclesia"*.

Although theological faith as such then cannot err, the believer can still have erroneous opinions since all his thoughts do not spring from faith. Not all the ideas which circulate among the People of God are compatible with the faith. This is all the more so given that people can be swayed by a public opinion influenced by modern communications media. Not without reason did the Second Vatican Council emphasize the indissoluble bond between the *"sensus fidei"* and the guidance of the People of God by the Magisterium of the pastors. These two realities cannot be separated.

Pope Francis, Address to the Members of
the International Theological Commission,
December 6, 2013

Through the gift of the Holy Spirit, the members of the
Church possess the "sense of the faith". It is a kind of
"spiritual instinct" which allows them to *sentire cum Ecclesia*
and to discern what conforms to the Apostolic faith and to
the spirit of the Gospel. Of course, it is clear that the *sensus
fidelium* must not be confused with the sociological reality
of majority opinion. It is something else.

CONTRIBUTORS

Walter Cardinal Brandmüller is former President of the Pontifical Committee for Historical Sciences.

Raymond Leo Cardinal Burke is Prefect of the Supreme Tribunal of the Apostolic Signatura.

Carlo Cardinal Caffarra is Archbishop of Bologna.

Velasio Cardinal De Paolis, C.S., is Emeritus President of the Prefecture of Economic Affairs of the Holy See.

Robert Dodaro, O.S.A., is President of the Patristic Institute, *Augustinianum*, Rome.

Paul Mankowski, S.J., is Scholar-in-Residence at the Lumen Christi Institute, Chicago.

Gerhard Ludwig Cardinal Müller is Prefect of the Congregation for the Doctrine of the Faith.

John M. Rist is Emeritus Professor of Classics and Philosophy at the University of Toronto, and former holder of the Kurt Pritzl, O.P., Chair of Philosophy at the Catholic University of America.

Archbishop Cyril Vasil', S.J., is Secretary of the Congregation for Oriental Churches.

INDEX